# Louisiana Entertains

## Menus and Recipes

## from

## The Rapides Symphony Guild

## Alexandria, Louisiana

Edited by Hope J. Norman and Louise A. Simon
Illustrations by Madelyn R. Waters
Wine Selections by Virginia and Jeems White

Proceeds from the sale of this book will be used to benefit the Rapides Symphony Orchestra.

Copyright © 1978 by
Rapides Symphony Guild, Alexandria, Louisiana

| | | |
|---|---|---|
| First printing | November 1978 | 20,000 |
| Second printing | July 1980 | 40,000 |

Library of Congress Catalog Card Number: 78 64496

ISBN: 0-9603758-0-5

Copies may be obtained from *Louisiana Entertains,* Rapides Symphony Guild, P.O. Box 4172, Alexandria, Louisiana, 71301. (Coupon in back of book.)

*Printed by*
Wimmer Brothers
Memphis, TN 38118

FOR

BILL AND SYLVIA KUSHNER

who entertain our ears
our minds
and always most deeply
our hearts

# Table of Contents

# INTRODUCTION

Louisiana entertaining is inseparable from food. The hospitable nature of the Bayou State residents and their devotion to a good table combine to create a cuisine which assails all of the senses—taste, sight, smell, touch and even sound. Real love is shown in creating and serving savory specialties. Food is a favorite topic of conversation both at the table, kitchen or dining room, and in the parlor.

Louisiana's culinary delicacies are an important part of the heritage and tradition of this unusual state, synthesizing the essence of classic structured French cuisine, the savor of local fish and game, the zest of Spanish and Italian spices, and the magic African use of herbs in creating nuances of flavor. The Creole heritage of New Orleans, the *joie de vivre* of Cajun south Louisiana, the graciousness of river plantations and the down-home goodness of Southern cooking further contribute to the uniqueness of taste and style that is Louisiana.

This book was developed from a series of parties hosted over a three year period by Central Louisianians in their homes to support the Rapides Symphony Orchestra, founded in 1967 and masterfully directed by William Kushner of Lake Charles. (The orchestra's name is derived from that of the parish, or county, of Rapides; in turn, the name Rapides arose from the French word for the rapids which were noted nearby in the Red River by early explorers.) The menus of these symphony parties were analyzed, tested and augmented to include a balance of multiple occasions, varying in size and degree of formality and taking into consideration season of the year, number of guests, tone of the occasion, textures, colors, taste and appearance of foods, ease of last-minute preparation teamed with careful advance labors, and the realities of present-day life styles. Local cooks, male and female and of all ages and backgrounds, selected recipes from their personal collections. Many specialties are family treasures, geared to today's kitchens. In the selection of these recipes and their arrangement into practical menu form, Southern tradition and Louisiana's unique flavor were stressed in the acknowledgement that this combination is what makes Louisiana's cuisine unsurpassed.

These menus are designed for those who wish to eschew everyday routine and to present a more imaginative bill of fare. It is assumed that the creative cook will use only the best of all ingredients: the freshest of fruits, vegetables and herbs, homemade stocks and mayonnaise, and newly-ground spices. Each recipe is adjusted to serve the number of portions indicated in the menu where the recipe occurs. Recipes starred in the menus appear in the text.

The menu arrangement of this book dictates that a thorough index be included. The use of this index enables the cook to adapt the recipes and menus to meet individual needs. The first three sections, Morning, Midday, and Evening, each begin with a menu for two and progress to larger occasions. The fourth section, Celebrations, follows a chronological progression of important events occurring throughout the year. The reader will quickly discern the adaptability of these recipes and the versatility of the menus.

The Rapides Symphony Guild acknowledges with deep appreciation the countless members and friends who have contributed their time, talents, energy and interest in support of this endeavor.

# WINE AND ENTERTAINING

The art of gracious entertaining is a refinement of the historic practice of sharing food and drink with other people. Sharing sustenance is universally symbolic of friendship; particularly in Louisiana with our curious and unique admixture of cultures, the warmth of hospitality often overwhelms newcomers. Whether the occasion is plain or fancy the host wishes the guest to "pass a good time" with food and wine being the vehicle for communication.

*PLANNING:* Gracious entertaining begins in the mind; the key is to relax. Gracious entertaining requires intelligent selection of the right foods for the occasion and the wine or wines to complement both. The pace and timing of the beginning, middle and end of a meal are often more important than what you serve. The host provides setting and sustenance, but the success of the occasion comes only from the guests. Corollary: planning the guest list is more important than planning the food and drink.

*WHY WINE?* Wine and food served together are infinitely more enjoyable than either by itself, and wine is the true mealtime beverage with a natural affinity for food that enhances the flavor of food as does no other beverage. Wine aids digestion and provides a sense of well-being which is virtually indispensable to gracious entertaining. Visual presentation is highly important in the enjoyment of a meal. Wine adds greatly to this pleasure. Since wine is highly symbolic of life, happiness and optimism, sharing wine with friends is meaningful, romantic, even exhilarating to the spirit. The leisurely and ample flow of wine throughout a meal adds continuity and a graceful rhythm, but the most important reason for serving wine when entertaining friends is that wine is delicious.

*BASIC WINE SELECTION:* Serve simple wines with simple fare and at casual occasions while reserving the richer wines for more elaborate preparations, but always be guided by your own tastes and those of your guests. "White wine with white meat and red wine with red meat" is simple enough, but there are plenty of exceptions. When the recipe calls for wine, serving the same wine at table is traditional and highly practical. Ethnic cuisine calls for wine from the same region or one of that style. Sparkling wines are perfect for festive affairs because their effervescence matches the mood as no other wines can. Aperitif wines greatly enhance the meal to follow. Dessert wines are frequently overlooked as a component of elegant dining. Remember port, liqueurs and brandies with or instead of the coffee.

*MORE THAN ONE WINE:* Multiple course meals are usually accompanied by several wines. It is just as easy to serve one bottle of two different wines as to serve two bottles of the same wine. Selecting two or more wines for a dinner is no more difficult than selecting each wine to complement the dish with which it will be served. The guidelines for serving two or more wines are quite simple: white before red, light before heavy, dry before sweet, young before old, lesser before better. Serving two or three wines of similar style with the same course stimulates the most remarkable conversations.

*PITFALLS:* Gracious dining is not enhanced by prolonged and/or excessive drinking before the meal. Avoid vinegar by substituting lemon juice in equal amounts in the recipe or serving the dish late in the meal after the wines have been served. Highly spiced foods (and there are many in Louisiana cuisine) may overwhelm the wine. Be especially careful with curry. Sweet preparations are not enhanced by dry table wines although desserts are marvelous with a luscious dessert wine.

*THE POCKETBOOK:* The most expensive wine is not always the best wine in its class or for the occasion, but generally you should serve the best wine you can afford. A sufficient quantity of sound inexpensive wine is highly more satisfactory than skimpy allotments of famous and costly wine. If your budget is limited, try serving three or more inexpensive wines with dinner and you will be amazed at the transformation of simple fare into real elegance! Your guests will be delighted but probably not realize why the meal was so exciting.

*WINE SERVICE:* Use large (at least 8 ounce) stemmed clear glasses which are tapered slightly at the top and which are filled about halfway. Chill white wines and rosé, but not too much, and serve reds at room temperature, except perhaps very light red wines which may be slightly chilled in the summer. Although most of the other conventions of wine etiquette and traditional service are reasonable enough and have merit, they are unnecessary for the enjoyment of wine. The real key to drinking wine with food is just to do what comes naturally and feels comfortable.

We hope these wine suggestions will help you to "pass a good time" with *Louisiana Entertains.*

*Virginia and Jeems White*

# Morning

# TABLE FOR TWO                              *(Serves 2)*

An extraordinary beginning.

*\*Mimosa*

*\*Eggs Sardou   or   \*Eggs Stravinsky*
*French Bread*

*\*Dessert Pancake*

*\*French-dripped Coffee*

## Mimosa

8   ounces orange juice, chilled        6½ ounces champagne, chilled

Combine in pitcher; serve in oversized frosted wine glasses.


## Eggs Sardou

1½ tablespoons butter              ¼   teaspoon pepper
10  ounces spinach, cooked and     ¼   teaspoon nutmeg
    well-drained                   ¼   teaspoon sugar
1   tablespoon flour               4   artichoke bottoms, warmed in
¼   cup cream                          salt water
½   teaspoon salt                  4   eggs, poached

Melt butter in saucepan; add spinach and cook 3 minutes. Sprinkle with the flour, stir and add cream. Cook 5 minutes over low heat. Add seasonings. Spinach sauce may be made ahead and refrigerated. Reheat gently when ready to assemble the dish.

Put spinach on serving plates and place 2 artichoke bottoms on each serving, each artichoke topped with a poached egg. Cover with Hollandaise sauce.

*Martha B. Walker*


## Eggs Stravinsky

2   English muffins, split and     2   ounces black caviar
    toasted                        4   eggs, poached

Spread muffin halves with caviar; top with eggs. Cover with Hollandaise sauce.

*Lillie G. Goldstein*

### Hollandaise Sauce

¼  pound butter, divided into thirds          ⅛  teaspoon salt
4   egg yolks, beaten                               ⅛  teaspoon cayenne
2   tablespoons lemon juice

Place one piece of the butter in the top of a double boiler over hot but not boiling water. Beat in egg yolks and lemon juice. When butter is completely melted, add another piece and beat until melted. Repeat with third piece of butter. Proper consistency should be reached by the time all butter is melted. Remove from heat and add seasonings. Keeps for a short time over warm water. If mixture separates and looks curdled, add a small amount of boiling water while beating constantly until sauce "returns"

## Dessert Pancake

⅓  cup flour                                    2   tablespoons butter or margarine
¼  teaspoon baking powder              Confectioners' sugar
⅓  cup milk                                     Lemon wedges
2   eggs, beaten

Combine flour and baking powder. Beat in milk and eggs, leaving batter a bit lumpy. Melt butter in a 10-inch cast iron skillet. When butter is melted, pour in batter all at once in the center. Bake at 425° for 15 to 18 minutes until pancake is golden. (It will rise up the sides and puff.) Remove from oven and immediately sprinkle with the confectioners' sugar (generously) and squeeze lemon wedges over it all. *Do not* double the recipe. Serve immediately.

Yield: 2 large servings or 4 small servings

*Fred Simon*

## French-dripped Coffee

1   cup drip grind dark roast coffee
     (or coffee and chicory)
4   cups boiling water

Fill "basket" with grounds and assemble pot.

Set coffee pot in a pan of simmering water on stove. Wet grounds by pouring ⅛ cup cold water into top of pot. When this has settled into grounds, begin dripping coffee by pouring boiling water into pot, no more than ⅛ cup at a time. Each time wait until the grounds have ceased to bubble before adding more boiling water.

Leftover coffee may be stored indefinitely in refrigerator and used for *café au lait.*

Yield: 8 demitasse

# BREAKFAST IN BED                    (Serves 2)

Continental breakfast on a tray.

## Orange Juice
## *Brioche
## *Mayhaw Jelly      *Kumquat Marmalade
## *Café au Lait

## Brioche

| | |
|---|---|
| 1   cup milk | 4   eggs, beaten |
| ¼   pound butter | 1   teaspoon grated lemon peel |
| 1   teaspoon salt | 5   to 6 cups flour |
| ½   cup sugar | 1   egg yolk |
| 2   packages yeast | 1   tablespoon milk |
| ¼   cup warm water | |

Scald milk; stir in butter, salt and sugar. Cool to lukewarm. Sprinkle yeast on warm water; stir to dissolve. Combine eggs and lemon peel and add to this the yeast and milk mixtures. Beat in flour a cup at a time; the dough will be soft to handle and will not be kneaded. Grease top of dough, cover and let rise in a warm place until doubled (1½ to 2 hours).

Punch down and refrigerate 4 to 6 hours until dough can be handled.

Shape ⅔ of the dough into smooth balls about 1½ inches in diameter. Shape remaining dough into ½ inch balls. Work quickly as dough will soften. Place large balls in greased muffin tins. Make a dent with finger and place small ball on top. Brush with egg yolk mixed with 1 tablespoon milk. Cover and let rise until doubled (1 hour).

Bake at 425° for about 10 minutes until brown. Remove from pans at once and place on wire rack. Serve warm or reheat in foil. Freezes well.

Yield: 2 dozen rolls

*Audrey G. Hammill*

## Mayhaw Jelly

The mayhaw, or Riverflat Hawthorn, is a small thorny tree widely found in Southern swamps and wetlands. From May to June it produces shiny reddish fruits ½ to ¾ inches in diameter that make a fine tart jelly.

Juice:

| | |
|---|---|
| 1 gallon mayhaws, washed, drained, stems removed | Water to cover |

Boil slowly in large pot until berries are soft. Pour off juice and reserve; then add half as much water as at the first cooking and boil again for about 45 minutes. Strain juice through cheesecloth. Allow berries to drip through cloth overnight if possible. Squeeze out pulp and reserve for making mayhaw pies (recipe page 163). Pulp may be frozen. Combine juice from both cookings and strain again.

Jelly:

| | |
|---|---|
| 4 cups mayhaw juice | 2 to 4 cups sugar, depending on |
| 1 tablespoon grain alcohol (optional) | alcohol test |

Test juice by mixing grain alcohol with 1 tablespoon juice. If juice is very thin and runny, use half as much sugar as juice, i.e., 2 cups sugar to 4 cups juice. If fairly thin, use 3 cups sugar to each 4 cups juice; if firm, use cup for cup. Test is optional but helpful.

Measure juice into large pot; add sugar and cook slowly to 220° on candy thermometer. Test by dipping a metal spoon into mixture and observing that 2 drops remain briefly on spoon when held above boiling jelly. Pour into hot sterilized jars and seal.

Yield: 28 ounces jelly

*Annie Lou S. McBride*

## Kumquat Marmalade

Kumquats are small tropical citrus fruits introduced to Louisiana in the early 18th century.

Wash, slice, and seed kumquats. Run through food processor in one quick on-off motion. Do not purée. For each 2 cups chopped kumquats, use 1 cup sugar and ½ cup water. Cover and simmer until desired thickness, about 1½ to 2 hours. Pour into sterilized jars.

*Betty Fay W. Lipsey*

## Café au Lait

| | |
|---|---|
| 2 cups strong black dripped coffee, heated to boiling | 2 cups milk, heated Sugar to taste |

Pour each cup half full of coffee; add an equal amount of milk. Sweeten as desired.

Yield: 4 cups

# PAIN PERDU                                   (Serves 4)

Pain perdu, literally "lost bread," originated as a use for leftover stale bread. Ribbon cane syrup, made from Louisiana sugar cane, is the choice for Louisiana tables.

### *Broiled Grapefruit*

### *Pain Perdu*   or   *French Toast*
### Ribbon Cane Syrup

### Coffee

## Broiled Grapefruit

2   grapefruit, halved                    4   maraschino cherries
4   teaspoons grenadine

Pour 1 teaspoon of grenadine over each grapefruit half and top with a cherry. Broil until golden and bubbly. Serve immediately.

## Pain Perdu

1   egg, beaten                          ¼   teaspoon salt
1   teaspoon vanilla                     ½   teaspoon cinnamon
2   tablespoons sugar                    6   slices day-old bread, halved
1   cup milk                             ¼   pound margarine

Beat together first 6 ingredients; dip bread slices into mixture. In a small skillet, melt margarine and fry bread slices over medium-high heat until golden brown and crusty.

## French Toast

3   eggs                                 ¼   teaspoon salt
1   cup milk                             6   slices white bread, halved
2   tablespoons Grand Marnier            ¼   cup vegetable oil
1   tablespoon sugar                     Confectioners' sugar for topping
½   teaspoon vanilla

Beat together eggs, milk and flavorings. Arrange bread slices in a flat dish and pour liquid over them, making sure each slice is well saturated. Cover and refrigerate overnight. Sauté until golden in hot oil and sprinkle with confectioners' sugar.

# COMPANY BREAKFAST  (Serves 6)

Visitors to Louisiana may expect to be served fresh figs during the brief midsummer harvesting season or may sample the wealth of preserved figs from the pantry. Fig trees are well-adapted to Gulf Coast states. The "Celeste" variety, the most popular in Louisiana, yields an abundant crop.

### Fresh Figs or Pineapple

### *Spicy Breakfast Casserole

### *Raisin Bran Muffins
### or
### *Refrigerator Muffins
### *Strawberry-Fig Jelly     *Fig-Lemon Conserve

### Coffee or Tea

## Spicy Breakfast Casserole

| | |
|---|---|
| 1 pound bulk pork sausage, cooked, crumbled, and drained | Salt and pepper to taste |
| 1 dozen eggs, beaten | 1 4-ounce can green chilies, chopped and drained |
| ¾ cup milk | 4 ounces Cheddar cheese, grated |

Combine eggs and seasonings. Place sausage in a 1½-quart baking dish. Pour egg mixture over sausage. Sprinkle with chilies, then cheese. Bake uncovered at 325° for 20 to 25 minutes. (Sausage may be cooked ahead and dish assembled easily before breakfast.)

*Irma S. Boyer*

## Raisin Bran Muffins

| | |
|---|---|
| 5 cups sifted flour | 1 15-ounce box Raisin Bran |
| 4 teaspoons baking soda | 4 eggs, beaten |
| 3 cups sugar | 1 quart buttermilk |
| 2 teaspoons salt | 1 cup melted shortening |

Resift flour with soda in a large bowl. Add remaining ingredients and mix well. May be refrigerated at this point up to 1 month. Half-fill greased muffin cups. Bake at 400° for 30 to 45 minutes or until lightly browned.

*Sarah B. Willis*

## Refrigerator Muffins

| | |
|---|---|
| 2 cups boiling water | 1 cup corn oil |
| 2 cups Nabisco 100% Bran | 3 cups sugar |
| 5 cups sifted flour | 4 eggs |
| 5 teaspoons baking soda | 4 cups Kellogg's All-Bran |
| 1 teaspoon salt | 1 quart buttermilk |

Mix water and Nabisco Bran and let stand. Sift flour, soda, and salt; add oil and sugar. Beat in eggs, 1 at a time. Combine with first mixture and add remaining ingredients, mixing well. Store in refrigerator.

Bake as needed in greased muffin cups 15 to 20 minutes at 375°. May be baked ahead and frozen.

*Ouita B. Steel*


## Strawberry-Fig Jelly

| | |
|---|---|
| 6 cups figs | 4 3-ounce packages strawberry |
| 6 cups sugar | gelatin dessert |
| 2 tablespoons lemon juice (optional) | |

Mix first 3 ingredients and let stand for several hours or overnight. Add gelatin to fig mixture in a 5-quart saucepan. Place on low heat, bring to a boil and continue to boil for 20 minutes. Pour into sterilized jars and seal.

Yield: 8 6-ounce jars

*Helen S. Juneau*


## Fig-Lemon Conserve

| | |
|---|---|
| 4 cups quartered fully-ripe figs | 1 3-ounce package lemon gelatin |
| 4 cups sugar | dessert |

Mix figs and sugar in a heavy saucepan. Cook on low heat for 15 minutes. Add gelatin; mix well and seal in hot jars.

Yield: 2 pints

*Betty Fay W. Lipsey*

# BIRTHDAY CELEBRATION *(Serves 6)*

A Louisiana senator's favorite.

### *Honeydew Melon*
### *\*Wild Doves*
### *\*Cheese Grits    \*Banana Fritters*
### *\*Biscuits*
### *\*Pear Preserves    \*Fig Preserves*
### *Coffee    Tea*

## Wild Doves

| | |
|---|---|
| 8 doves | 1 green pepper, finely chopped |
| Lemon-pepper | 4 tablespoons bacon drippings |
| Garlic salt | 1 orange or tangerine, peeled, |
| 1 cup flour | seeded and chopped |
| 2 onions, finely chopped | Peeling of one orange or tangerine, |
| 6 ribs celery, including tops, finely chopped | chopped |

Season doves inside and out with lemon-pepper and garlic salt. Coat each bird with flour. Stuff with a small amount of the vegetables. Brown doves in fat in iron Dutch oven. Pour off excess grease; add remaining vegetables, fruit pieces and peel. Cover tightly and bake in 300° oven for 1 hour. Do not lift lid during cooking time.

*Mary G. Johnston*

## Cheese Grits

| | |
|---|---|
| 1 cup grits | ¼ pound margarine |
| 4 cups boiling water | 1 6-ounce roll garlic cheese |
| ½ teaspoon salt | 2 eggs, separated |

Stir grits and salt into water. Cook, stirring occasionally, 4 minutes. Add margarine, cheese, and beaten egg yolks. Beat egg whites until stiff and fold into grits. Pour into a buttered 2-quart casserole and bake at 350° for 45 minutes or until brown and bubbly.

*Bee H. Randolph*

## Banana Fritters

1   cup sifted flour
1¼ teaspoons baking powder
¼  teaspoon salt
1   egg, beaten

⅓  cup milk
2   teaspoons salad oil
3   bananas, quartered
Salad oil for frying

Combine dry ingredients. Beat egg with milk and oil; stir into dry mixture. Coat bananas in batter and fry in deep fat at 375° until brown. Drain and serve hot.

*Betsy B. Hardin*

## Biscuits

2   cups flour
3   teaspoons baking powder
1   teaspoon salt

¾  cup shortening
¾  cup milk

Sift together dry ingredients. Cut in shortening, then add milk all at once and stir with a fork. Knead lightly on a floured board or wax paper. Roll out dough to approximately ½ inch thick and cut into rounds. Bake at 450° for 8 to 12 minutes.
Yield:  18  2½-inch rounds

*Jean A. Lafleur*

## Pear Preserves

24  cups sliced green pears (18 to
      19 pounds or 36 pears)
7½ cups sugar

⅜  cup lemon juice
¾  cup water

Peel, core and slice pears into medium sized pieces. Combine all ingredients and cook in enameled pan until pears are clear (transparent) and juice is thickened, stirring frequently. If pears become clear before juice is thickened, remove pears and continue cooking juice. Return pears to juice and reheat before placing in sterilized jars.
Yield:  4 to 5 pints

*Bernice C. Woods*

## Fig Preserves

2  gallons figs
2  gallons water
½ cup baking soda

5  pounds sugar
1½ to 2 lemons, thinly sliced

Dissolve soda in water and soak figs 15 minutes; rinse thoroughly and drain. Put figs in a heavy saucepan with sugar and lemons. Start cooking on very lowest heat until sugar melts, stirring to prevent sticking. Gradually increase heat to medium and allow mixture to simmer, uncovered, for 3 hours, or until mixture reaches desired consistency. Pour into hot jars and seal immediately.

Yield:  8 to 9 pints

*Betty Fay W. Lipsey*

# SLUMBER PARTY BREAKFAST          *(Serves 8)*

For a houseful of overnight guests, serve a "specialty of the house": homemade sausage. The custom of making one's own sausage in Louisiana derives from the Acadian *boucherie*, or butchering, when families gathered to prepare meat for the winter.

### *Fresh Fruits*

### *\*Homemade Sausage Patties*

### *\*Pick of Pancakes*
### *\*Fruit Syrups and Sauces*

### *Cold Milk      Hot Chocolate*


## *Homemade Sausage Patties*

| | |
|---|---|
| 5  pounds semi-coarsely ground pork | 1  tablespoon sugar |
| 2  tablespoons salt | 1  tablespoon black pepper |
| | 2  tablespoons fennel seed or sage |

Add seasonings to pork. Stuff into casings or form into patties. Fry until done. Freezes well.

*Joseph Rizzo*


## *Fluffy Pancakes*

| | |
|---|---|
| 2  cups flour | 2  cups milk |
| ½  teaspoon salt | 4  rounded tablespoons sour |
| 2  tablespoons sugar | cream |
| 2  tablespoons baking powder | 4  tablespoons melted butter, |
| 2  eggs | cooled |

Mix dry ingredients in a large bowl. Combine eggs, milk, and sour cream and pour into the dry ingredients slowly, beating with a whisk to prevent lumping. Add butter and beat until smooth. Batter may be kept several days in the refrigerator, covered. It will thicken, so, before cooking, add about 4 tablespoons of milk in which 1 teaspoon of baking powder has been dissolved. These may be frozen and reheated.

Yield: 2 dozen pancakes

## Nutritious Pancakes

2  cups cottage cheese  
6  eggs, beaten  
½ teaspoon salt

4  tablespoons butter or margarine  
½ cup sifted flour

Blend cottage cheese until smooth. Add remaining ingredients and beat until well blended.  
Yield: 2 dozen pancakes

## Griddle Cakes

2  cups flour  
2  tablespoons sugar  
2  teaspoons salt  
2  teaspoons baking powder

2  eggs  
1½ cups milk  
6  tablespoons melted shortening

Mix dry ingredients. Beat eggs and milk together and add to flour mixture. Add shortening and blend well. If too thick, add up to ½ cup more milk.  
Yield: 2 dozen pancakes

## Apple Syrup

1  cup apple juice  
2  cups sugar

Cinnamon stick

Bring to boil, stirring. Cool and seal in sterilized jars.

## Berry Syrup

1  10-ounce package frozen  
   berries

2  cups sugar  
½ cup water

Bring all ingredients to boil, stirring. Skim off foam with metal spoon. Pour into sterilized jars and seal.

## Orange or Grape Syrup

1  cup orange or grape juice  
2  cups sugar

2  tablespoons lemon juice

Combine juice and sugar and bring to boil, stirring. Skim off foam with metal spoon, add lemon juice and seal in jars.

## Brown Sugar Syrup

1   cup brown sugar                      4   tablespoons butter
Pinch salt                                    ¼   teaspoon vanilla
½   cup water

   Combine first 4 ingredients. Cook until thick; add flavoring.

## Colonial Syrup

1   cup maple syrup                     ½   teaspoon cinnamon
½   cup honey                             ½   cup crushed caraway seeds

   Mix together and bring to a hard boil, stirring. Cool.

## Cream and Honey Sauce

⅔   cup light honey                      ⅛   teaspoon cloves
⅔   cup heavy cream or evaporated   ⅛   teaspoon allspice
     milk                                    ⅛   teaspoon nutmeg
¼   teaspoon cinnamon

   Bring honey to a hard boil. Remove from heat and add remaining ingredients, blending well. Return to heat and stir until sauce reaches boiling point. Cool.

## Burnt Sugar Sauce

1   cup granulated sugar               ½   cup warm water

   Over high heat in a black iron skillet, stir and scrape the sugar with a wooden spoon until it forms lumps. When it begins to melt, lower heat; continue stirring and scraping until clear and golden brown, resembling a syrup. Add water all at once. Continue stirring over low heat until mixture has no lumps and reaches a thin syrup consistency. Do not overcook. This will thicken as it stands.

# CHRISTMAS MORNING (Serves 8)

Setting the scene for a festive day with Southern flair.

*Milk Punch   or   *Eggnog

*Sausage Coffee Cake   or   *Louisiana Coffee Cake

*Holiday Baked Apples

Coffee

## Milk Punch

10 to 12 ice cubes, depending
    on size
6 ounces whiskey or brandy

4 cups milk
4 tablespoons sugar
Nutmeg to taste

The above ingredients are sufficient for 2 batches in an electric blender.
Place ice in blender with liquor. Add milk and sugar. Frappé well. Strain.
Sprinkle with nutmeg.

*Conway E. Crossland*

## Eggnog

10 eggs, separated
¾ cup sugar
1¼ cups bourbon

1 quart heavy cream
Nutmeg to taste

Beat egg yolks until thick and creamy. Mix in sugar. Add whiskey very
slowly. Beat egg whites until stiff. Fold yolk mixture into whites. Whip cream
until it forms peaks and fold into egg mixture. Sprinkle with freshly ground
nutmeg.
Yield: 8 7-ounce servings

*Tollie C. Alexander*

## Sausage Coffee Cake

1   pound bulk sausage
½ cup chopped onions
¼ cup grated Parmesan cheese
½ cup grated Swiss cheese
1   egg, beaten
¼ teaspoon Tabasco
1½ teaspoons salt

2   tablespoons chopped parsley
2   cups Bisquick
¾ cup milk
¼ cup mayonnaise
1   egg yolk
1   tablespoon water

Brown sausage and onions; drain. Add next 6 ingredients. Make batter of Bisquick, milk and mayonnaise. Spread half of batter in 9×9×2-inch greased pan. Pour in sausage mixture, then spread remaining batter on top. Mix egg yolk and water and brush top. Bake at 400° for 25 to 30 minutes or until cake leaves edges of pan. Cool 5 minutes before cutting into 3-inch squares. This recipe doubles easily in a 9 × 13-inch pan. Freezes well.

*Joan K. Kaye*

## Louisiana Coffee Cake

½ pound butter
1   cup sugar
3   eggs
1   cup sour cream
2½ cups sifted cake flour
1   tablespoon baking powder
1   teaspoon baking soda

Pinch of salt
1   teaspoon vanilla
1   teaspoon lemon extract
1   cup toasted chopped nuts
½ cup sugar
2   teaspoons cinnamon
4   tablespoons butter

Cream together butter and sugar. Add eggs 1 at a time, then sour cream, continuing to beat. Resift and gradually add 2 cups of the flour. Resift the remaining ½ cup flour with baking powder, soda, and salt and fold into batter by hand. Fold in flavorings. Pour half the batter into a greased and floured 8½×12-inch pan.

Combine nuts, sugar, and cinnamon. Sprinkle half of this mixture over batter in pan. Cover with remaining batter and sprinkle the other half of the nut mixture on top. Dot with butter. Bake at 350° for 30 minutes. Cool in pan, refrigerate, and reheat when ready to serve. Freezes well.

*Miriam W. Levy*

## *Holiday Baked Apples*

¾  cup raisins
1½ cups white wine
8   cooking apples, cored

¼  teaspoon grated lemon peel
4   tablespoons sugar
1½ tablespoons butter

Soak raisins in wine for ½ hour. Drain, reserving wine. Stuff apples with raisins. Sprinkle with lemon peel and sugar. Dot with butter and add wine. Bake at 400° for 35 minutes. Serve hot or cold.

*Leda B. Mazzoli*

# HOUSE PARTY                                    *(Serves 8)*

Prepared at home and easily transported to a weekend vacation spot for last minute baking. A basket of satsumas, a variety of tangerine with special sweetness grown alongside the Mississippi River below New Orleans, is an added treat.

*Bloody Marys*
*Cheese Krispies*     Louisiana Satsumas

*Sausage Soufflé*
*Baked Tomatoes*     *Anadama Bread*

*Coffee*

## Bloody Marys

46  ounces tomato juice
¼  cup lemon juice
¼  cup Worcestershire sauce
1   teaspoon Tabasco sauce

1½ teaspoons salt
1   teaspoon pepper
2   cups vodka
1   tablespoon celery seeds

Mix first 6 ingredients and chill. When ready to serve, stir in vodka. Sprinkle each serving with celery seeds.
Yield: 11  6-ounce drinks

## Cheese Krispies

½  pound margarine, softened
2   cups grated sharp cheese
2   cups sifted flour
½  teaspoon salt

1   teaspoon cayenne
2   cups Rice Krispies
1   cup pecan halves (optional)

Cream margarine and cheese. Add flour, salt and pepper. Stir cereal in by hand. Shape into small balls and place on ungreased cookie sheet. Flatten each ball with a fork. Top with pecan half if desired. Bake at 300° for 20 minutes. Store tightly covered. Freezes well.
Yield: 6 dozen

*Elia E. Thomas*

## Sausage Soufflé

| | |
|---|---|
| 1 pound bulk pork sausage, cooked, crumbled, and drained | 5 eggs |
| | 2 cups half and half |
| 6 slices bread, crusts removed | 1 teaspoon salt |
| 3 tablespoons butter | 1 teaspoon dry mustard |
| 1½ cups grated Cheddar cheese | |

Butter bread and cut into cubes. Place in 9×13-inch baking dish. Sprinkle with sausage; top with cheese. Beat remaining ingredients together and pour over sausage mixture. Chill overnight. Bake uncovered at 350° for 40 to 45 minutes.

Variation: 2 cups diced ham may be substituted for sausage.

*Nancy C. Weems*

## Baked Tomatoes

| | |
|---|---|
| 8 tomatoes | 4 tablespoons butter |
| Salt and pepper to taste | Garlic salt to taste |
| 2 cups Italian-seasoned bread crumbs | |

Halve tomatoes and sprinkle with salt and pepper. Cover the cut side thickly with bread crumbs. Dot with butter; sprinkle with garlic salt. Bake for 15 minutes at 375°. Do not overcook as tomatoes will get mushy.

*Clarice S. Johns*

## Anadama Bread

| | |
|---|---|
| 6 to 7 cups whole wheat flour | 1½ cups water |
| ½ cup corn meal | 3 tablespoons butter |
| 1 teaspoon salt | 1 cup milk |
| 3 packages yeast | ½ cup unsulphured molasses |

In large bowl thoroughly mix 2½ cups flour, corn meal, salt, and yeast. Heat water, butter, and milk to 120° and add to mixture. Stir in molasses and beat 2 minutes at medium speed, scraping bowl occasionally. Stir in additional flour to make a stiff dough. Knead on a lightly floured board until smooth and elastic. Divide dough in half and cover with plastic wrap to rise until doubled in bulk. Place in 2 greased 9×5×3-inch loaf pans. Bake at 350° for about an hour, until loaf pulls slightly away from pan edges.

*Cherry C. Grosz*

# EARLY ON A FROSTY MORNIN'     *(Serves 10)*

An impressive all-in-one entrée made from what's in the cupboard.

### *Homegrown Tomato Juice*
### *Hidden Treasure*
### *Sautéed Apple Rings*
### Coffee

## Homegrown Tomato Juice

10  pounds fully ripe tomatoes,          1  cup chopped carrots
    quartered                        1  cup chopped celery
2  cups chopped onion                    Salt and pepper to taste
2  cups chopped green papper

Combine ingredients in large cooking pot. Simmer, covered, for 45 to 60 minutes, until vegetables are mushy. Press through sieve or colander, extracting all juice from cooked mixture. Place juice in pan and heat to boiling. Pour into scalded jars and seal.
Chill and stir well before serving.
Yield: 2 quarts

*Juanita M. Wilson*
*Burt W. Sperry*

## Hidden Treasure

10  slices bread                         12  ounces Cheddar cheese, sliced
5   tablespoons butter                   15  slices bacon, halved and
10  eggs                                     partially cooked

Butter bread and place on cookie sheet. Separate eggs, placing yolk in center of each slice. Surround yolk with pieces of cheese, enough to cover bread to edges. Beat egg whites to a stiff meringue; spread over top of bread, yolk and cheese—like frosting, piling to edge of crust. Top with bacon. Bake at 375° for 15 minutes.

*Persis J. Crawford*

## Sautéed Apple Rings

6  MacIntosh apples, cored and
   sliced into rings
¼  pound butter
½  cup sugar
3  tablespoons water
Lemon juice (optional)

In a large skillet, melt butter and add apple slices. Sprinkle each slice with ½ teaspoon sugar and sauté for 2 minutes. Turn slices, sprinkle each with another ½ teaspoon sugar, and sauté for 2 minutes. Remove apples to serving dish. Add water to skillet, swirl, and heat until water evaporates. Spoon sauce over apples. If apples are bland, sprinkle slices with lemon juice before adding sugar.

*Audrey G. Hammill*

# BELLES CALAS! TOUT CHAUD!          *(Serves 10)*

Hot calas add a New Orleans flavor to this brunch. Calas are fluffy fried rice cakes whose name is derived from their African origins. Hungry churchgoers on French Quarter streets after Mass welcomed the cry "Belles calas! tout chaud!" from the turbanned calas women who balanced on their heads baskets of the hot cakes.

### *Orange Champagne Cocktail*

#### *Ham Alexandria*
#### *Poached Pears*

#### *Calas*
#### Coffee

## Orange Champagne Cocktail

1   quart champagne, chilled
1   quart ginger ale, chilled

2   cups orange juice, chilled
1   pint strawberries, sliced

Combine liquids in a pitcher. Serve in glasses topped with a few slices of strawberries as a garnish.

## Ham Alexandria

6    tablespoons butter
½    pound mushrooms, sliced
2    14-ounce cans artichoke hearts, drained and quartered
3    tablespoons flour
2    cups milk
1    cup grated Swiss cheese

Salt and pepper to taste
5    English muffins, halved and toasted
10   slices baked ham
2    eggs, hard-boiled and sliced
20   pimiento strips

In a skillet melt 2 tablespoons butter. Add mushrooms and sauté 2 to 3 minutes. Add artichokes and sauté for another 3 minutes. Transfer to a bowl. In the same skillet, melt remaining butter; add flour and stir until smooth. Gradually add milk, stirring until thickened. Stir in cheese until melted. Mix with mushrooms and artichokes. Season to taste.

Arrange muffin halves on a platter; layer with ham slices; cover generously with sauce mixture. Garnish with eggs and pimientoes.

*Audrey G. Hammill*

## Poached Pears

5   pears, peeled, cored and halved     1½ cups red wine
¾  cup sugar                              2   cinnamon sticks
½  cup water

Combine sugar, wine, water and cinnamon sticks in large saucepan. Boil 5 minutes. Add pears; simmer, covered, for 15 minutes or until tender when pierced. Remove pears. Boil down syrup until thick. Pour syrup over pears and refrigerate. Will keep for several days. Serve hot or cold.
Variation: Mix peaches with pears.

*Theodosia M. Nolan*

## Calas

3   cups boiling water        6   tablespoons flour
½  cup rice                   ½  teaspoon vanilla
½  package yeast              Cinnamon and nutmeg to taste
½  cup lukewarm water         Vegetable oil for deep frying
2   eggs, beaten             Confectioners' sugar
½  cup sugar

Add rice to boiling water, cover and reduce heat; cook about 25 minutes or until rice is soft and mushy. Drain and cool. Mix yeast with warm water. Mash rice and mix well with yeast. Set in a warm place to rise overnight or about 12 hours.

Add eggs to rice mixture; stir in sugar, flour, and flavorings. Allow to rise 15 minutes. Shape into balls or cakes. Fry in deep fat (370°) until brown. Drain; sprinkle with confectioners' sugar and serve hot.

*Jacque S. Caplan*

# VERSATILE CARTE                                    *(Serves 10)*

A light and attractive brunch or late supper.

## *Quiche Soufflé   or   *Spinach Quiche
### *Brandied Peaches
### *Blonde Brownies
### Coffee

*Meursault or California Pinot Blanc*

## Quiche Soufflé

2   9-inch pie shells, baked 7          1   teaspoon salt
    minutes and cooled                 ¼   teaspoon nutmeg (optional)
8   eggs, separated                    3   cups grated Swiss cheese
3   cups half and half

Combine egg yolks, cream, salt and nutmeg. Fold into stiffly beaten egg whites. Add grated cheese and pour into pie shells. Bake at 350° for 40 to 45 minutes. Let stand 5 minutes before serving. Top with crab sauce.

### Crab Sauce

2   cups crabmeat                      1   teaspoon salt
4   tablespoons butter, melted         2   cups half and half
4   tablespoons flour                  Cayenne or black pepper to taste

Heat crabmeat in butter. Blend in flour and salt. Add cream and season to taste. Cook over medium heat, stirring constantly until thickened.
Variation: 2 cups cooked shrimp may be substituted for crabmeat.

*Susan R. Chadwick*

## Spinach Quiche

2   9-inch pie shells, baked 7          2   teaspoons salt
    minutes and cooled                 ½   teaspoon pepper
½   cup diced onion                    Dash of nutmeg
2   cups shredded Mozzarella           20  ounces spinach, cooked and
    cheese                                 well-drained.
4   eggs, beaten                       4   tablespoons grated Parmesan
2   cups plain yogurt                      cheese (optional)
2   tablespoons flour

Sprinkle onion and cheese over bottom of pie shells. Add yogurt, flour and seasonings to eggs. Stir spinach into egg mixture and pour into pie shells. Sprinkle with Parmesan cheese and bake at 350° for 35 minutes.

*Ruth O. Prince*

## Brandied Peaches

2   29-ounce cans peach halves
¾ to 1 cup brandy
¾  cup firmly packed brown sugar
½  cup cider vinegar
3   sticks cinnamon
1   tablespoon whole cloves

Drain syrup from peaches and reserve. Decrease amount of syrup by as much brandy as you plan to use. Add brandy to syrup and combine with sugar, vinegar and spices. Simmer for 5 minutes and pour over peaches. Marinate in refrigerator for several hours. Serve cold.

*Suzonne K. Hunter*

## Blonde Brownies

4   cups flour
2   teaspoons baking powder
½  teaspoon baking soda
2   teaspoons salt
1⅓ cups margarine, melted
4   cups brown sugar
4   eggs, beaten
2   teaspoons vanilla
1   12-ounce package chocolate chips
1   cup chopped pecans (optional)

Sift flour with baking powder, soda and salt. Combine brown sugar with margarine; cool, and stir in eggs and vanilla. Mix with the dry ingredients and spread in 2 greased, floured 9×12-inch pans. Mix nuts and chocolate chips and sprinkle on top of batter. Bake at 325° for 35 to 40 minutes.

Variation: Substitute butterscotch chips for chocolate chips, or combine in equal amounts.

Yield: 8 dozen 1½-inch squares

*David J. Norman*

# AFTER THE HUNT                    *(Serves 10)*

Hearty midmorning fare.

**\*Bloody Bulls**

**\*Oysters in Patty Shells**

**\*Quail**
**\*Apricot Rice        \*Popovers**

**\*Fruit Coupe**
**Coffee**

## Bloody Bulls

3   quarts tomato juice
2   10½-ounce cans beef broth
3   cups vodka
1½ teaspoons salt
1½ teaspoons pepper

½ cup lemon juice
½ cup Worcestershire sauce
1½ teaspoons celery salt
1½ teaspoons Tabasco

Mix and serve cold over ice.

*Leta'dele B. Defee*
*Frances M. Cox*

## Oysters in Patty Shells

3   pints oysters, drained, liquor
    reserved
8   tablespoons finely chopped
    green onions and tops
8   tablespoons finely chopped
    celery
8   tablespoons butter
8   tablespoons flour

2½ to 3 cups cream
2   teaspoons salt
1   teaspoon paprika
Pepper to taste
4   teaspoons lemon juice
2   teaspoons Worcestershire sauce
8   tablespoons minced parsley
10  patty shells

Sauté onions and celery in butter until limp. Add flour, and, when bubbly, add cream and oyster liquor. Cook, stirring, until thick and smooth. Add seasonings and oysters. Bring to the boiling point, but do not allow to boil. Remove from fire, stir in parsley, spoon into patty shells and serve immediately.

*Susan R. Chadwick*

## Quail

| | | | |
|---|---|---|---|
| 2 | cloves garlic, pressed | 4 | tablespoons soy sauce |
| 4 | tablespoons brown sugar | 2 | teaspoons oregano |
| 1 | cup salad oil | 2 | teaspoons marjoram |
| 1 | cup white wine | 10 | quail |

Combine first 7 ingredients and pour over quail. Marinate for at least an hour. Bake in a Dutch oven at 325° for 1 hour or until tender.

*Smitty G. Bowdon*

## Apricot Rice

| | | | |
|---|---|---|---|
| 6 | ounces dried apricots | 3 | cups cooked rice |
| ½ | cup finely chopped onion | 1 | teaspoon salt |
| 1 | cup finely chopped celery | | White pepper to taste |
| 4 | tablespoons butter | ¼ | cup chopped parsley |

Soak fruit in water to cover for 30 minutes. Drain and mince. Steam onions and celery in butter in a tightly covered saucepan until wilted. Combine with remaining ingredients and blend well. Bake 40 minutes at 375° in a greased 1½-quart casserole.

## Popovers

| | | | |
|---|---|---|---|
| 2 | cups milk | 4 | tablespoons melted butter, |
| 2 | cups sifted flour | | cooled |
| 4 | eggs | 1 | teaspoon salt |

In a blender, mix all ingredients until the batter is just combined. Half fill 12 greased muffin cups with the batter. Bake on a preheated baking sheet at 425° for 30 minutes or until well-puffed and crisp. Serve immediately.

*Audrey G. Hammill*

## Fruit Coupe

| | | | |
|---|---|---|---|
| 1 | pint yogurt | 1 | pint strawberries |
| 1 | 20-ounce can pineapple chunks, drained and chilled | ½ | cup flaked or shredded coconut |
| 1 | 20-ounce can fruit cocktail, drained and chilled | 4 | tablespoons honey |

Mix yogurt, fruit, ¼ cup of coconut and 2 tablespoons honey. Chill. When ready to serve, dribble with remaining honey and coconut.

*Alexandria General Nutrition Center*

# BRUNCH À LA CREOLE                    *(Serves 12)*

A true Creole is a descendant of early French and Spanish settlers in Louisiana. Today the word has come to be associated with the cooking indigenous to New Orleans and south Louisiana. Here is the epitome of a Creole brunch.

Basic to the majority of Creole dishes is a roux, that rich mixture of fat and flour browned slowly together to a dark chocolate color.

### *Creamy Milk Punch*

### *Grillades*
### *Grits Casserole*      *Baked Bananas*
### *Cheese Biscuits*

### *Pecan Pie*
### Café au Lait

*Gamay Rosé or a light Beaujolais*

## Creamy Milk Punch

| | |
|---|---|
| 2   quarts vanilla ice cream | 2   teaspoons vanilla |
| 1½ cups brandy | 2   cups cold milk (approximate) |
| 4   tablespoons sugar | Nutmeg |

The above ingredients are sufficient for 2 batches in an electric blender.

Place 1 quart ice cream in blender. Add ¾ cup brandy, 2 tablespoons sugar and 1 teaspoon vanilla. Blend 5 seconds or until well mixed. Add 1 cup milk to full mark on jar and blend 5 seconds more. Serve in chilled julep cups. Sprinkle with nutmeg. Repeat.

Yield:  About 64 ounces

*Coates Stuckey*

## Grillades

| | |
|---|---|
| 6   pounds veal round ¼-inch thick, cut into serving pieces | 3   cups chopped green onions |
| 1½ tablespoons salt | 3   cloves garlic, minced |
| 1   teaspoon pepper | 3   cups chopped tomatoes (or |
| ¾  cup bacon drippings | less) |
| ½  cup flour | 1   teaspoon thyme |
| 2   cups chopped onions | 3   bay leaves |
| ¾  cup chopped celery (ribs and leaves) | Tabasco to taste |
| | Worcestershire to taste |
| 6   thinly sliced green peppers | 1½ cups warm water |
| | ¾  cup parsley |

Salt and pepper veal. In a heavy Dutch oven, brown meat in 4 tablespoons of the drippings. Remove veal; keep covered and warm. Add remaining drippings and flour to Dutch oven, stirring constantly over low heat to make a chocolate brown roux. Add celery, peppers, onions and garlic. Sauté until limp. Add only enough of the tomatoes to add a pink tint to the roux which should retain its brown color. Add seasonings and stir in water.

Place meat in roux, cover and cook slowly about 1 hour. Remove bay leaves and stir in parsley. Serve piping hot, spooned over grits with lots of gravy.

Overnight refrigeration enhances the flavor of the sauce. To reheat, add a small amount of warm water or beef stock. If veal is unavailable, tender beef round is a good substitute.

*Joy N. Hodges*

## Grits Casserole

6   cups water
4   teaspoons salt
2   cups grits

2   cups milk
4   tablespoons butter
4   eggs, beaten

In a saucepan, bring water and salt to a rolling boil. Slowly add grits, stirring constantly. Turn heat to low, cover and cook for 20 to 25 minutes or until water is absorbed. Remove from heat and allow to cool. Heat milk and butter together and add to lukewarm grits. Stir until smooth. Add eggs, mixing thoroughly. Spoon into a 2-quart greased ovenproof dish and bake at 350° for 1 hour 15 minutes or until light brown.

*Florence L. Hall*

## Baked Bananas

12  firm bananas, cut into thirds
3   tablespoons lemon juice
1   teaspoon grated orange peel
½   teaspoon cinnamon

¼   teaspoon nutmeg
⅓   cup granulated brown sugar
¼   pound butter, cut into pats
Salt to taste

Place banana sections in 13×9×2-inch baking dish. Sprinkle with juices, peel, spices and brown sugar. Dot with butter and salt lightly. Bake at 350° for 45 minutes, basting occasionally. Serve hot. May be prepared and refrigerated several hours before baking, in which case add 5 minutes to cooking time.

Variation: Roll each banana section in crushed corn flakes before proceeding with directions. If plantains (a larger, starchier cousin to the banana) are used, increase the sugar and cooking time.

*Florence L. Hall*

## Cheese Biscuits

| | |
|---|---|
| 3   cups sifted flour | 1   cup grated sharp cheese |
| 5   teaspoons baking powder | ¼  cup chopped pimiento |
| 1½ teaspoons salt | 1 to 1½ cups cold milk |
| ½  teaspoon cayenne | Melted butter (optional) |
| ½  cup shortening | Sesame seeds (optional) |

Sift dry ingredients together. Cut in shortening, cheese and pimiento. Add milk to make a soft dough. Roll out on a floured board to ½-inch thickness. Fold over and roll again. Cut with a 2-inch biscuit cutter and place on greased cookie sheet, leaving space between so that all sides can brown. Bake at 450° about 15 minutes. If desired, brush with melted butter and sprinkle with sesame seeds before baking. Freezes well.

Yield: About 36

*Aimée C. Whatley*

## Pecan Pie

| | |
|---|---|
| 1   pound light brown sugar | ½ cup milk |
| ¼  pound butter | 1   cup chopped pecans |
| 4   eggs, beaten | 2   8-inch pie shells |

Melt sugar and butter together. Add eggs, milk and nuts. Stir until blended. Divide filling between pie shells and bake at 300° for 1 hour. Cool on wire racks.

*Phyllis N. Dunbar*

### Double Pie Crust

| | |
|---|---|
| 1½ cups flour | 1   egg, beaten |
| ½  teaspoon baking powder | 2½ tablespoons ice water |
| ½  teaspoon salt | 1   teaspoon vinegar |
| ⅔  cup shortening | |

Blend dry ingredients with shortening in mixer. Add egg and liquids. Form into 2 flattened balls. Wrap and chill 15 to 20 minutes. Roll out each ball on a floured board and fit into an 8-inch pie pan.

*Vera W. Daspit*

# TWELFTH NIGHT BRUNCH                    *(Serves 16)*

King's Cake is traditionally served on the twelfth day after Christmas (January 6), setting off a round of parties for the Mardi Gras season.

### *Artichoke-Oyster Soup*

### *Chicken Livers and Canadian Bacon*
### *Spoon Bread*
### *Creole Eggplant*

### *Oranges Bayou Boeuf*

### *King's Cake*
### *Coffee*

*Châteauneuf-du-Pape or Petite Sirah*

## *Artichoke-Oyster Soup*

| | |
|---|---|
| ¼ pound butter | Cayenne to taste |
| 2 bunches green onions, chopped | 1 teaspoon salt |
| 3 ribs celery, chopped | 1 tablespoon Worcestershire |
| 3 cloves garlic, pressed | sauce |
| 2 14-ounce cans artichoke hearts, washed, drained, and quartered | 1 quart oysters, drained and chopped, liquor reserved |
| 3 tablespoons flour | 1 cup evaporated milk |
| 1 to 1½ quarts chicken stock | 1 cup milk |

Melt butter in a heavy 4-quart pot. Sauté onions, celery and garlic until soft. Add artichokes. Sprinkle with flour and stir to coat well, but do not brown. Add stock and seasonings. Cover and simmer 1 hour. Add oysters and liquor. Simmer for 10 minutes, but *do not boil*. Stir in milk and refrigerate at least 8 hours, or up to 3 days. Reheat gently and serve.

Yield: 2 quarts

*Joseph Rizzo*

## Chicken Livers and Canadian Bacon

2  pounds chicken livers            4  tablespoons margarine
1  cup chopped green onions         16  slices Canadian bacon

Sauté livers and onions lightly in margarine for 10 minutes. Add bacon slices and cook 5 minutes more.


## Spoon Bread

6  cups milk                        2  tablespoons salt
2¼ cups corn meal                   2  tablespoons sugar
12 tablespoons butter               12 eggs, separated

Bring milk to a boil, then add corn meal and cook to the consistency of mush. Remove from heat; add butter, salt and sugar. Cool. Add beaten egg yolks. (May be made ahead up to this point; cover and refrigerate.)

Beat egg whites until stiff and fold into corn meal mixture. Pour into 2 buttered 3-quart casseroles. Bake uncovered 30 minutes at 375°.

*Susan R. Chadwick*


## Creole Eggplant

3  eggplants, peeled and sliced     Salt and pepper to taste
3  onions, sliced                   Parmesan cheese
6  tomatoes, peeled and sliced      6  tablespoons butter, melted
3  green peppers, sliced into rings

Layer vegetables alternately in 2 greased 8×13-inch casserole dishes, seasoning each layer. Sprinkle top with cheese, then pour butter over all. Cover and bake at 350° for 45 minutes, then uncover and bake 10 more minutes.


## Oranges Bayou Boeuf

8  navel oranges                    1  cup Grand Marnier
2  quarts orange sherbet, softened

Scoop out oranges, remove seeds and mix pulp with sherbet and liqueur. Fill each shell with mixture and freeze. Remove oranges from freezer 30 minutes before serving.

*Dorothy I. Stuckey*

## King's Cake

1   package yeast
¼   cup warm water
6   tablespoons milk, scalded and
       cooled
4 to 5 cups flour
½   pound butter
¾   cup sugar
¼   teaspoon salt
4   eggs
2   tablespoons melted butter

Small plastic doll (or bean) to
   designate the "monarch"
Light corn syrup for topping
Green, yellow, purple granulated
   sugar for topping (To color
   sugar, shake with a few drops of
   food coloring in a tightly
   covered jar until desired color is
   obtained)

Dissolve yeast in warm water. Add milk and about ½ cup of flour. In a large bowl, blend butter, sugar, salt and eggs. Add yeast dough and mix thoroughly. Gradually add 2½ cups flour to make a medium dough. Place in greased bowl and brush with melted butter. Cover with a damp cloth and allow to rise until doubled—about 3 hours. Use 1 cup (or more) flour to knead dough and roll into a 4 to 5 foot long rope. Form into an oval on a 14×17-inch greased cookie sheet, connecting ends of rope with a few drops of water. Press the doll (or bean) into the dough from underneath. Cover with a damp cloth and let rise until doubled—about 1 hour. Bake at 325° 35 to 45 minutes or until lightly browned. Brush top of cake with corn syrup and sprinkle with alternating bands of colored sugar. Freezes well.

Traditionally, the person served the doll or bean is the next ruler and must give the next week's party at which a new king's cake chooses a new monarch.

# SUNDAY BRUNCH                                    *(Serves 18)*

Elegant enough for any occasion.

## *Kir

## *Orange Walnut Chicken
## *Rice Ring        *Blanched Broccoli
## *Jelly Muffins

## *Lemon Freeze
## or
## *Creole Cream Cheese Ice Cream

## Coffee

## Kir

1   cup crème de Cassis              1   gallon Chablis

Mix and chill.
Yield: 34 4-ounce servings

## Orange Walnut Chicken

9   pounds fryer pieces              1   cup broken walnuts
Salt and pepper to taste            1   cup raisins
3   tablespoons curry powder        ¾   teaspoon cinnamon
1   cup melted butter or margarine  6   navel oranges, peeled, sliced
3   teaspoons grated orange peel        and cut to center on 1 side
2¼  cups orange juice               ½   cup warm water
3   8½-ounce cans pineapple         3   tablespoons flour
    tidbits, undrained              3   teaspoons soy sauce

Sprinkle chicken pieces on all sides with salt, pepper and curry. Rub seasonings well into flesh. Dip pieces in butter and place skin side down in large shallow baking pan. Bake at 400° for 10 minutes. Turn pieces and repeat. Meanwhile, heat to boiling the orange peel, juice, pineapple, nuts, raisins and cinnamon. Pour hot mixture over chicken and reduce oven temperature to 350°. Bake 30 to 40 minutes more. Remove chicken to warm serving platter, reserving pan with drippings. (Chicken may be deboned at this point.) Twist orange slices and arrange over chicken. In a small saucepan, gradually add water to flour, stirring constantly. Add soy sauce and pour into baking pan. Simmer over low heat 1 to 2 minutes, scraping pan constantly. When well mixed with drippings, pour mixture over garnished chicken.

*Sally E. Bennett*

## Rice Ring

6  cups cooked rice
4  tablespoons margarine, melted

2  teaspoons celery salt
⅔  cup chopped chives

Heat rice in margarine; add seasonings. Pack into greased 3-quart ring mold. Place mold in pan of hot water and keep warm in oven until serving time. To unmold, run a spatula around edges and invert onto heated platter.

## Blanched Broccoli

3  bunches broccoli, cut into
   serving-sized pieces
3  quarts water
2  tablespoons sugar

2  tablespoons salt
1¼ pound butter, melted
4-ounce jar pimientos (optional)

Place first 4 ingredients in a large boiler, making certain broccoli is covered with water. Bring to a rolling boil. Remove from heat. With tongs, arrange broccoli on a serving platter. Pour melted butter over all. Garnish with pimientos. Serve immediately.

*Florence L. Hall*

## Jelly Muffins

2  cups sifted flour
2  cups corn meal
2½ tablespoons baking powder
4  tablespoons sugar
2  teaspoons salt

2  eggs, beaten
2  cups milk
½  cup cooking oil
4  ounces jelly

Sift dry ingredients together. Combine eggs, milk and oil. Stir into dry ingredients, mixing only until moist. Half-fill greased muffin cups. Spoon 1 teaspoon jelly onto center of each uncooked muffin. Bake at 425° for 20 minutes.
Yield: 24 muffins

*Betsy B. Hardin*

## Lemon Freeze

4   lemons                              2   cups heavy cream, whipped
6   eggs, separated                     2½ cups vanilla wafer crumbs
1   cup sugar

Squeeze lemons, reserving juice; grate peel. Beat egg yolks slightly and combine with juice, peel and sugar. Cook over hot water, stirring constantly, until the consistency of heavy syrup. Remove from heat. Cool. Beat egg whites until stiff and fold into lemon mixture. Fold in cream. Sprinkle half of crumbs in bottom of a 3-quart oblong casserole. Add lemon mixture and top with remaining crumbs. Freeze. To serve, cut into squares.

*Susan R. Chadwick*

## Creole Cream Cheese Ice Cream

2   11-ounce cartons Creole cream      1   pint heavy cream
    cheese                             1   8-ounce can crushed pineapple,
1¼ cups sugar                              drained
1½ teaspoons almond (or vanilla)       Maraschino cherries
    extract

Beat cream cheese with mixer until smooth. Add 1 cup sugar and extract. In another bowl whip cream until stiff, gradually mixing in ¼ cup sugar; fold into cheese mixture. Pour into 8-inch square cake pan and freeze 1 hour. Decorate top with fruits. Return to freezer to firm. Remove 15 minutes before serving. Cut into squares.

Cottage cheese may be substituted for Creole cream cheese, but the flavor will not be as unusual.

*Estha W. Heyman*

# BRUNCH BON VIVANT

(*Serves 36*)

A Louisiana good time!

### *Orange Blossoms*

### *Creole Eggs*
### *Broiled Bacon and Sausage Links*
### *Home-baked Bread*      *Crystal Fruit Bowl*

### *Coconut Pecan Bars*
### Coffee

*California Gamay or Côtes du Rhône*

## Orange Blossoms

2   fifths gin, chilled
1   fifth apricot brandy, chilled
48 ounces orange juice, chilled

1   cup lemon juice, chilled
Orange bitters (optional)

Mix all ingredients in a glass punch bowl.
Yield: 36 4-ounce servings

*Dorothy I. Stuckey*

## Creole Eggs

¾  pound butter
3   cups chopped onions
2   cups chopped green pepper
3   cups chopped celery
3   cups sliced mushrooms
3   10¾-ounce cans cream of tomato soup
3   10¾-ounce cans cream of mushroom soup
3   tablespoons chili powder
4½ tablespoons Worcestershire sauce

1   tablespoon MSG
1   tablespoon Beau Monde seasoning
Salt, pepper and Evangeline hot sauce to taste
45 eggs, hard-boiled the day of the party
6   cups grated sharp Cheddar cheese
4½ cups Ritz cracker crumbs

In butter, sauté onions, mushrooms, green pepper and celery. Add soups and seasonings. Simmer until well blended. Sauce will keep several days in refrigerator, but does not freeze well.

Cut eggs into halves and divide equally into 3 lightly greased, oblong 3-quart casserole dishes. Pour sauce over eggs. Top each casserole with cheese and crumbs. Bake at 450° for 15 minutes.

*Marilyn K. Banks*

## Home-Baked Bread

| | |
|---|---|
| 1   package yeast | 2   teaspoons baking powder |
| ⅔ cup lukewarm water | 1   cup sugar |
| 1½ cups milk (or water) | 4 to 5 cups flour |
| ½ cup cooking oil | Softened butter |
| 2   teaspoons salt | |

In a large bowl, dissolve yeast in water. Add milk (or water), oil, salt, baking powder and sugar. Stir until dissolved, then add ½ cup flour at a time until a soft dough is formed and all flour blended in. On floured board, knead dough about 3 minutes. Place in a large bowl, cover with a damp cloth and allow to rise in a warm location, about 1½ hours or until doubled in size. Knead again slightly. Form into 3 loaves and place in 9¼×5¼×3-inch greased bread pans. Let rise again for about 45 minutes. Bake at 350° for about 30 to 40 minutes or until dark golden brown. Brush with soft butter. Freezes well.
    Yield:  3 large loaves

*Madeline N. Jeansonne*


## Crystal Fruit Bowl

| | |
|---|---|
| 4   pineapples cut into 1-inch chunks | 5   lemons |
| 9   pints strawberries | 9   avocados, sliced |
| 1   pound powdered sugar | ½ cup sugar |
| 4   cantaloupes scooped into 1-inch balls | |

Toss pineapple chunks and strawberries with powdered sugar. Add cantaloupe. Chill. Reserving half a lemon, squeeze juice of remaining lemons on avocados. Chill. To serve, rub the reserved lemon half around the rim of a clear glass bowl. Sprinkle sugar on a tea towel and invert bowl on sugar to form a crust around the rim. Toss fruits together gently in prepared bowl. Serve ice cold.

*Susan R. Chadwick*

## Coconut Pecan Bars

½  pound butter
1   cup dark brown sugar
2   cups flour
4   eggs
2   cups light brown sugar
1   cup grated coconut

2   tablespoons flour
1½ cups chopped pecans
¼  teaspoon salt
2   teaspoons vanilla
Confectioners' sugar

Cream butter and dark brown sugar, add the 2 cups flour and mix well. Divide dough and press into two 9-inch square pans. Bake in 350° oven for 20 minutes. Beat the eggs until frothy and pale yellow. Gradually add the light brown sugar and beat until thick. Toss coconut in the 2 tablespoons flour and stir in. Add pecans, salt and vanilla. Spread over the baked crusts and bake 20 minutes more or until browned. When cool, dust with confectioners' sugar and cut into 1½-inch squares.

Yield: 6 dozen

*Eileen M. Fuhrer*

# GARDEN PARTY BRUNCH                    *(Serves 50)*

Hospitality pre-prepared!

*Pineapple Punch*     *Tangy Bloody Marys*

*Marinated Ham Slices*    *Brunch Scrambled Eggs*
*Coarse-ground Grits*    *Fresh Fruit Compote*
*Herb and *White Bread*
*Miniature Bran Muffins*

*Fudge*     *Caramel Brownies*
Coffee

## Pineapple Punch

3   cups sugar
3   cups water
2   42-ounce cans pineapple juice
6   6-ounce cans frozen lemonade
    concentrate

1½ cups water
4   quarts ginger ale, chilled

Bring sugar and 3 cups water to a boil; stir until sugar melts; cool. Mix with next 3 ingredients and chill at least 12 hours. When ready to serve, add ginger ale.
    Yield: 75   4-ounce servings

*Jane T. Sharp*

## Tangy Bloody Marys

8   46-ounce cans V-8 juice
1   gallon vodka
2½ cups lemon juice
1¾ cups Worcestershire sauce

3   tablespoons salt
2   teaspoons Tabasco
2   teaspoons pepper

Mix in a 5-gallon container and chill. May be stored for a week in refrigerator.
    Yield: 90   6-ounce drinks

*Franklin H. Mikell*

## Marinated Ham Slices

10 pounds ham slices
1   fifth red wine

20 ounces plum or crabapple jelly

Melt jelly; add wine and pour over ham slices. Refrigerate at least 24 hours. Serve at room temperature.

## Brunch Scrambled Eggs

| | | | |
|---|---|---|---|
| 1 | pound butter | 1 | teaspoon curry powder |
| 4 | cups minced green onions | 1 | teaspoon white pepper |
| 1 | cup flour | 1 | teaspoon cayenne |
| 5 | cups evaporated milk | 1 | teaspoon dry mustard |
| 5 | cups homogenized milk | 6 | dozen eggs |
| 4 | cups grated sharp cheese | 4 | cups water |
| 2 | cups sherry | | Salt and pepper to taste |
| 2 | teaspoons seasoned salt | 8 | tablespoons safflower oil |

Melt half the butter in a large saucepan. Sauté onions lightly and stir in flour. Gradually add milk and cook, stirring constantly, until thickened. Blend in cheese; remove from heat and stir in sherry and next 5 ingredients. Measure and set aside to cool.

Beat 1½ dozen eggs with 1 cup water and season lightly with salt and pepper. Melt 4 tablespoons butter in a skillet and add 2 tablespoons oil. Scramble eggs until they barely hold together. Set aside to cool. Repeat 3 times with remaining eggs.

Grease 4 3-quart casseroles lightly and pour ⅛ of the white sauce into the bottom of each casserole dish. Place scrambled eggs evenly on top of sauce and cover with remainder of sauce. Entire top and bottom of eggs must be covered. Cover tightly and refrigerate (up to 2 days).

Bring casseroles to room temperature. Bake covered at 275° for about 1 hour. Keep warm over hot water until ready to serve.

*Gerry J. Sperry*

## Fresh Fruit Compote

| | | | |
|---|---|---|---|
| 2 | cups sliced oranges | 3 | cups strawberries |
| 3 | cups pineapple chunks | 3 | cups sliced bananas |
| 2 | cups sliced apples | 2 | cups grapes |
| ½ | cup grated lemon peel | 2 | cups sliced pears |
| 1 | cup brandy | 3 | cups sliced peaches |

Mix first 3 fruits. Sprinkle with lemon peel and brandy; refrigerate. On day of party, add other fruits. Serve very cold.

## Coarse-ground Grits

5 cups coarse-ground grits
4 quarts chicken stock

2 to 3 teaspoons salt
4 tablespoons butter

Cook grits in chicken stock seasoned with salt and butter for length of time specified on package.

## Herb Bread

1½ cups milk, scalded
4 tablespoons sugar
4 tablespoons margarine
3 teaspoons salt
1 teaspoon nutmeg
2 teaspoons sage
4 teaspoons caraway seeds

1 tablespoon poppy seeds
1 tablespoon dried onion
2 packages yeast
½ cup warm water
2 eggs, beaten
6 to 7 cups flour

Mix first 9 ingredients together while milk is still warm; set aside to cool. Dissolve yeast in water; add eggs. Beat into milk mixture. Gradually beat in flour and knead until smooth. Let rise, covered, in a greased bowl until doubled. Punch down and knead again. Place in a greased bundt pan, or halve and place in 2 5½×9½×2-inch pans. Let rise again. Bake at 350° for 50 minutes for bundt pan, 30 minutes for bread pans. Freezes well.

*Joyce G. Hayne*

## White Bread

1 package yeast
6 cups Wondra flour
1 tablespoon salt

2 tablespoons margarine
2¼ cups skim milk
2 tablespoons honey

In a large bowl mix yeast, 2 cups flour and salt. Heat margarine, milk and honey together to 120°. Add to the dry mixture and mix thoroughly. Add remaining flour, using more if necessary. Knead quickly until smooth and elastic. Place dough in a greased bowl, cover, and let rise until doubled, about 1 hour.

Punch down the dough, knead for 1 minute, and divide in half. Pat into loaf shape and place in greased 9×5×2¾-inch bread pans. Cover and let rise again until dough fills the pans and is rounded at the top.

Bake at 400° for about 40 minutes or until done.

Yield: 2 loaves weighing about 1¼ pounds each

*Frances B. Davis*

## Miniature Bran Muffins

1¼ cups flour
3   teaspoons baking powder
½ teaspoon salt
½ cup sugar
2½ cups 40% Bran Flakes

1¼ cups milk
1   egg
⅓ cup vegetable oil
1   8-ounce jar orange marmalade

Stir together flour, baking powder, salt and sugar. Set aside. Combine bran flakes and milk in mixing bowl. Let stand until cereal softens, about 2 minutes. Add egg and oil. Beat well. Add dry ingredients to cereal mixture, stirring only until combined. Portion batter evenly into 40 greased miniature cups. Spoon a drop of marmalade into center of batter. Bake at 400° for 15 minutes or until golden brown. Freezes well.

*Cathy S. Long*

## Fudge

2   cups sugar
⅔ cup unsweetened cocoa
¼ pound butter
½ cup milk

2   tablespoons light corn syrup
2   teaspoons vanilla
1   cup chopped nuts (optional)
5½ cups confectioners' sugar, sifted

Mix sugar, cocoa, butter, milk and corn syrup in a saucepan. Slowly bring to a boil, stirring constantly. Boil 1 minute. Remove from heat. Add vanilla and nuts *immediately. Quickly* stir in confectioners' sugar, 1 cup at a time. Scrape into a 9×13-inch pan. Pat smooth with fingers. Cool. Cut into squares.

*Fred Simon*

## Caramel Brownies

7   ounces butter
1   pound brown sugar
2   eggs, beaten
1½ cups flour

2   teaspoons baking powder
2   teaspoons vanilla
1½ cups chopped pecans

Melt butter and brown sugar in the top of a double boiler. Remove from heat and blend in next 4 ingredients in order listed, stirring until smooth. Add nuts. Pour into 11×14-inch pan which has been lined with lightly buttered foil. Bake at 350° for about 30 minutes or until a cake tester comes out clean. Cool in pan. Remove, peel off foil and cut into squares.

*Josephine S. Kellogg*

# OLD WORLD COFFEE                          *(Serves 50)*

Delicate aromas set the stage for this unusual fête. Display on an easel near the serving table the various coffee recipes for guests to follow. A collection of fine old cups, a treasured cloth, and antique decanters will add flair.

## *Variety of Coffees*

### *Strudel*
### *Rum Fruit Cakes*        *Danish Bars*
### *Armenian Spice Cake*        *Date Loaf Candy*

## *Coffees*

2   30-cup urns hot coffee
10  quarts milk, heated
4   cups heavy cream, whipped
    with 4 tablespoons
    confectioners' sugar and 2
    teaspoons vanilla
Sugar
50  cinnamon sticks

1 to 2 ounces grated nutmeg
2 to 3 cups grated semi-sweet
    chocolate
Peel of 5 lemons, cut in strips
1   pint cognac or brandy
1   pint Kahlua, Tia Maria, or
    Crème de Cacao

Tuscano Coffee:  Coffee, sugar, lemon peel, brandy
Viennese Coffee:  Coffee, cognac, whipped cream, nutmeg
Cappucino:  ½ coffee, ½ hot milk, cinnamon stick, nutmeg, sugar
Café au Lait:  ½ coffee, ½ hot milk, sugar
Fiesta Coffee:  Coffee, cinnamon stick, whipped cream, grated chocolate,
                Kahlua

## Strudel

| | |
|---|---|
| ½ pound margarine, melted and cooled | 3 tablespoons apricot preserves |
| 1 cup sour cream | 1 cup yellow raisins |
| 2 cups flour | 1½ cups apricot preserves |
| 1 cup dried apricots | ¾ cup chopped pecans |
| ½ cup chopped yellow raisins | 1 cup flaked coconut |
| ¾ cup sugar | 2 teaspoons cinnamon |

Mix margarine with sour cream; blend in flour. Shape loosely into 5 rectangles about 3×5 inches each. Sprinkle well with flour and wrap each in floured wax paper. Refrigerate overnight.

Cover chopped raisins and apricots with water; simmer for 15 minutes and let cool. Drain and mash well. Add 3 tablespoons preserves and ¼ cup sugar. Refrigerate.

Soak 1 cup raisins in warm water for a few minutes. Drain and refrigerate.

Remove rectangles of dough from refrigerator 5 minutes before ready to roll. Place each on a sheet of floured wax paper and press out with fingers, keeping rectangular shape and turning so that both sides are floured. Cover with another sheet of wax paper and roll out until the dough measures approximately 8×13 inches. Carefully remove top piece of paper. Take care not to roll too thin and not to let wax paper wrinkle. Any hole in the pastry will allow filling to run out and burn while baking.

Spread 3 or 4 tablespoons of preserves on each piece of rolled dough, leaving a margin of at least 1 inch on each long side and across seam end. Top with an equal amount of prepared apricot filling. Sprinkle one-fifth of the pecans, coconut, and raisins on each. Do not overfill.

Lift end of paper and start rolling strudel slowly. (It will separate from the paper as you roll.) Fold ends of strudel in on the next to last turn. Place seam side down on foil-lined baking sheet. Take care in placing strudel on foil as it cannot be moved.

Score across each roll at ½-inch intervals. Bake 30 to 35 minutes at 350°. Mix cinnamon with remaining sugar; sprinkle rolls and bake 10 to 15 minutes more. (It will not be brown.) Remove immediately to cutting board and separate into scored sections with a sharp knife.

Yield: 90 small pieces

Variation: Use kumquat marmalade (recipe p. 7) in place of apricot preserves.

*Audrey G. Hammill*

## Armenian Spice Cake

| | |
|---|---|
| 2 cups brown sugar | 1 egg, beaten |
| 2 cups flour | 1 teaspoon nutmeg |
| ¼ pound butter | Chopped pecans |
| 1 cup sour cream | Cinnamon |
| 1 teaspoon baking soda | |

Blend first 3 ingredients; halve and set aside. Mix sour cream and baking soda; add egg and nutmeg and blend into half of the sugar-flour mixture. Spread the remaining sugar-flour mixture evenly over the bottom of a greased 10-inch square pan. Pour batter over this. Sprinkle the top generously with the pecans and cinnamon. Bake at 350° for about 40 minutes. Do not open oven during the first half hour of baking.

*Dorothy G. Portier*

## Rum Fruit Cakes

| | |
|---|---|
| ¼ pound butter | 1 cup pineapple chunks, chopped and dredged in flour |
| 1 cup sugar | |
| 1 egg | 1 cup cherries, chopped and dredged in flour |
| 1 cup unsweetened applesauce | |
| 2 cups flour | 1 cup pecans, chopped and dredged in flour |
| 2 tablespoons cocoa | |
| 1 teaspoon allspice | 2 teaspoons rum extract |
| 1 teaspoon cloves | 2 tablespoons sherry |
| 1 teaspoon cinnamon | 1 tablespoon whiskey |
| ⅛ teaspoon salt | 2 tablespoons butter, softened |
| 1 teaspoon baking soda, dissolved in ½ cup hot water | 1 cup confectioners' sugar |
| | 1 to 2 teaspoons rum extract |
| 1 cup raisins, chopped and dredged in flour | 1 tablespoon milk |

Cream the ¼ pound butter and sugar together. Add next 16 ingredients in order, mixing well. Spoon into miniature paper baking cups placed close together on cookie sheets. Bake at 450° for 12 to 15 minutes. Cool.
Mix remaining ingredients and spread on cakes.
Yield: 12 dozen

*Suzonne S. Kellogg*

## Danish Bars

| | |
|---|---|
| ¼ pound butter | ¼ teaspoon salt |
| 1 cup flour | ½ cup flaked coconut |
| 2 eggs | ½ cup finely chopped walnuts |
| 1½ cups firmly-packed brown sugar | 2 cups confectioners' sugar |
| | 2 tablespoons orange juice |
| 1 teaspoon vanilla | 2 tablespoons melted butter |
| 2 tablespoons flour | 1 tablespoon lemon juice |
| ¼ teaspoon baking powder | 1 teaspoon almond extract |

Cut butter into 1 cup flour with a pastry blender. Press mixture into the bottom of an 8×10-inch or 7×11-inch pan. Bake at 350° for 10 to 15 minutes. Meanwhile, blend together eggs, brown sugar, vanilla, 2 tablespoons flour, baking powder and salt. Stir in coconut and walnuts. Spread this mixture on the baked pastry and return to oven for 25 minutes or until golden. Cool.

Mix remaining ingredients together. Spread on cake.

Yield: 48 squares

*Clarice S. Johns*

## Date Loaf Candy

| | |
|---|---|
| ¾ cup sugar | 1 cup chopped pecans |
| ¼ cup evaporated milk | Pecan halves (optional) |
| 1 8-ounce package dates, chopped | |

Heat the milk and sugar in a heavy saucepan until sugar is dissolved. Add dates and cook 3 minutes longer, stirring frequently. Remove from heat and fold in chopped nuts. Pour onto buttered wax paper or foil and shape into 2 loaves. Decorate with pecan halves. Slice.

*Lois Hazel Edwards*

# HARVEST COFFEE                    *(Serves 100)*

Natchitoches, on the Cane River in northwest Louisiana, is the oldest settlement in the entire Louisiana Purchase. Its spicy meat pies make a delectable contribution to Louisiana cuisine.

*Meat Pies*

*Cheese Tray*     *Devilled Pecans*

*Prune Cake*      *Apricot Dainties*
*Apple Cake*      *Candied Coconut*

*Cold Apple Cider*     *Hot Buttered Rum*
*Spiced Tea*

## Meat Pies

18 ounces cream cheese, softened
1½ pounds margarine, softened
6 to 7 cups flour
2½ pounds ground chuck, browned and drained
2 packages Chef Boyardee spaghetti sauce mix complete with tomato base and cheese

2 teaspoons chili powder
1 cup chopped ripe olives
2 to 3 jalapeño peppers, seeded and chopped fine

Blend first 3 ingredients with mixer or pastry blender. Chill thoroughly. Mix remaining ingredients. Cover and chill at least 12 hours.

Roll dough thin between lightly floured sheets of wax paper. Use biscuit cutter about 2¼ inches wide to cut circles. Put 1 teaspoon of meat mixture on circle, fold over and pinch edges together. Prick tops with fork. Freeze on cookie sheets for several hours. Remove and place in containers between layers of wax paper. Bake frozen at 425° for 10 to 12 minutes or until pastry is golden brown.

Yield: About 20 dozen

*Ruth O. Prince*

## Cheese Tray

7 to 10 pounds assorted cheeses
4 10-ounce boxes assorted crackers

## Devilled Pecans

| | |
|---|---|
| 2 cups vegetable oil | 2 teaspoons salt |
| 4 pounds pecan halves | 1 teaspoon cayenne |
| 4 teaspoons celery salt | |

Sauté nuts slowly in oil, stirring constantly, until they are crisp. Drain on paper towels. Combine salts and pepper in a large bowl, add nuts, and toss well while nuts are still warm.

*Janice R. Roy*

## Prune Cake

| | |
|---|---|
| 1 cup prunes, prepared ahead as directed below | 1 teaspoon baking soda |
| 2 cups sugar | 1 teaspoon salt |
| 1 cup vegetable oil | 1 teaspoon cinnamon |
| 3 eggs, beaten | ½ teaspoon ground cloves |
| 1 cup buttermilk | 1 teaspoon nutmeg |
| 2 cups flour | 1 teaspoon vanilla |
| | 1 cup chopped pecans |

Cook prunes in water to cover for 30 minutes. Refrigerate at least 24 hours in juices. Drain and chop prunes.

Mix sugar and oil together, add eggs and mix well. Blend in buttermilk and prunes. Sift together flour, soda, salt and spices; stir into above mixture. Add vanilla and pecans. Bake in greased and floured tube or bundt pan for 55 to 60 minutes at 350°.

*Betsy B. Hardin*

## Apricot Dainties

| | |
|---|---|
| 2 6-ounce packages dried apricots | 1 cup pecan meal or finely ground pecans |
| 2 cups sugar | Confectioners' sugar |
| 6 tablespoons orange juice | |

Place apricots, sugar and orange juice in the top of a double boiler and cook until sugar dissolves and apricots are soft. Cool mixture and shape fruit into balls with a little pecan meal in the center of each. Roll balls in pecan meal, then in confectioners' sugar.

*Ruby L. Wright*

## Apple Cake

3   cups chopped, peeled            1   teaspoon salt
    apples (4 large apples)         1   teaspoon baking soda
1   cup chopped pecans              ½   teaspoon cinnamon
½   cup chopped dates               ½   teaspoon allspice
½   cup raisins                     ½   teaspoon ginger
1   cup flour                       ¼   teaspoon nutmeg
1   cup vegetable oil               1   teaspoon vanilla
1   cup light brown sugar           ¼   pound butter
1   cup dark brown sugar            ⅔   cup sugar
2   eggs                            1   5.33-ounce can evaporated
2   cups flour                          milk

Dredge fruits and nuts in 1 cup flour. Mix oil, brown sugar and eggs. Sift next 7 ingredients together and add to fruit mixture. Combine with egg mixture and vanilla. Pour into greased and floured tube pan or 3 8×4×2½-inch loaf pans. Bake at 350° for 1 hour 10 minutes.

Combine remaining ingredients and cook over medium heat, stirring constantly for 8 to 10 minutes. Pour over warm cake.

*Markay S. Sherrill*

## Candied Coconut

1   coconut                         1   cup water
2   cups sugar

Pierce holes in coconut and drain the milk. Crack the shell with a hammer and peel off brown skin with potato peeler. Sliver coconut meat and set aside.

In a heavy saucepan, boil sugar and water until it spins a thread or reaches 275° on a candy thermometer. Stir in coconut, reduce heat, cover, and steam for 10 minutes. Uncover and stir until crystallized. Pour onto wax paper and separate into pieces. Store in a well-ventilated container.

*Marjorie K. McBride*

## Cold Apple Cider

3  gallons apple cider              12  sticks cinnamon
2  ounces whole cloves             Mint sprigs for garnish

Bring ingredients to a boil. Allow to set for 1 hour. Remove spices and chill. Add sprig of mint to each serving.
Yield: 64  6-ounce servings

*Alexandria Junior League*


## Hot Buttered Rum

2  gallons apple cider             2  ounces whole cloves
1  quart dark rum                  1  pound butter
72 cinnamon sticks

Combine cider and rum and heat to boiling. Heat serving mugs and, into each, place 1 cinnamon stick and 3 cloves. Fill with hot rum mixture. Top with ½ tablespoon butter.
Yield: 72  4-ounce servings

*Ray A. Whatley*


## Spiced Tea

1  1-pound 2-ounce jar            2  cups sugar
   orange-flavored Tang           2  teaspoons cinnamon
2  12-ounce envelopes Wyler's     1  teaspoon ground cloves
   lemonade mix                   Boiling water
1  cup instant tea powder

Combine dry ingredients and mix thoroughly. Store in covered container.
Allow 1 cup of dry mix for each 1½ quarts of boiling water or 3 rounded teaspoons for each cup.

*Kathryn M. Harris*

# COUNTRY COFFEE                          *(Serves 200)*

Natural foods, home-baked breads, and fresh produce evoke a homespun atmosphere. Serve the spreads and jellies in simple crocks, the breads on boards, and the goodies in baskets. Oversized stoneware mixing bowls may be used for punch. Jugs filled with fresh wildflowers on tables covered with heirloom quilts will add to the charm. Allow 3 or 4 slices per person of the various breads.

**\*Assorted Breads**
**Apple Slices      Grapes**
**Cream Cheese      Butter and Jellies**
**\*Natural Tidbits**
**\*Fried Coconut**

**\*Sherry-Pineapple Julep      \*Milk Punch for a Crowd**
**Coffee**

## Applesauce Bread

| | |
|---|---|
| ½ cup honey | 1  teaspoon allspice |
| ¼ cup safflower oil | 1  teaspoon cinnamon |
| 1  egg, beaten | 1  cup chunky applesauce |
| 2¼ cups whole wheat | 1  cup broken nuts |
| flour | 1  cup golden raisins |
| 1  teaspoon baking soda | ½ cup chopped dates |
| ¼ teaspoon salt | ¾ cup coconut |
| ½ teaspoon nutmeg | |

Blend honey and oil. Add egg. Sift 1¾ cups flour with soda, salt and spices and stir into honey mixture gradually, beating until smooth. Dredge nuts, raisins and dates in remaining ½ cup flour and add to mixture. Blend in applesauce and coconut. Pour into an 8-inch oiled tube pan and bake at 325° for 45 to 50 minutes or until a cake straw tests clean. Slide knife around edges to loosen. Cool on a wire rack.

*Suzonne K. Hunter*

## *Banana Nut Bread*

1¾ cups flour
2 teaspoons baking powder
¼ teaspoon baking soda
½ teaspoon salt
⅓ cup shortening

⅔ cup sugar
2 eggs, beaten
1 cup mashed ripe
 bananas
½ cup chopped nuts

Sift together flour, baking powder, soda and salt. Beat shortening until creamy. Add sugar gradually and continue beating until light and fluffy. Blend in eggs. Add flour mixture alternately with bananas, a little at a time, beating after each addition until smooth. Stir in nuts. Bake in a greased 9×5-inch bread pan at 350° about 1 hour 10 minutes.

*Betsy B. Hardin*

## *Orange Nut Bread*

1 orange
Boiling water
2 tablespoons shortening
1 teaspoon vanilla
1 egg, beaten
2 cups flour

¼ teaspoon salt
1 teaspoon baking powder
½ teaspoon baking soda
1 cup sugar
½ cup finely chopped nuts

Squeeze orange; remove all membranes and grind peel. Measure juice and add boiling water to make 1 cup. Combine shortening, orange juice, peel, egg and vanilla. Add dry ingredients and mix well. Stir in nuts. Bake in 2 8×4-inch greased loaf pans at 350° for 50 to 60 minutes. Cool in pans. Refrigerate several hours before slicing. Freezes well.

*Betsy B. Hardin*

## *Pumpkin Bread*

3 cups flour
1 teaspoon baking soda
1 teaspoon salt
3 teaspoons cinnamon
2 cups sugar

2 cups cooked, mashed
 pumpkin
4 eggs, beaten
1¼ cups vegetable oil
1 cup chopped pecans (optional)

Sift dry ingredients together in a large bowl. Stir pumpkin, eggs and oil together. Make a well in the dry ingredients, add pumpkin mixture, and stir until smooth. Add pecans if desired. Pour into 2 9½×5½×2-inch greased loaf pans and bake at 325° for 45 minutes or until a cake tester comes out clean.

*Sara M. Burnside*

## Dill Bread

| | |
|---|---|
| 1 package yeast | 2 teaspoons dill seed |
| ¼ cup warm water | ¼ cup melted shortening |
| 1 cup creamed cottage | 1 egg |
|   cheese | ¼ teaspoon baking soda |
| 2 tablespoons sugar | 1 teaspoon salt |
| 1 tablespoon instant minced | 2¼ cups flour |
|   onion | |

Soften yeast in water. Heat cheese to lukewarm and combine in large mixing bowl with sugar, onion, dill, shortening, egg and yeast. Sift together salt, soda and flour and gradually add to bowl, using electric mixer and beating well. Let rise until almost doubled in bulk (about 2 hours). Punch down dough. Put in buttered 1½-quart round casserole. Let rise until light (about 1 hour). Bake at 350° for 40 minutes. Freezes well.

*Nancy C. Weems*

## Sweet Potato Bread

| | |
|---|---|
| ¼ pound butter | 3 cups sugar |
| ½ cup yogurt | 2 teaspoons baking soda |
| ½ cup honey | 2 teaspoons salt |
| 1 teaspoon cinnamon | 1 teaspoon nutmeg |
| 1½ cups chopped pecans | 1 teaspoon cinnamon |
| 2 cups grated raw sweet | 1 cup cooking oil |
|   potatoes | ¾ cup water |
| 3½ cups flour | 4 eggs, beaten |

Combine first 4 ingredients in a saucepan and boil 1 minute. Stir in 1 cup pecans. Cool.

Mix remaining pecans with sweet potatoes. In a large mixing bowl combine dry ingredients and stir in potato-nut mixture. Blend oil, water and eggs and add, mixing only enough to moisten.

Line 2 9×5-inch loaf pans with greased foil. Place 1 cup batter in each pan. Top each with ½ cup of cooled butter mixture, cover with another cup of batter, then another ½ cup of butter mixture, and finish with topping of batter. Bake at 350° for 65 to 75 minutes until center of crack is dry to touch. Cool 15 minutes. Remove from pan and store overnight, wrapped in foil, before slicing. Will keep 1 month in refrigerator; freezes well.

*Jacque S. Caplan*

## Sausage Bread

| | |
|---|---|
| 1 pound bulk pork sausage | 1 teaspoon nutmeg |
| 1½ cups liquid brown sugar | ¼ teaspoon salt |
| 1 egg, beaten | 1 cup strong black coffee |
| 3¼ cups flour | 2 teaspoons vanilla |
| 2 teaspoons baking soda | 3 ounces chopped almonds, |
| 3 teaspoons baking powder | dredged in flour |
| 2 teaspoons cinnamon | 1 cup raisins, dredged in flour |

Blend sugar and sausage together; add egg. Sift dry ingredients into sausage mixture alternately with coffee and vanilla. Mix thoroughly. Fold in nuts and raisins. Bake in greased bundt pan for 1½ hours at 350°.

## Natural Tidbits

| | |
|---|---|
| 3 cups sunflower kernels | 3 cups dried apples or apricots, |
| 3 cups pumpkin kernels | chopped |
| 3 cups almonds or peanuts | 3 cups shredded coconut |
| 3 cups golden raisins | (optional) |
| 3 cups raisins | Salt to taste |

Mix all ingredients and store in tightly covered containers.

*Marguerite D. Jacobson*

## Fried Coconut

8 to 10 coconuts
Vegetable oil

Puncture "eyes" of coconut and drain the milk. Crack open and remove meat, slicing lengthwise to make long strips.

Heat oil to 375° and fry strips a few at a time. When pieces float to the top and are slightly golden, remove and drain on brown paper. Sprinkle lightly with salt. Do not overcook. Will keep several days in an airtight container.

*Nurit P. Wahlder*

## Sherry-Pineapple Julep

4   46-ounce cans pineapple juice
4   fifths dry sherry
2   cups orange juice

2   28-ounce bottles Collins Mix,
    chilled
Mint sprigs for garnish

Combine pineapple juice, sherry and orange juice. Cover and chill 24 hours to blend and mellow flavors. When ready to serve, pour into punch bowl and add Collins Mix.
    Yield: 2¾ gallons

*Jean A. Gamburg*

## Milk Punch for a Crowd

5   pounds sugar
3 to 4 cups boiling water
25  quarts half and half
1   gallon brandy or bourbon

10  ounces vanilla
3½ gallons vanilla ice cream
1½ ounces nutmeg

Completely dissolve sugar in water. Combine with half and half, brandy and vanilla. May be stored at this point.
    When ready to serve, put scoops of vanilla ice cream in bottom of each pitcher or punch bowl. Pour in milk punch. Ice cream will add flavor and keep punch cold. Serve sprinkled with nutmeg.
    Yield: 8½ gallons

*Teecy D. Wagner*

# Midday

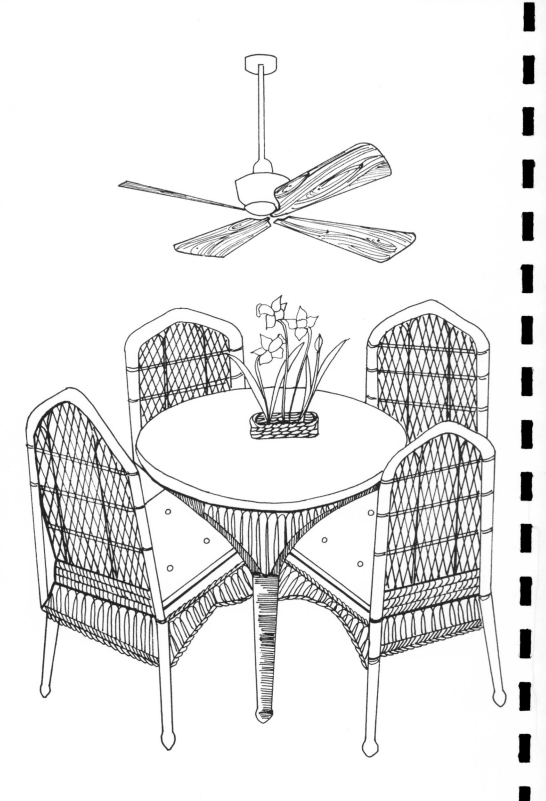

# DÉJEUNER À DEUX                    *(Serves 2)*

When the occasion calls for an important luncheon for two.

### *Trout Evangeline   or   *Veal Etruscan
### *Tossed Green Salad
### *Toasted French Bread Slices

### *Apple Tarts
### Coffee

*Macon Blanc or California Chardonnay with trout*
*Grignolino or Bardolino with veal*

## Trout Evangeline

3   cups water
½   teaspoon salt
¼   teaspoon white pepper
2 to 3 slices lemon
1   onion, quartered
2   teaspoons minced parsley
2   ribs celery, chopped
12  ounces fresh trout, redfish or
     bass fillets, boned and skinned
2   tablespoons butter
¼   cup chopped green onions

2   tablespoons flour
2   tablespoons white wine
Salt, pepper and Tabasco to taste
1   egg yolk, beaten
6   shrimp, cooked and peeled
6   oysters
1   teaspoon minced parsley
¼   cup lump crabmeat
Paprika, lemon slices and parsley
     for garnish

Combine the first 7 ingredients; simmer for 10 minutes. Add fish fillets; poach for 5 to 10 minutes until tender. Remove fish to individual 8×4-inch oval casserole dishes. Cover and refrigerate. Simmer stock an additional 5 to 10 minutes. Strain and reserve.

Melt butter and sauté green onions until tender. Blend in flour; cook slowly for 5 minutes. Stir constantly; do not brown. Remove from heat; add 1 cup fish stock, wine and seasonings, stirring until smooth. Return to low heat; stir constantly until thick. Add 2 tablespoons sauce to egg yolk; stir egg mixture back into sauce, blending well. Continue cooking gently; add shrimp, oysters, crabmeat and parsley. Heat thoroughly until oysters curl, 5 to 10 minutes. Pour sauce over fillets in casserole dishes, which may now be refrigerated again until time to reheat.

Heat at 325°, uncovered, for 20 to 25 minutes if sauce has been refrigerated, for 10 to 15 minutes if it has not, or until hot throughout and bubbly around sides of dish. Before serving, each dish may be topped with lemon slices, a sprinkle of paprika, and parsley.

*Mary Frances L. James*

## Veal Etruscan

| | |
|---|---|
| ½ tablespoon butter | ¼ cup white wine |
| 2 tablespoons olive oil | 1 onion, sliced |
| 1 clove garlic, pressed | ¼ pound mushrooms, sliced |
| ¾ to 1 pound *white* veal | 1 green pepper, quartered |
|    tenderloin, thinly sliced in | 1 8-ounce can tomato sauce |
|    medallions | ½ cup water |
| Salt, black pepper, cayenne and | |
|    rosemary to taste | |

In a heavy skillet, sauté garlic in butter and olive oil. Add veal and sauté *very lightly and quickly* on both sides; season. Cook slowly for 10 minutes over low heat. Add wine; simmer for approximately 5 more minutes. Add onions, mushrooms and pepper. Continue cooking until vegetables wilt. Add tomato sauce and water; cook for 10 to 15 minutes, or until meat and vegetables are tender.

*Dee B. Basignani*

## Toasted French Bread Slices

1 loaf French bread
¼ pound butter, softened

Slice bread very thin; butter lightly on one side. Toast on a cookie sheet at 225° for 2½ hours. Serve hot. Keeps for days in tightly covered container.

## Apple Tarts

| | |
|---|---|
| 1½ cups grated apples | 2 individual tart shells, baked |
| ½ cup sugar | ½ cup heavy cream, whipped |
| ½ teaspoon freshly grated nutmeg | |

Mix apples, sugar and nutmeg. Store in refrigerator overnight or for several days. Immediately before serving, spoon apple mixture into shells. Top with whipped cream.

Variation: Serve apple mixture in sherbet dishes instead of pastry shells; toasted pecans may be added.

*Ledoux R. Provosty, Jr.*

# SALAD LUNCHEON *(Serves 4)*

Easy to serve after a busy morning.

### *Vegetable Medley Salad or *Chef Salad
### Hot Rolls
### *Toffee Bars or *Delicate Lemon Fingers
### Iced Tea

*Green Hungarian or Emerald Riesling*

## Vegetable Medley Salad

½ head lettuce and ½ head
   Romaine, torn
2 medium carrots, grated
1 8-ounce can green peas,
   drained

1 8-ounce can Blue Lake green
   beans, drained
2 tomatoes, quartered
1 avocado, peeled and sliced
2 hard-boiled eggs, sliced

Mix greens and carrots. Toss with remaining ingredients. Serve with the following dressing.

### Buttermilk Dressing

1 cup mayonnaise
½ cup catsup
½ cup buttermilk

Pinch of garlic powder
1 teaspoon paprika
½ teaspoon Worcestershire sauce

Blend ingredients together.
Yield: 1 pint

*Peggy E. Brian*

## Chef Salad

1 6-ounce jar marinated artichoke
   hearts
1 clove garlic, pressed
1 teaspoon salt
2 tablespoons lemon juice
1 16-ounce can mixed bean
   salad, drained

1 cucumber, sliced
1 cup Cheddar cheese cubes
2 tomatoes, cut into pieces
1 cup diced ham, turkey or
   chicken
Cayenne to taste
Lettuce

Drain artichoke hearts and reserve oil. Combine with next 9 ingredients in salad bowl. Refrigerate for 24 hours. Toss with reserved oil and serve on bed of lettuce.

*Howard N. Nugent, Jr.*

## Toffee Bars

¼  pound butter
¼  pound margarine
½  cup sugar
1   16-ounce box Keebler's
     Graham Crackers, divided at
     perforations

1   cup slivered or chopped
     almonds

Line shallow cookie sheets (with sides) with graham cracker squares. Melt butter and margarine in saucepan, then stir in sugar. Bring to slow boil and cook for 2 minutes; spoon syrup over crackers. Sprinkle with almonds. Bake exactly 10 minutes at 350°. Remove with spatula while hot to aluminum foil sheet. Cool.

*Margaret D. Ratelle*

## Delicate Lemon Fingers

¼  pound butter
1   cup sifted flour
¼  cup confectioners' sugar
1   cup sugar

2   tablespoons flour
½  teaspoon baking powder
2   eggs
3   tablespoons lemon juice

Mix first 3 ingredients together and press evenly into 9×9×2-inch pan (moisten fingers to avoid sticking). Bake for 15 minutes at 350°.

Mix remaining ingredients and pour over baked bottom layer. Return to oven for 20 to 25 minutes. Do not overcook. Top should be a little soft. Cut into fingers or squares when cool and sprinkle with additional confectioners' sugar.

*Bess L. Foster*

# SIMPLE BUT SPECIAL                              *(Serves 4)*

A tasty and attractive luncheon which can be skillfully executed by even an inexperienced cook.

### Tray of Raw Relishes
### *Tomato Juice Cocktail

### *Cheese Soufflé
### *Avocado, Grapefruit and Orange Salad
### Rolls

### Ice Cream with *Melba Sauce
### Coffee

*Entre-Deux-Mers or California Chablis*

## Tomato Juice Cocktail

20  ounces tomato juice
1   tablespoon vinegar
1   tablespoon lemon juice
1   teaspoon Worcestershire sauce

Salt, pepper, garlic salt, and
    Tabasco to taste
1   teaspoon horseradish (optional)

Mix well ahead and chill.

*Ellen I. Latham*

## Cheese Soufflé

1   cup milk
1   tablespoon cornstarch
1¼  cups grated sharp cheese
    (¼ pound)

Pinch of salt
3   eggs, separated

Cook milk and cornstarch together slowly, blending well. Add cheese a little at a time, stirring until cheese is completely melted. Add salt. Beat egg yolks until fluffy and add hot cheese mixture. Mix thoroughly. Fold in stiffly beaten egg whites. Pour into well-greased soufflé dish or 1½-quart casserole. Place in pan of hot water. Bake 40 minutes at 375°.
*Serve immediately.*

*Fanny D. Simon*

## Avocado, Grapefruit and Orange Salad

| | |
|---|---|
| 1 avocado, peeled and sliced | 1 grapefruit |
| 1 tablespoon lemon juice | Lettuce leaves |
| 1 orange | |

Sprinkle avocado slices with lemon juice. Using a sharp paring knife, peel the skin and outer pulp from the orange and grapefruit. Slice toward the center along the side of each membrane and remove fruit sections.

Arrange the avocado and fruit sections on lettuce leaves. Serve with celery seed dressing.

### Celery Seed Dressing

| | |
|---|---|
| ¾ to 1 cup sugar | ½ teaspoon celery salt |
| 1 teaspoon salt | ⅓ cup white vinegar |
| 1 teaspoon dry mustard | 1 cup salad oil |
| 3 tablespoons grated onion | 2 tablespoons celery seed |

Combine first 7 ingredients in blender and, on low speed, add oil a little at a time. Stir in celery seed.

Yield: 1 pint

## Melba Sauce

| | |
|---|---|
| 1 10-ounce package frozen raspberries | ¼ cup sugar |
| ¾ cup black currant jelly | ½ teaspoon lemon juice |

Cook first 3 ingredients over moderate heat, stirring until mixture comes to a boil. Simmer, stirring occasionally, for 20 minutes. Strain and cool. Add lemon juice. Chill.

Yield: 1 cup

*Caroline K. Gilliland*

# SPRINGTIME IN LOUISIANA *(Serves 6)*

Louisiana cuisine is prominently identified with the crawfish, those small pugnacious crustaceans found throughout the state in every roadside ditch. Recreational crawfishing is a familiar sign of springtime. Cooked imaginatively and eaten with delight, crawfish dishes epitomize Louisiana.

*Crawfish Pie*
*Fresh Asparagus*
*French Bread*

*Mile-high Cake*
*Louisiana Strawberries*
*Coffee*

*Muscadet or Chenin Blanc*

## Crawfish Pie

| | |
|---|---|
| 4 tablespoons butter | ½ to 1 cup basic brown sauce (see following) |
| ½ cup peanut oil | |
| ½ cup chopped onion | 1 tablespoon Worcestershire sauce |
| 1 cup chopped celery | |
| ¼ cup chopped green pepper | ½ teaspoon Tabasco |
| ¼ cup chopped green onions | Salt and pepper to taste |
| ½ cup minced parsley | 2 teaspoons Beau Monde seasoning (optional) |
| 2 cups sliced mushrooms | |
| 2 cups cooked and peeled crawfish tails (1 pound) | 1 baked 8-inch pie shell or 6 individual shells, about 4 ounce capacity each |
| ½ cup sliced water chestnuts | |

Heat butter and oil in heavy skillet. Add onions, celery and peppers; sauté until limp and transparent. Add green onions, parsley and mushrooms; sauté until vegetables are wilted. Add crawfish tails, water chestnuts, brown sauce and seasonings, stirring and cooking just to blend. Pour into shell or shells and serve.

Variation: 2 cups cooked, peeled shrimp may be substituted for crawfish.

*Dorothy I. Stuckey*

### Brown Sauce

2 to 3 tablespoons oil  
2   tablespoons diced carrots  
2   tablespoons diced onions  
1   tablespoon diced celery  

1½ tablespoons flour  
1½ tablespoons tomato paste  
2½ cups beef stock  
1½ cups red wine  

In heavy skillet heat oil; add vegetables. Cook until they begin to brown. Remove from heat; stir in flour, tomato paste, and stock. Return to heat and bring to a boil; simmer about 30 minutes with pan half-covered. Add wine and cook uncovered for 20 minutes. Strain and use as required. Freezes well.

Yield: 2½ to 3 cups

## Mile-high Cake

2   cups sifted flour  
1½ cups sugar  
3   teaspoons baking powder  
1   teaspoon salt  
½  cup vegetable oil  
¾  cup water  

7   eggs at room temperature,  
    separated  
1   teaspoon vanilla  
1   teaspoon almond extract  
½  teaspoon cream of tartar  
Confectioners' sugar  

Mix dry ingredients in a bowl, making a well in center. Pour oil, water, egg yolks and flavorings into well. Beat 7 to 10 minutes at medium speed on mixer. In separate bowl, add cream of tartar to egg whites and beat until stiff but not dry. Fold batter gently into whites. Bake in ungreased tube pan at 325° for 45 minutes, at 350° for an additional 10 minutes. Invert on a funnel or bottle until cool. Loosen around rim and turn out onto cake plate. Dust with confectioners' sugar.

*Lillie G. Goldstein*

# SUMMER SEAFOOD                                    *(Serves 6)*

The shrimp industry is one of Louisiana's most important fisheries resources. Year-round availability of these shellfish from the Gulf of Mexico inspires an immense repertoire of shrimp dishes.

### *Green Peppers Stuffed with Shrimp*
### *Herb-marinated Tomatoes*
### *Cool-rise White Bread*

### *Cheese Cake  or  *Sherry Cooler*
### Iced Tea

*Grenache Rosé or Sylvaner*

## *Green Peppers Stuffed with Shrimp*

| | |
|---|---|
| 3   onions, chopped | 3½ cups dry French bread crumbs |
| ½ cup chopped celery | ½ teaspoon cayenne |
| ½ cup chopped green pepper | Salt and pepper to taste |
| 1 clove garlic, pressed | 6   green peppers, halved, seeded |
| ¼ pound margarine | and scalded |
| 2   pounds peeled raw shrimp | 2   tablespoons margarine |

Sauté onions, celery, chopped pepper and garlic in margarine until wilted. Add shrimp, stirring only to mix. Cover and cook very slowly for 15 minutes. Reserve ½ cup bread crumbs, adding remainder to seafood mixture. Add up to ½ cup water, if necessary. Season to taste. Stuff into pepper shells and sprinkle with reserved bread crumbs. Dot with additional margarine and bake at 300° for 15 minutes.

Crawfish is an excellent substitute for shrimp but, when adding to wilted vegetables, cook only 5 minutes.

*Hope J. Norman*

## Herb-marinated Tomatoes

¼ cup tarragon vinegar
⅔ cup salad oil
1 teaspoon salt
¼ teaspoon pepper
½ teaspoon thyme or marjoram

¼ cup chopped parsley
¼ cup minced chives
6 to 8 tomatoes, peeled and
   quartered

Mix first 7 ingredients and pour over tomatoes. Marinate in covered dish for 24 hours in refrigerator. Stir occasionally.

*Bootsie P. Voelker*

## Cool-rise White Bread

2 packages yeast
½ cup warm water
2 tablespoons sugar
1 teaspoon salt
3 tablespoons margarine or
   shortening

1¾ cups warm milk
5½ to 6 cups flour
Vegetable oil
Melted margarine

Sprinkle yeast over warm water in a large mixer bowl. Stir until dissolved. Add sugar, salt, margarine, milk and 2 cups flour. Beat with mixer at medium speed until smooth and bubbly. Add 1 cup flour and beat 150 strokes by hand. Gradually add remaining flour, working it in to make a soft dough which leaves the side of the pan. Turn out on a lightly floured board. Knead 5 to 10 minutes until smooth and springy. Cover dough and allow to rest for 20 minutes.

To shape loaves, punch down and divide dough in half. Roll and shape each half into a 12×8-inch rectangle. Break down air bubbles. Beginning with upper 8-inch end, roll, seal ends, and fold under. Place loaves seam side down in center of greased 8½×4½×2⅝-inch loaf pans. Brush with a little vegetable oil and cover loosely with plastic wrap. Allow to rise in refrigerator 2 to 24 hours.

Remove from refrigerator, uncover, and let stand 10 minutes. Break any gas bubbles with a greased toothpick. Bake 30 to 40 minutes at 400°. Remove from pans, brush with margarine, and cool on wire racks.

*Laura F. Waring*

## Cheese Cake

| | |
|---|---|
| 16 ounces cream cheese at room temperature | 1 teaspoon vanilla |
| 4 eggs | ½ pint sour cream |
| 1 cup sugar | ¼ cup sugar |
| Pinch of salt | ¼ teaspoon almond extract |
| | Maraschino cherries (optional) |

Beat cream cheese with mixer until fluffy. Add eggs, 1 at a time, beating constantly. When thoroughly mixed, blend 1 cup sugar, salt and vanilla in slowly. Pour mixture into an 8-inch square greased pan. Bake 45 minutes at 350°. Cool.

Mix sour cream with remaining sugar and almond extract. Spread over cooled cake. Return to oven and bake 15 minutes at 350°. Cool again and chill several hours, overnight or longer. Cut into serving pieces and top with cherries.

*Izy R. Steinschulte*


## Sherry Cooler

| | |
|---|---|
| 2 tablespoons gelatin | 3 tablespoons lemon juice |
| 1 cup cold water | 1 lemon, thinly sliced |
| 1 cup sugar | ½ pint heavy cream, whipped, for topping |
| 1 cup boiling water | |
| 1½ cups sherry | |

Soak gelatin in cold water; dissolve sugar and gelatin mixture in boiling water. Add sherry and lemon juice. Pour into a 2-quart serving dish and float lemon slices on top. (Here is an excellent opportunity to use your favorite crystal bowl.) Chill until set. Ladle whipped cream on top and serve at the table.

*Eva Lou E. Wellborn*

# OYSTER LOAVES  (Serves 6)

Perfect any time of day for a small, informal group. Oysters are an all time favorite eaten either raw or cooked in an infinite variety of ways. The brackish waters from the Gulf of Mexico mingle with the fresh water lakes and rivers to give Louisiana bivalves a special taste.

### *Pumpkin Soup

### *Oyster Loaves

### *Lime Sherbet      *Brownies
### Coffee

*California Sauvignon Blanc or Sancerre*

## Pumpkin Soup

| | |
|---|---|
| 2    tablespoons butter | 1    teaspoon salt |
| ¼ cup chopped onion | ⅛ teaspoon pepper |
| 1¼ teaspoons curry powder | ¼ teaspoon MSG (optional) |
| 1    tablespoon flour | 3½ cups chicken broth |
| 2    cups cooked pumpkin | 2    cups cream |
| 1    teaspoon brown sugar | Minced parsley for garnish |
| ⅛ teaspoon nutmeg or mace | |

In 4 quart heavy saucepan melt butter. Add onion, curry powder and flour; sauté 2 or 3 minutes. Stir in pumpkin and next 5 ingredients which have been combined. Add chicken broth. Bring to a simmer. Remove from heat a few minutes to blend flavors. Stir in cream and bring back just to simmer. Adjust seasonings; sprinkle with parsley.

*Dorothy I. Stuckey*

## Oyster Loaves

| | |
|---|---|
| 2    cups corn flour or yellow corn meal | 1    quart peanut oil, heated to 350° |
| 1½ teaspoons salt | 2    loaves French bread, each 20 inches long |
| ½ teaspoon black pepper | ¼ pound butter, softened |
| ½ teaspoon cayenne | 2    cloves garlic, pressed |
| 4    dozen oysters, drained | 2    tablespoons minced parsley |

Season corn meal or corn flour with salt and pepper; shake oysters in mixture. Fry quickly in hot oil until oysters float (about 1½ minutes). Allow oil to reheat before adding more oysters.

Split French bread loaves horizontally and cut into thirds. Scoop out centers. Blend butter with garlic and parsley; spread onto bread. Broil 2 minutes. Pile the oysters on and serve at once with:

| | |
|---|---|
| Sliced tomatoes | Catsup |
| Shredded lettuce | Tabasco |
| Mayonnaise | Lemon wedges |
| Tartar sauce | Horseradish |

*James D. Neilson. Jr.*

## Lime Sherbet

| | |
|---|---|
| 1 teaspoon gelatin | ½ cup plus 1 tablespoon lime juice |
| 4 teaspoons cold water | 2 cups milk |
| ½ cup plus 1 tablespoon sugar | Dash of salt |
| 2 tablespoons water | 1 cup heavy cream |
| ½ cup light corn syrup | 2 drops green food coloring |

Soak gelatin in the 4 teaspoons of cold water 5 minutes. In a heavy saucepan bring sugar, 2 tablespoons water and corn syrup to boiling over medium heat. Add gelatin mixture; cool. Add lime juice, milk and salt slowly to mixture. Freeze partially. Whip cream and add food coloring. Combine with gelatin mixture. Beat until frothy and return to freezer.

*Susan R. Chadwick*

## Brownies

| | |
|---|---|
| ½ pound butter | Pinch of salt |
| 4 ounces unsweetened chocolate | 4 eggs |
| 2 cups sugar | 2 teaspoons vanilla |
| 1½ cups sifted flour | 1½ cups chopped nuts |

Melt the butter and chocolate; cool. Blend in sugar. Add flour and salt alternately with the eggs. Add vanilla and nuts. Pour into a greased 9×12-inch pan. Bake 30 to 40 minutes at 350°. Do not overbake. Brownies should be sticky. Let cool in pan; cut into squares.

Yield: 3 dozen

*Amelia K. Levine*

# QUICHE LUNCHEON *(Serves 6)*

An unusual use for one of Louisiana's most popular seafoods.

*Oyster-Spinach Quiche*
*Spiced Oranges*
**French Bread**

*Coffee-Toffee Dessert*
**Coffee**

*Graves or Blanc Fumé*

## Oyster-Spinach Quiche

| | |
|---|---|
| 1 white onion, chopped | Cayenne to taste (optional) |
| 2 tablespoons butter | 2 eggs, beaten |
| 1 10-ounce package frozen creamed spinach, thawed | 1 cup half and half |
| 2 tablespoons flour | 2 tablespoons grated Parmesan cheese |
| 1 teaspoon salt | 1 dozen oysters, drained |
| ¼ teaspoon pepper | 1 9-inch pie shell, baked |
| ¼ teaspoon nutmeg | |

Sauté onion in butter; stir in spinach and cook 2 minutes. Add flour and seasonings. Combine eggs with cream and cheese; beat well and stir into spinach mixture. Place oysters in pie shell and cover with spinach mixture. Bake at 400° for 50 to 55 minutes.

*Nancy C. Weems*

## Spiced Oranges

| | |
|---|---|
| ¾ cup sugar | 2 cinnamon sticks |
| 1 cup water | 4 lemon slices |
| 1 cup dry red wine | 6 navel oranges, peeled and sectioned |
| 5 cloves | |

Combine all ingredients except oranges in heavy saucepan and bring to a boil. Simmer 10 minutes. Pour over oranges and refrigerate.

*JoAnn W. Kellogg*

## *Coffee-Toffee Dessert*

¼ cup dark brown sugar, firmly
   packed
¾ cup finely chopped pecans
1 ounce unsweetened chocolate,
   grated
1 stick piecrust mix, finely
   crumbled
1 tablespoon water
1 teaspoon vanilla
¼ pound butter

¾ cup sugar
1 ounce unsweetened chocolate,
   melted and cooled
3 teaspoons instant coffee
   powder
2 eggs
1 teaspoon rum extract
1 tablespoon confectioners' sugar
½ teaspoon rum extract
½ pint heavy cream, whipped

Mix brown sugar, pecans, grated chocolate and piecrust mix. Add water
and vanilla. Mix well. Moisten fingers with cool water and press mixture firmly
into bottom and sides of a well-buttered 8-inch pie pan. Bake at 350° for 15
minutes. Cool.

Cream butter, gradually adding sugar. Stir in melted chocolate and 2 teaspoons coffee. Add eggs, 1 at a time, beating at medium speed for 5 minutes
after each addition. Add rum extract.

Break cooled crust into bite-sized pieces. Fold into coffee mixture. Spoon
into crystal dessert dishes. Refrigerate.

Fold 1 teaspoon coffee, confectioners' sugar and rum extract into whipped
cream. Chill. Immediately before serving desserts, add dollop of topping to
each.

Variation: Pour filling into cooled crust. Refrigerate. Immediately before
serving, cut into wedges and add topping.

*Florence B. Crowell*

# FRIENDS GATHER

Good for a day of cards or sports.

### *Curried Lima Bean Soup*

### *Brown Derby Salad   or   *Sardis Salad*
### *No-knead Bread*
### *Cherokee Plantation Tea*

### *Lemon Chiffon Pie   or   *Coeur de Creme*
### Coffee

*Chenin Blanc or Pouilly-Fuissé/Vinzelles*

## Curried Lima Bean Soup

| | |
|---|---|
| 1   10-ounce package frozen lima. beans | ⅛ teaspoon pepper |
| 2   tablespoons butter or margarine | ½ teaspoon tarragon |
| ⅓ cup sliced green onions | 4   sprigs parsley |
| 1   teaspoon curry powder | 1½ cups chicken broth |
| ½ teaspoon salt | ½ cup cream |

In a saucepan combine beans, butter, onions and curry powder with the amount of water directed on package and cook until soft. Purée in blender with salt, pepper, tarragon and parsley. Return to saucepan, add chicken broth and cream, and heat gently. Serve hot or cold. Louisianians often serve appetizer soups in a *demitasse* before coming to the table.

Yield: 28 ounces

*Fredda D. Texada*

## Brown Derby Salad

| | |
|---|---|
| ½ head of lettuce, shredded | ¾ cup crumbled Roquefort cheese (3 ounces) |
| 6   halves chicken breasts, cooked and diced | 2   medium avocados, peeled and cut into wedges |
| 2   tomatoes, peeled and diced | 1   small stalk endive, sliced |
| 3   hard-boiled eggs, chopped | 1   tablespoon chopped chives |
| 6   slices crisp bacon, crumbled | |

Place lettuce in a large salad bowl. Arrange chicken, tomatoes, eggs, bacon and cheese on top. Garnish with avocado and endive. Sprinkle with chives. Toss at the table with French dressing.

### French Dressing

¾ cup salad oil                          Salt and pepper to taste
¼ cup vinegar or lemon juice

   Mix together and chill.

*Terry H. Easterling*

## Sardis Salad

6  halves chicken breasts, cooked       1  cup cooked green peas, drained
   and diced                            1  cup chopped pecans
3  tablespoons chopped green            1  cup mayonnaise
   onions                               1  cup sour cream
½  to 1 cup chopped celery,             Salt, pepper and Tabasco to taste
   including leaves                      Paprika for garnish
3  tablespoons capers, drained          8 lettuce leaves
1  cup chopped parsley

   Mix first 7 ingredients; chill. In a separate bowl blend mayonnaise, sour
cream and seasonings; chill. When ready to serve, combine and mound on
lettuce. Sprinkle with paprika.
   Variation: 4 cups lump crabmeat may be substituted for chicken.

*Margaret D. Ratelle*

## No-knead Bread

2  cups warm water                      6½ to 7 cups flour
2  packages yeast                       1  egg
½  cup sugar                            ¼  cup shortening
2  teaspoons salt

   In a large mixer bowl dissolve yeast in water. Add sugar, salt and about half
the flour. Beat thoroughly at medium speed for 2 minutes. Add egg and
shortening; beat in the remaining flour gradually until smooth. At this point
the dough may be covered with plastic wrap and stored in the refrigerator
until ready to continue preparation.
   About 2 hours before baking, shape into round or long loaves or rolls, and
place on a greased baking sheet or into 2  8½×4½×2⅝-inch greased loaf
pans. Cover with greased plastic wrap. Let rise in a warm place 1½ to 2
hours. Bake at 375° for 12 to 15 minutes for rolls, 35 to 45 minutes for
loaves.
   Yield: 2 loaves or 3 dozen pocketbook rolls

*Merrill C. Rush*

## Cherokee Plantation Tea

| | |
|---|---|
| 3 tablespoons tea leaves | 4½ quarts boiling water |
| 3 cups boiling water | ¾ cup lemon juice |
| 6 handfuls mint leaves and stalks | 6 to 8 mint sprigs for garnish |
| ¾ cup sugar | |

Place tea in a large warmed ceramic pot. Add 3 cups boiling water and swirl around to "dust" tea, then pour off and discard water. Add mint and sugar. Pour in the 4½ quarts boiling water, cover, and steep 7 minutes. Strain and add lemon juice. Serve over ice in chilled julep cups, garnished with mint sprigs.

Yield: 12    12-ounce glasses

*Theodosia M. Nolan*


## Lemon Chiffon Pie

| | |
|---|---|
| 4 eggs, separated | 1 teaspoon grated lemon peel |
| ½ cup lemon juice | ½ pint heavy cream, whipped and |
| ½ teaspoon salt | sweetened to taste |
| ¾ cup sugar | |
| 1 tablespoon gelatin softened in ¼ cup cold water | |

Beat egg yolks in the top of a double boiler with the lemon juice, salt, and ¼ cup of the sugar. Cook, stirring constantly, over hot, not boiling, water until of custard consistency. Add the softened gelatin and stir until completely dissolved. Stir in lemon peel. Cool. When mixture begins to thicken, fold in egg whites which have been stiffly beaten with the remaining ½ cup sugar. Fill the following baked pie shell and chill. Top with whipped cream.

### Pie Shell

| | |
|---|---|
| 1 cup flour | ⅓ cup well-chilled shortening |
| ½ teaspoon salt | 2 to 3 tablespoons cold water |

Sift flour and salt into a large mixing bowl. Cut shortening into flour mixture rapidly. When shortening is the size of tiny peas, add water gradually, mixing lightly until dough holds together. Shape into a ball and refrigerate 30 minutes. Place on a floured surface and roll to ⅛-inch thickness, 2 inches larger than 10-inch pie pan. Transfer to pan; trim edges and flute. Prick pastry with a fork and bake at 400° approximately 10 minutes or until golden brown.

*Virginia B. Klock*

## *Coeur de Crème*

9   ounces cream cheese at room        ⅛   teaspoon salt
    temperature                        1   cup heavy cream, whipped
2   tablespoons milk

Beat first 3 ingredients together until soft and fluffy. Fold into the whipped cream. Place in a wet heart-shaped mold and chill thoroughly. Serve with fresh berries or the following sauce.

### *Cherry Sauce*

1   16½-ounce can dark sweet          2 to 3 tablespoons arrowroot
    pitted cherries in heavy syrup

Heat cherries and syrup. Slowly blend in arrowroot and stir until thickened. Purée in blender. Chill.

*Louise A. Simon*

# HEARTY SOUP AND SANDWICH *(Serves 8)*

A satisfying meal for the healthiest of appetites.

## *Black Bean Soup*
## *Spedini*
## *Orange Apricot Sherbet*
## *Heirloom Cookies*
## *Coffee*

## Black Bean Soup

| | |
|---|---|
| 1 pound dried black beans, rinsed and drained | 2 teaspoons Worcestershire sauce |
| 2 quarts water | 2 tablespoons lemon juice |
| ½ pound salt pork or ham hocks | Salt and pepper to taste |
| 1 yellow onion, quartered | 2 tablespoons sherry |
| 4 tablespoons chopped celery | 2 cups hot chicken stock (optional) |
| 4 tablespoons minced parsley | 8 lemon slices studded with cloves |
| 4 whole cloves | |

In a large pot combine first 7 ingredients. Simmer over low heat until tender (about 3 hours). Remove meat and cloves; dice meat. Purée soup in blender at low speed; add chicken stock if thinner soup is desired and return to heat. Add remaining seasonings, sherry and meat. Serve hot, garnished with lemon slices.

*Jane Ann F. Jarrell*

## Spedini

| | |
|---|---|
| 2 20-inch loaves of French bread | 2 tablespoons poppy seeds |
| ½ cup chopped yellow onion | 1 pound Swiss cheese, sliced |
| ¼ pound butter | 16 slices bacon |
| 3 to 4 tablespoons prepared mustard | |

Remove most of crust from top of bread. Slice at 1-inch intervals almost through. Sauté onion in butter; add mustard and poppy seeds. Spoon this mixture into cuts in loaf. Insert slices of Swiss cheese. Arrange bacon over top of loaf. May be wrapped in foil and frozen at this point. Bake uncovered at 350° for 10 to 15 minutes (30 minutes if frozen) or until cheese melts and bacon is crisp.

*Peggy E. Brian*

## *Orange Apricot Sherbet*

2½ cups sugar
2   tablespoons flour
2   cups orange juice
6   tablespoons lemon juice

1   16-ounce can apricots, drained
    and mashed
1½ cups heavy cream

Combine all ingredients. Freeze until almost hard. Remove from freezer and whip well. Refreeze in mold. Let set at room temperature 10 to 15 minutes before serving.

*Willie L. Morgan*


## *Heirloom Cookies*

½   pound butter
1   tablespoon vanilla
1   cup confectioners' sugar
½   teaspoon salt
1¼ cups ground almonds

2   cups sifted flour
French decorets or ½ cup
    confectioners' sugar mixed with
    2 teaspoons cinnamon, for
    topping

Cream butter, vanilla, sugar and salt. Add almonds. Blend in flour. Shape dough into small balls. To decorate before baking, roll shaped dough in decorets. Bake on ungreased cookie sheet at 325°, for 15 to 18 minutes. (Cookies will not brown). To decorate after baking, roll warm cookies in cinnamon and sugar mixture.
    Yield: 4½ dozen

*Terry H. Easterling*

# GULF SHRIMP SALADS (Serves 8)

A cold seafood luncheon featuring shrimp, usually abundant in Louisiana markets.

*Eggplant Soup*

*Shrimp Salad or *Shrimp Aspic*
*Melba Toast*

*Lemon Cake Pudding*
*Coffee*

*Grey Riesling or Alsatian Riesling*

## Eggplant Soup

| | |
|---|---|
| 2 tablespoons butter | 1¼ teaspoons curry powder |
| 2 tablespoons oil | ⅛ teaspoon thyme |
| 1 cup chopped onion | ⅛ teaspoon basil |
| ¾ cup chopped celery | 1 teaspoon salt |
| 2 pounds eggplant, peeled and diced | Freshly ground black pepper |
| | 6 to 7 cups chicken stock |
| 2 cups peeled, thinly sliced potatoes | Pinch cayenne |
| | 2 cups heavy cream |

Steam onion and celery in hot oil and butter in tightly covered pot for 10 minutes over low heat. Add eggplant and potatoes; steam 15 minutes more until vegetables soften. Stir in next 6 ingredients. Bring to a boil; lower heat and simmer 30 minutes. Cool for 10 minutes. Purée in blender. Add cayenne and cream. Serve hot or cold. Freezes well.

Yield: 1½ to 2 quarts

*Margaret D. Ratelle*

## Shrimp Salad

3   pounds headless shrimp
2   quarts water
1   teaspoon salt
1   lemon, thinly sliced
1   onion, thinly sliced
1   7¼-ounce can pitted black
    olives, drained
1   16-ounce can green beans,
    drained
½   cup lemon juice

¼   cup salad oil
1   tablespoon wine or tarragon
    vinegar
1   clove garlic, pressed
1   bay leaf
1   tablespoon dry mustard
1   teaspoon salt
½   teaspoon cayenne
Freshly ground black pepper
1   head lettuce

Bring water and salt to boil; add shrimp and cook 5 to 10 minutes after water returns to boil. Drain immediately; peel and devein. Combine shrimp with lemon and onion slices, olives and green beans; toss lightly. Make dressing of next 8 ingredients; pour over shrimp and vegetables. Marinate at least 2 hours in refrigerator. Just before serving, tear lettuce and toss with shrimp mixture.

*Frances B. Davis*

## Shrimp Aspic

2   tablespoons gelatin
½   cup cold water
2½  cups tomato juice
2   tablespoons lemon juice
1   teaspoon Worcestershire sauce
1   tablespoon fresh onion juice
1   teaspoon salt
Cayenne to taste

1   teaspoon horseradish
¼   cup minced celery, including
    leaves
¼   cup minced green pepper
¼   cup chopped avocado
    (optional)
1½  cups cooked shrimp

Soften gelatin in cold water. Heat, do not boil, 1 cup tomato juice and pour over gelatin, stirring until completely dissolved. Add remaining tomato juice and seasonings; chill an hour or until mixture begins to thicken. Stir in remaining ingredients. Pour mixture into an oiled 4 or 5 cup ring mold which has been placed in freezer for 30 minutes before use. Refrigerate for several hours or overnight. Unmold on a cold serving plate 30 minutes before serving and return to refrigerator to firm. Serve with the following mayonnaise.
    Variation: Omit shrimp.

*Emily S. French*

### Tangy Mayonnaise

| | |
|---|---|
| 2 egg yolks | 3 tablespoons lemon juice |
| 1 teaspoon prepared mustard | 1½ cups salad oil |
| 1 teaspoon salt | Cayenne |

Place egg yolks, mustard, salt, lemon juice and ½ cup oil in blender. Cover; blend a few seconds until smooth. Without stopping blender, pour remaining oil into center of egg mixture *very slowly*. Blend just until oil is added and mixture is thick and smooth.

Yield: 1 pint

*Terry H. Easterling*


## Lemon Cake Pudding

| | |
|---|---|
| 1 cup sugar | Grated peel of 1 lemon |
| 4 tablespoons flour | 3 eggs, separated |
| ⅛ teaspoon salt | 1½ cups milk |
| 2 tablespoons melted margarine | 1 cup heavy cream, whipped |
| 5 tablespoons lemon juice | (optional) |

Combine first 4 ingredients. Add lemon juice and peel. Combine egg yolks and milk and add, mixing well. Fold stiffly beaten egg whites into mixture. Pour into 9×12-inch greased casserole. Place in pan of hot water and bake at 300° for 45 minutes. May also be baked in 8 individual custard cups for 30 minutes. Serve warm or chilled. Garnish with whipped cream.

*Persis M. Johns*

# PATIO PARTY

(Serves 8)

Louisiana is justly proud of its splendid supply of crabs and their delicate flavor. Epicureans relish the numerous ways of serving this seafood.

**\*Marinated Crabmeat   or   \*Crab Vinaigrette**

**Rolls**

**\*Peach Crumble   or   \*Rum Cream Pie**
**Iced Tea or Coffee**

## Marinated Crabmeat

2   pounds lump crabmeat
2   onions, thinly sliced
1   cup vegetable oil
1   cup vinegar

1   cup ice water
Salt and pepper to taste
Lettuce, tomatoes and hard-boiled
    eggs

Mix oil, vinegar and water. Pour over crabmeat and onion. Store covered in refrigerator for several hours. (Better if prepared a day ahead.) Drain well; serve on bed of lettuce garnished with quartered eggs and sliced tomatoes.

Variation: Serve with tomato aspic. Use the shrimp aspic recipe, p. 84, omitting shrimp.

*Frances B. Davis*

## Crab Vinaigrette

2   0.6-ounce envelopes Good
    Seasons Old Fashion French
    Salad Dressing Mix
½ cup dry white wine
1   cup salad oil
½ to ¾ cup white wine vinegar (or
    lemon juice)
6   tablespoons sliced green onions

6   tablespoons minced green
    pepper
4   tablespoons chopped parsley
6   tablespoons capers
2   pounds lump crabmeat
Lettuce, tomatoes and hard-boiled
    eggs for garnish

Combine wine with dressing mix in a jar; shake well. Add next 6 ingredients and shake again. Arrange crabmeat on lettuce leaves. Spoon the sauce generously over the crabmeat and garnish. Top with the following mayonnaise.

### Tart Mayonnaise

| | |
|---|---|
| 1 egg | 1½ teaspoons prepared mustard |
| 1 tablespoon lemon juice | Cayenne to taste |
| 1 teaspoon confectioners' sugar | 1 cup salad oil |
| ½ teaspoon salt | 1 tablespoon lemon juice |

Blend first 6 ingredients just until mixed. Turn blender to medium high speed and *slowly* add oil. Add the remaining lemon juice.

Yield: 1¼ cups

*Dorothy G. Portier*

## Peach Crumble

| | |
|---|---|
| 1 cup sugar | 1½ cups milk |
| 1 egg, beaten | 2 cups peeled, diced peaches, |
| 1 cup chopped walnuts | sprinkled with lemon juice |
| 1 5⅝-ounce package instant | 8 tablespoons sherry (optional) |
| vanilla pudding mix | 8 tablespoons whipped cream |
| 1½ cups sour cream | (optional) |

Combine sugar, egg and nuts. Line a 15×10×½-inch baking pan with greased foil. Spread nut mixture in pan. Bake at 350° for 18 to 20 minutes until golden brown; cool to room temperature. Coarsely crumble baked mixture. Divide half of the crumbs among 8 sherbet glasses. Combine pudding mix, sour cream and milk. Beat at low speed with mixer 1 or 2 minutes until well blended. Fold in peaches. Spoon the mixture over crumbs; top with remaining crumbs. Chill several hours. Spoon 1 tablespoon of sherry over each portion. Top with whipped cream.

*Terry H. Easterling*

## Rum Cream Pie

| | |
|---|---|
| 1 tablespoon gelatin | 1 pint heavy cream, whipped |
| ½ cup water | ⅓ to ½ cup dark rum |
| 6 egg yolks | 1 10-inch pastry shell, baked |
| 1 cup sugar | Semi-sweet chocolate shavings |

Soak gelatin in water. Bring to a boil over low heat. Beat egg yolks until very light in color. Add sugar, then stir in hot gelatin. Fold mixture into whipped cream. Add rum. When cool, but not set, pour into shell. Garnish with chocolate.

*Terry H. Easterling*

# SATURDAY LUNCH                    *(Serves 8)*

Good for the college crowd.

*\*Sangria*

*\*Chili Olé   or   \*Pizza*
*\*Overnight Coleslaw*

*\*Buttermilk Pound Cake*
*\*Heavenly Hash Cake*

## Sangria

| | |
|---|---|
| 2 lemons, sliced | 2 quarts red wine |
| 1 orange, sliced | 1 cup brandy |
| 2 limes, sliced | 2 quarts lemon-lime soda, chilled |
| 2 tablespoons sugar | Fruit slices for garnish (optional) |
| 1 teaspoon cinnamon | |

Place fruit in a large glass pitcher. Sprinkle with cinnamon and sugar. Allow to stand 1 hour. Mash fruit to extract juices. Add wine and brandy; chill. Just before serving, stir in soda. Serve in large wine glasses over ice.

Yield: 4½ quarts

*Karen N. Norman*

## Chili Olé

| | |
|---|---|
| 2 pounds ground chuck | 1 teaspoon cumin |
| 1½ cups chopped onion | 1 bay leaf |
| ½ cup chopped green pepper | ½ teaspoon cayenne |
| 1 clove garlic, pressed | 1 quart water |
| 1 28-ounce can Italian-style tomatoes | 3 tablespoons flour blended with ½ cup water for thickening (optional) |
| 1 15-ounce can Italian-style tomato sauce | 1 11-ounce can ranch style beans (optional) |
| 2 teaspoons salt | 1 pound sharp Cheddar cheese, cubed |
| 6 tablespoons chili powder | |
| 3 whole cloves | |

In a 3 or 4-quart Dutch oven, cook first 4 ingredients until meat is lightly browned. Add tomatoes, sauce, seasonings and water. Cover and simmer 1 hour. Skim fat. Remove bay leaf and cloves. Thicken with flour paste or add beans, if preferred. Serve hot garnished with cheese cubes.

*Mary Frances P. Ewing*

## Pizza

1 13¾-ounce package hot roll mix
2 tablespoons butter or margarine
½ pound mushrooms, sliced
1½ to 2 pounds bulk pork sausage
½ cup minced onion
1 8-ounce can tomato sauce

1 6-ounce can tomato paste
1 teaspoon oregano
½ pound Mozzarella cheese, grated
½ pound Parmesan cheese, grated
½ cup minced parsley

Prepare roll mix as label directs. Let rise in warm place until light (30 to 60 minutes). Sauté mushrooms in butter lightly. Remove and set aside. In same skillet, fry sausage until pink color disappears. Remove meat; pour off all drippings except 1 tablespoon and sauté onions until tender. Add tomato sauce, paste and oregano.

When dough is light, divide into 4 parts. Flatten each into a 10-inch pie pan. Sprinkle half the Mozzarella on dough. Cover with tomato mixture. Add remaining Mozzarella and sausage. Top with Parmesan cheese, parsley and mushrooms. Bake at 450° for 15 to 20 minutes.

Freezes well uncooked; add 15 minutes more baking time. May also be frozen after baking.

*Joyce M. Brewer*

## Overnight Coleslaw

1 head cabbage, shredded
1 to 2 onions, thinly sliced
⅓ to ½ cup sugar
1 cup white vinegar
2 teaspoons dry mustard

2½ teaspoons salt
1 teaspoon celery seed
2 to 3 tablespoons salad onions (optional)
1 cup salad oil

Layer cabbage and onions in a large container, sprinkling each layer with sugar. In a saucepan, bring next 5 ingredients to a boil. Remove from heat. Beat in oil. Heat again, but do not boil. Pour over cabbage mixture. Cover tightly and refrigerate at least 24 hours. Keeps well up to a week. Serve with a slotted spoon.

*Nina L. Ginsberg*

## Buttermilk Pound Cake

½ pound butter
2¾ cups sugar
4 eggs
3 cups sifted flour

¼ teaspoon baking soda
1 cup buttermilk
1 teaspoon vanilla, almond or
  lemon flavoring

Cream butter and sugar. Add eggs, 1 at a time, beating well after each addition. Resift flour with soda. Add alternately with buttermilk and flavoring. Bake in well-greased tube or bundt pan at 350° for 1 hour. Cool slightly. Invert on wire rack. Freezes well.

*Agatha B. Flowers*


## Heavenly Hash Cake

½ pound butter
4 tablespoons cocoa
4 eggs
2 cups sugar
1½ cups cake flour
2 cups toasted nuts, chopped

25 marshmallows, halved
1 pound confectioners' sugar
6 tablespoons cocoa
6 tablespoons butter
¾ cup evaporated milk

Melt ½ pound butter with 4 tablespoons cocoa. Beat eggs into sugar and add to chocolate mixture. Add flour and nuts. Bake in a 13×9×2-inch greased pan at 350° for 30 minutes. Immediately upon removing cake from oven, press marshmallows into cake to cover.

Sift confectioners' sugar with cocoa. Melt butter in milk. Add to chocolate mixture. Pour over warm cake.

*Amelia K. Levine*

# SPECIAL OCCASION *(Serves 10)*

Decorative and delicious; prepared a day ahead.

### *\*Zucchini Soup*

### *\*Centerpiece Salad*
### *\*Whole Wheat Bread*

### *\*Sunshine Cake*
### *Coffee*

*California or Alsatian Gewurztraminer*

## *Zucchini Soup*

| | |
|---|---|
| 4 tablespoons butter or margarine | White pepper to taste |
| 5 zucchini, sliced | 1 cup milk |
| 1 onion, sliced | 3 cups chicken stock |
| 1 potato, peeled and sliced | 1 13-ounce can evaporated milk |
| 1½ teaspoons salt | or equal amount of cream |
| ½ teaspoon soy sauce | Nutmeg (optional) |
| 1 teaspoon sugar | |

Sauté vegetables in butter until tender but not browned. Add salt, pepper, soy sauce and sugar. Purée with ¼ cup of milk in a blender. Return to saucepan and add stock, remaining milk, and canned milk. Correct seasonings. Serve hot or cold with a dash of nutmeg. Freezes well.

Yield: 3 quarts

*Margaret D. Ratelle*

## Centerpiece Salad

8   red potatoes, boiled, peeled and chopped
2   hard-boiled eggs, chopped
¼   cup chopped celery
2   dill pickles, chopped
½   cup mayonnaise
1   tablespoon prepared mustard
Salt and pepper to taste
½   onion minced (optional)
1   head lettuce
6   ounces sliced Muenster or Swiss cheese
6   tomatoes, cut into wedges

3   cucumbers, quartered and cut into 3 inch sticks
5   avocados, peeled and cut into wedges, drizzled with lemon juice
2   cups cubed ham or cooked shrimp
1   7¼-ounce can pitted ripe olives, drained
2   green peppers, cut into rings
1   bunch radishes
½   teaspoon oregano
½   cup salad oil
½   cup wine vinegar

Combine first 8 ingredients to make potato salad. Line a 14-inch platter with large lettuce leaves. Mound potato salad in center. Shred the rest of the head of lettuce over the salad. Cover lettuce with sliced cheese. Starting at the base of the salad mound, place alternating rings of tomato wedges, cucumber sticks and avocado wedges. Place ham cubes or shrimp between wedges. Decorate with pepper rings, olives and radishes. Sprinkle with crushed oregano. Cover tightly with plastic wrap and refrigerate. When ready to serve, drizzle with mixture of oil and vinegar. Serve in wedges cut at the table with a serrated pie server.

*Joyce M. Brewer*

## Whole Wheat Bread

2   cups flour
2   packages yeast
3   tablespoons sugar
1   teaspoon salt

2   cups milk
3   tablespoons vegetable oil
3½ to 4 cups whole wheat flour

Combine first 4 ingredients. Heat milk and oil to 115° and pour into dry ingredients. Beat until smooth. Add remaining flour to mixture gradually, beating well after each addition, until a soft dough forms. Knead 8 minutes on a lightly floured board. Cover and let rest 20 minutes. Divide in half and shape loaves. Place in 2 greased 8½×4½×2⅝-inch pans, cover with plastic wrap and refrigerate 2 to 24 hours. Let stand at room temperature for 10 minutes. Bake 30 to 35 minutes at 350°.

*Laura F. Waring*

## Sunshine Cake

8  eggs, separated
1  teaspoon cream of tartar
Pinch of salt
1¼ cups extra fine sugar
2  teaspoons vanilla
¼ to ½ teaspoon almond extract
1  cup sifted cake flour

1¼ cups sugar
½  cup flour
2½ cups milk, scalded
1  tablespoon gelatin softened in
   ½ cup cold water
3  cups heavy cream, whipped

Beat egg whites at low speed until foamy. Add salt and cream of tartar, then beat at high speed until stiff but not dry. Continue beating, gradually adding the extra fine sugar, 1 teaspoon vanilla and the almond extract. Gently fold in 4 beaten egg yolks. Fold in flour by sifting a little at a time on top of mixture until all flour is used. Bake in ungreased tube pan 40 to 50 minutes at 350°. Invert pan on a rack to cool. Remove cake from pan only after it is thoroughly cool.

Add sugar to 4 remaining egg yolks a little at a time, beating continuously until thick and creamy. Blend in flour gradually and beat until smooth. Stir in milk in small amounts. Cook over low heat, continuing to stir constantly, until custard thickens. Remove from heat and add gelatin, mixing until it dissolves. Cool; refrigerate until chilled but not set, stirring occasionally as it cools. When thoroughly chilled but not congealed, fold in whipped cream which has been flavored with remaining 1 teaspoon vanilla.

To assemble, cut cake into 3 layers and fill between layers with custard mixture. Frost top, sides and center hole of cake. Refrigerate for several hours before serving. This cake improves with age and is still delicious 48 hours after having been made.

*Miriam W. Wilkins*

# NEW ORLEANS FARE

*(Serves 10)*

Traditional Monday lunch in south Louisiana.

### *Red Beans 'n' Rice*
### *Green Salad*
### *French Bread*

### *Praline Sundaes*
### *Coffee*

*Zinfandel or Chianti*

## Red Beans 'n' Rice

| | |
|---|---|
| 1  pound red kidney beans, rinsed and drained | 1  teaspoon coarsely ground black pepper |
| 1  ham bone, plus left-over ham bits, cut up | 3  quarts water |
| 2  cups chopped red onion | 1  tablespoon salt |
| 2 to 3 cloves garlic, minced | 1  dried red pepper pod (or 1 teaspoon cayenne) |
| 2  cups chopped celery, including leaves | 1  pound smoked sausage, sliced, sautéed and drained |

In large Dutch oven, bring all ingredients except sausage to a boil; simmer 4 to 5 hours until beans are soft and liquid is thick. Stir in sausage for the last 30 minutes of cooking. Adjust seasonings. Serve over hot rice.

*Hope J. Norman*

### *Fluffy Rice*

| | |
|---|---|
| 2  cups water | 2  teaspoons salt |
| 2  cups long grain rice, rinsed | |

Place all ingredients in the top of a double boiler and cook over boiling water for 1 hour. Remove from pot with a fork, fluffing on plates or platter. Can be cooked ahead and reheated.

*Persis M. Johns*

## French Bread

| | | | |
|---|---|---|---|
| 5 | pound bag unbleached flour | 4 | tablespoons sugar |
| 5 | cups warm water | 2 | tablespoons salt |
| 2 | packages yeast | 2 | egg whites |

In order to keep flour contained, place flour bag in a large grocery sack while working. In a large mixer bowl dissolve yeast in water and stir in salt and sugar. Gradually add flour with mixer on low speed. Continue using mixer as long as possible while working in the flour. Remove dough to floured board and continue adding up to a total of 14 cups of flour, working dough as flour is added. When dough will take no more flour, knead by hand for 10 minutes. Place dough in a large greased bowl, turning dough to grease on all sides. Cover with a moist towel and let rise in a warm place away from drafts until doubled in bulk (about 1½ to 2 hours). Punch down, let rest a few minutes, then knead 3 or 4 times to remove air. Divide into 8 equal pieces, shape into loaves, place into well-greased French bread pans, and slash diagonally several times with a sharp knife. Lightly beat the egg whites and brush tops of loaves. Let rise again in a warm place until loaves fill pans completely (2 hours or more). Bake at 450° for 15 minutes, then lower temperature to 350° and bake an additional 30 minutes. Remove from pans and cool on rack. Wrap individually in aluminum foil and freeze.

To serve, warm in foil for 15 minutes at 350°, open foil and return to oven for 5 minutes longer, or until loaf is crisp and crust feels crunchy. The French bread pans specified in this recipe are of corrugated steel, double rounded and 18 inches long.

Yield: 8 loaves.

*Robertson L. Gilliland*

## Praline Sundaes

| | | | |
|---|---|---|---|
| ⅓ | cup water | ⅛ | teaspoon rum extract |
| ⅓ | cup brown sugar | ⅛ | teaspoon maple extract |
| 1 | cup white corn syrup | 10 | servings vanilla ice cream |
| 1 | cup chopped pecans | | |

Combine water, sugar and corn syrup in saucepan; cook slowly until mixture comes to a boil. Add nuts and flavorings. Cool. Cover and refrigerate.

To serve, spoon sauce over ice cream.

Yield: 1 pint sauce

*Jean A. Gamburg*

# OYSTER SPECIALTIES                          *(Serves 10)*

The special taste of Louisiana oysters has inspired gourmets for decades. Here are two dishes for which New Orleans has become world-renowned.

### *Creamy Tomato Soup*

### *Oysters Rockefeller   or   *Oysters Bienville*
### *Sourdough Bread*
### *Winter Salad*

### *Kahlua Mousse   or   *Apricot Mousse*
### Coffee

*Puligny-Montrachet or California Chardonnay*

## Creamy Tomato Soup

36  ounces tomato juice
8   ounces sour cream
4   tablespoons minced green
    onions
¼   teaspoon basil
¼   teaspoon curry
¼   teaspoon ginger

¼   teaspoon nutmeg
1   teaspoon salt
1   teaspoon sugar
2   tablespoons lemon juice
3   tablespoons catsup
Pepper to taste

Blend all ingredients together until thoroughly mixed. Chill at least 24 hours.
   Yield: 3 pints

*Norman A. Simon*

## Oysters Rockefeller

2   bunches green onions and tops,
    chopped
1   bunch parsley, minced
¼   pound butter or margarine
4   10-ounce packages chopped
    spinach, cooked, drained,
    puréed
1   tablespoon celery salt
¾   tablespoon anchovy paste
2   tablespoons Worcestershire
    sauce

2   tablespoons Tabasco
2   tablespoons horseradish
2   teaspoons basil
1   teaspoon marjoram
2   tablespoons absinthe (Pernod)
1   tablespoon Peychaud bitters
Salt to taste
5   dozen oysters, drained

Sauté onions and parsley in butter for 20 minutes in large Dutch oven. Cool. Remove and purée until smooth. Return to pan; add spinach and seasonings and bring to a full boil. Remove from heat; add absinthe and bitters. This can be made ahead and kept in refrigerator. Freezes well.

Place 6 oysters in each ramekin and bake at 450° until edges of oysters curl (about 10 minutes). Remove from oven, pour off excess liquid, and top oysters with sauce. Return to oven and cook 5 to 10 minutes until slightly brown and bubbly on top. Serve immediately.

*Frances A. Morris*

## Oysters Bienville

| | |
|---|---|
| ¼ pound butter | 2 teaspoons salt |
| 16 green onions, chopped | ¼ teaspoon black pepper |
| ½ pound mushrooms, chopped | ¼ teaspoon cayenne |
| 4 tablespoons flour | 5 dozen oysters, drained |
| 1½ cups chicken broth | 2 cups bread crumbs |
| 2 cups cooked shrimp, chopped | ½ cup grated Parmesan cheese |
| 3 egg yolks | Paprika |
| ¾ cup white wine | |

Sauté onions and mushrooms lightly in butter. Blend in flour and gradually add broth; stir in shrimp. Beat egg yolks with wine and add to mixture, stirring constantly until thickened. Remove from heat and season. Sauce may be made ahead and refrigerated until time to cook oysters.

Place 6 oysters in each ramekin and bake at 450° about 10 minutes or until edges of oysters curl. Remove from oven and pour off excess liquid. Top with sauce; sprinkle with crumbs, cheese and paprika and return to oven. Bake 10 minutes longer at 450°.

Variation: Top poached fish with sauce and bake 15 to 20 minutes at 350°.

Yield: 1¼ quarts sauce

*Mabel P. Berlin*

## Sourdough Bread

4½ to 5½ cups unsifted flour  
1　tablespoon sugar  
2　teaspoons salt  
2　packages yeast  
1　12-ounce can malt liquor  

¼　cup water  
1　tablespoon margarine  
Cornmeal  
1　egg white, slightly beaten  
Sesame or poppy seeds  

Thoroughly combine 4½ cups flour, sugar, salt and yeast. Heat malt liquor, water and margarine until warm (120° to 130°; margarine need not melt). Gradually add to dry ingredients. Beat 2 minutes at medium speed with electric mixer, scraping bowl occasionally. Add ½ cup flour or enough to make thick batter. Beat at high speed for 2 minutes, scraping bowl occasion-ally. Stir in enough additional flour to make soft dough. Turn onto lightly floured board; knead until smooth and elastic, 8 to 10 minutes. Place in greased bowl, turning to grease all sides. Cover and let rise in warm place, free from drafts, until doubled in bulk, about 1 hour.

Punch dough down. Turn onto lightly floured board; divide in 2 parts and form each piece into smooth ball. Cover; let rest for 10 minutes. Roll each piece into a 12×7-inch rectangle. Bring 2 long sides together to form seam down center. Pinch seam tightly to seal. Place seam side down on greased baking sheets which have been sprinkled with cornmeal. Cover; let rise in warm place, free from draft until doubled in bulk. Brush loaves with beaten egg white and sprinkle with seeds. Slash tops diagonally in several places, 1 to 3-inches deep. Bake at 400° for 20 to 25 minutes. Cool on racks.

Yield: 2 large loaves

*Laura F. Waring*

## Winter Salad

6　carrots, peeled and thinly sliced  
1　6-ounce can pitted ripe olives,  
　　sliced  

½ cup French dressing  
Romaine lettuce leaves  

Steam carrots 3 to 5 minutes. Remove from heat, drain, and chill thoroughly. Toss carrots and olives with French dressing and arrange on lettuce leaves.

*Frances A. Morris*

## Kahlua Mousse

½ cup sugar
½ cup water
2 eggs
Dash of salt
1 6-ounce package chocolate
 chips

2 tablespoons cognac
3 tablespoons Kahlua
½ pint heavy cream, whipped
Toasted slivered almonds

Heat sugar in water until sugar dissolves; set aside. Mix eggs, salt and chocolate in blender. Add the sugar mixture slowly and blend until thick. Cool. Add cognac and Kahlua. Fold half of the cream into chocolate mixture. Chill several hours. Serve in small wineglasses, topped with remaining whipped cream and almonds.

*Dorothy I. Stuckey*

## Apricot Mousse

2 tablespoons gelatin
½ cup cold water
1 pound dried apricots
2 cups water

2 cups sugar
Peel of 1 lemon
6 egg whites, beaten until fluffy

Soften gelatin in cold water. Cook apricots with sugar and lemon peel in water until tender. Remove peel and add gelatin, stirring until dissolved. Cool; purée. Fold egg whites into apricot mixture. Pour into large ring mold and refrigerate at least overnight. Unmold and serve with Vanilla Sauce.

### Vanilla Sauce

2 cups milk, scalded
1 teaspoon vanilla
3 egg yolks, beaten

3 tablespoons flour
½ cup sugar

Add vanilla to milk and cool. Add sugar and flour to egg yolks and beat until smooth. Pour into cooled milk; strain. Cook over low heat, stirring constantly (about 10 minutes) until thick. Chill thoroughly.

*Carmelina M. del Valle*

# SHRIMP AND RICE                                    *(Serves 10)*

Two versions of shrimp prepared in well-seasoned sauces.

### *Shrimp Creole   or   *Creamy Shrimp Curry
### Steamed Rice
### Green Salad
### *Herbed French Bread

### *Pineapple Pound Cake
### *Crème de Menthe Glacée

### Coffee

*Dry Alsatian Muscat or Gewurztraminer*

## Shrimp Creole

| | |
|---|---|
| 1 cup corn oil | 32 ounces tomato sauce |
| 1 cup flour | ½ cup white wine (optional) |
| 4 pounds peeled, raw shrimp | ½ cup water |
| 2 cups chopped green onions | 1 tablespoon black pepper |
| 4 to 6 tablespoons chopped parsley | ½ teaspoon cayenne |
| 1 cup chopped green pepper | Salt to taste |
| 1 clove garlic, pressed | 1 bay leaf |

Make a roux by browning flour in oil over low heat, stirring constantly until dark brown. Stir in shrimp, coating them with roux. Add onions, parsley, green pepper and garlic; sauté lightly. Stir in remaining ingredients. Simmer for 30 minutes. Serve over steamed rice.

*Martha S. Paxton*

## Creamy Shrimp Curry

| | |
|---|---|
| 12 tablespoons margarine | 3 cups sour cream |
| 3 onions, chopped | 1 tablespoon lemon juice |
| 4 cloves garlic, pressed | Salt and cayenne to taste |
| 3 to 4 teaspoons curry powder | 4 pounds cooked, peeled shrimp |
| 3 10¾-ounce cans cream of mushroom soup | |

Sauté onion and garlic in margarine until soft. Stir in curry powder and soup, heating thoroughly. Remove from heat. Add sour cream, lemon juice, salt and cayenne. Immediately before serving, add shrimp and heat thoroughly. Serve over steamed rice, accompanied by the following condiments:

1½ cups raisins
1½ cups peanuts
1½ cups chopped apple
5 hard-boiled eggs, chopped
1½ cups chutney

1½ cups shredded coconut
1½ cups pineapple chunks
4 bananas, sliced
10 slices crisp bacon, crumbled

*Midget D. Lamkin*

## Herbed French Bread

1 loaf French bread
¼ pound margarine, softened

Garlic salt to taste
2 tablespoons minced parsley

Slice loaf lengthwise. Spread margarine generously over bread and sprinkle with garlic salt and parsley. Cut loaf diagonally, not completely through, into serving slices. Broil for 1 or 2 minutes, or until brown.

*Izy R. Steinschulte*

## Pineapple Pound Cake

½ cup shortening
½ pound butter or margarine
2¾ cups sugar
6 eggs
3 cups sifted flour
1 teaspoon baking powder
¼ cup milk

1 teaspoon vanilla
¾ cup undrained crushed pineapple
4 tablespoons butter or margarine
1½ cups confectioners' sugar
1 cup crushed pineapple, drained

Cream shortening, butter and sugar. Add eggs, 1 at a time, beating thoroughly after each addition. Gradually add flour sifted with baking powder, alternately with milk. Stir in vanilla and pineapple with juice. Pour batter into well-greased 10-inch tube pan. Place in cold oven. Turn oven to 325° and bake for 1½ hours or until top springs back when touched lightly. Let stand for few minutes in pan. Run knife around edges and remove carefully to rack.

Cream 4 tablespoons butter with confectioners' sugar; blend in drained pineapple; pour over cake while hot.

*W. Ellis Powell*

## Crème de Menthe Glacée

1 quart vanilla ice cream, softened slightly
1 quart pineapple sherbet, softened slightly

Green crème de menthe to taste
10 sprigs mint

Mix ice cream and sherbet, adding crème de menthe until mixture becomes light green. Spoon into sherbet dishes. Freeze. Garnish with mint leaves.

*Mary Alice C. Hill*

# CAJUN CLASSIC  *(Serves 12)*

Descendants of French Acadians exiled fron Nova Scotia in the mid 1700's, south Louisiana's Cajuns are truly unique "country folk" who have refused to let their heritage be engulfed by Americana. Their "joie de vivre" is legion, their language a picturesque patois, their music an oral tradition, and their cuisine an exciting synthesis. Here is their most popular method of preparing crawfish, a staple in Acadiana.

*Crawfish Étouffée*

*Spinach Salad with *Vermouth Dressing
French Bread

*Fresh Strawberry Pie
Coffee

German Trocken or Pinot Noir Rosé

## Crawfish Étouffée

¾ pound margarine
6 cups chopped onion
2 cups chopped celery
2 cups chopped green pepper (optional)
6 cloves garlic, pressed
4 teaspoons salt
1 teaspoon black pepper
1 teaspoon cayenne

1 teaspoon sugar
¼ cup tomato paste
3 tablespoons cornstarch
3 cups water (or 1½ cups water and 1½ cups white wine)
4 pounds boiled, peeled crawfish tails
1 green onion, chopped
1 teaspoon Kitchen Bouquet

In a heavy pot, melt margarine; sauté onion, celery, green pepper and garlic until soft. Stir in salt, black and cayenne pepper, sugar and tomato paste. Simmer, stirring occasionally, for 20 minutes. Dissolve cornstarch in water; add. Cook for 20 minutes, or until sauce thickens. Add crawfish, green onion and Kitchen Bouquet. Refrigerate overnight. Reheat and serve over steamed rice. Do not overcook.

Variation: Use shrimp instead of crawfish.

*Lokie D. Wynne*

## Spinach Salad

1½ pounds spinach
4   green onions and tops, chopped
2   teaspoons tarragon, crushed

2   tablespoons capers, drained
10  mushrooms, sliced
4   hard-boiled eggs, sliced
6   slices crisp bacon, crumbled

Wash and tear spinach, removing stems. Wrap in terry cloth towel and crisp in freezer five minutes. Remove to salad bowl. Toss with tarragon and green onions. Refrigerate. Just before serving, add eggs, bacon, capers and mushrooms. Toss with the following dressing.

## Vermouth Dressing

¼   cup lemon juice
¼   cup dry vermouth
2   teaspoons dry mustard
1   teaspoon pepper

1   clove garlic, pressed
2   teaspoons salt
¾   cup olive oil
¾   cup salad oil

Combine ingredients and shake well.

*Margaret D. Ratelle*

## Fresh Strawberry Pie

2   9-inch pie shells, baked
2   quarts strawberries
2   cups sugar

4   tablespoons cornstarch
2   cups heavy cream, whipped

Place half of the berries in pie shells. In saucepan mash remaining berries. Bring to a boil and add sugar which has been mixed with cornstarch. Cook slowly 10 minutes or until mixture is clear, stirring constantly. Let cool and pour over berries in shells. Chill and top with whipped cream.

*Billie B. Tibbets*

# MIDDAY DINNER
## AT GRANDMOTHER'S                    *(Serves 12)*

A beloved Southern custom: "dinner" at noon.

### *Fried Chicken*    *Rice and *Gravy*
### **Okra and Tomatoes*    *Skillet Corn*
### *Angel Biscuits*

### *Peach Cobbler*
### Buttermilk or Iced Tea

## Fried Chicken

3  cups flour
3  tablespoons salt
3  tablespoons paprika
¾  teaspoon pepper
1½ cups bread crumbs (optional
   for extra crispness)

3  eggs, beaten
½  cup milk
3  fryers, cut into pieces
Salad oil (enough to cover skillet
   to ¼ inch depth)

Combine first 5 ingredients in a paper sack. Beat eggs and milk together. Dip chicken pieces into milk mixture, then shake in sack containing flour mixture. Heat oil in large skillet to 350° and brown chicken pieces well on all sides, a few at a time. Return all chicken to skillet, reduce heat, cover and cook 30 minutes. Uncover and cook 15 minutes more. Reserve pan drippings for gravy (below).

*Mary Jane Brown*

## Gravy

2  tablespoons pan drippings from
   fried chicken
2  tablespoons flour
2  cups milk

1  cup chicken stock
1  teaspoon salt
Pepper to taste

Stir the flour into the drippings, mixing well. Blend in remaining ingredients and cook slowly 10 minutes until thickened.

## Rice

| | |
|---|---|
| 4   cups water | 2   cups long-grained rice |
| 2   teaspoons salt | ½   teaspoon salad oil |

In a heavy saucepan bring water and salt to a boil. Stir in rice and oil, reduce heat to low and simmer tightly covered for 20 minutes, or until liquid is absorbed. Place rice in a colander over simmering water, cover with a dish towel, and allow to steam until served.

## Okra and Tomatoes

| | |
|---|---|
| 2   onions, chopped | 2   bay leaves |
| 4   tablespoons salad oil | 1½ teaspoons salt |
| 3   pounds okra, sliced crosswise | ½   teaspoon pepper |
| 6   tomatoes, peeled and chopped | ½   cup dark brown sugar |

Sauté onions in oil until lightly browned. Stir in okra and cook, covered, 5 minutes on low heat. Add other ingredients, cover tightly and simmer 30 minutes.

## Skillet Corn

| | |
|---|---|
| 24 ears corn | 1½ teaspoons salt |
| ¼   pound margarine | ½   teaspoon pepper |
| ¼   cup flour | 1   tablespoon sugar |
| 1½ cups milk | |

Cut kernels from corn, scraping edge of knife over cob to extract as much juice as possible. Melt margarine in heavy skillet and sauté corn lightly (5 to 10 minutes). Combine a little of the milk with the flour and stir into corn. Add the other ingredients and remaining milk and simmer, covered, over *very* low heat 20 minutes, being careful not to scorch corn.

*Nena M. Love*

## Angel Biscuits

| | |
|---|---|
| 5   cups flour | 1   package yeast |
| ¼ cup sugar | 4   tablespoons warm water |
| 5   teaspoons baking powder | 2   cups buttermilk |
| 1   teaspoon baking soda | 4   tablespoons melted |
| 1½ teaspoons salt | margarine or butter |
| 1   cup shortening | |

Sift together dry ingredients. Cut in shortening with pastry blender. Dissolve yeast in warm water and add with the buttermilk to the other ingredients, mixing well. Roll out to ¼-inch thickness on lightly floured board. Cut into rounds with a 2-inch biscuit cutter, dip in melted butter, and bake on cookie sheet 15 minutes at 400°.

Dough may be refrigerated a day or so before baking, or biscuits may be slightly underbaked and frozen.

Yield:  100 biscuits

*Nancy C. Weems*

## Peach Cobbler

| | |
|---|---|
| 6   cups peeled, sliced fresh | 2   teaspoons cinnamon |
| peaches | 1½ cups flour |
| 2   cups sugar | ¼ teaspoon salt |
| ¼ teaspoon salt | 2   teaspoons sugar |
| 2   eggs, beaten | ¾ cup shortening |
| 2   teaspoons flour | 4   tablespoons ice water |
| 4   tablespoons butter | |

Combine first 5 ingredients and place in a flat, buttered 3-quart baking dish. Dot with butter and sprinkle with cinnamon.

Mix next 3 ingredients and cut in shortening with a pastry blender, adding water as needed. Roll out on a lightly floured board, cut into strips, and cover fruit with a latticed top. Bake at 400° for 30 minutes.

*Mabel Roshton*

# COMPANY FOR SUNDAY DINNER  (Serves 12)

Gathering after church with family and friends is a favorite Louisiana custom.

***Curried Pea Soup***

***Chicken Rosalie***
Rice      ***Apricot Casserole***
***Hearts of Palm Salad***
***Old-fashioned Rolls***

***Schaum Torte***
**Coffee**

### Curried Pea Soup

2  10-ounce packages frozen green peas
2  onions, sliced
2  carrots, sliced
2  cloves garlic, pressed
2  ribs celery, chopped, including leaves

2  potatoes, peeled and chopped
2  teaspoons salt
2  teaspoons curry powder
4  cups chicken stock
2  cups milk

Combine first 8 ingredients with 2 cups of stock. Bring to a boil; cover and simmer 15 minutes. Purée; add remaining stock and milk. Reheat slowly in top of double boiler over simmering water. Serve hot or cold.
Yield: 2½ quarts

*Dorothy I. Stuckey*

## Chicken Rosalie

12  halves chicken breasts, boned
    and skinned
¼  pound margarine
12  slices ham
1  cup mushrooms
1  10½-ounce can cream of
    chicken soup
1  10½-ounce can cream of
    mushroom soup

½  cup white wine
1  teaspoon poultry seasoning
1  teaspoon thyme
1  teaspoon sage
1  teaspoon paprika
1  teaspoon Tabasco
Minced parsley

Sauté chicken breasts lightly in margarine. Place each on a ham slice in a 9×12-inch greased baking dish. In same skillet used for browning chicken, sauté mushrooms. Add remaining ingredients, mix well and spoon over chicken and ham. Sprinkle with parsley and bake at 275° for 2½ hours.

*Hope J. Norman*

## Apricot Casserole

2  1-pound 13-ounce cans apricot
    halves, drained
24  Ritz crackers

¾  cup light brown sugar
6  tablespoons butter or
    margarine, melted

Place apricots in baking dish, cut sides up. Crumble crackers over top, sprinkle with sugar, and drizzle butter over all. Heat at 350° for 20 minutes.

*Ann S. Lomax*

## Hearts of Palm Salad

3  14-ounce cans hearts of palm,
    drained
1½ cups salad oil
1  cup red wine vinegar
3  tablespoons lemon juice
2  cloves garlic, pressed

¾  teaspoon salt
½  teaspoon pepper
Cayenne to taste
2  heads lettuce, torn
½  cup grated Parmesan cheese

Slice hearts of palm into serving-sized pieces. Combine next 7 ingredients and pour over hearts of palm. Marinate overnight. Just before serving toss with lettuce and cheese.
Variation: Hearts of artichokes may be substituted.

*Carol M. Hensel*

## Old-fashioned Rolls

| | |
|---|---|
| 2 cups milk, scalded | 5 cups flour, sifted |
| 7 tablespoons shortening | 1 teaspoon salt |
| ½ to ¾ cup sugar | ½ teaspoon baking soda |
| 1 package yeast | 4 tablespoons butter, melted |

Pour milk over shortening and sugar; stir until lukewarm. Add yeast and stir until dissolved. Sift 3 cups flour into large bowl and slowly add the liquid mixture. Beat until smooth. Cover and let rise in warm place for 2 hours. Sift in salt, soda, and remaining flour. Mix well. Knead dough on floured surface until satiny and elastic (10 to 15 minutes). Place dough in greased bowl, turning to coat all sides; refrigerate until thoroughly chilled.

Roll out on floured surface and cut into 2-inch rounds. Brush with melted butter and fold in half, sealing the edges lightly together. Place on greased baking sheet 1-inch apart. Cover and let rise 2 hours until doubled in size. Bake at 375° until brown (10 minutes). Dough will keep in refrigerator for 5 or 6 days.

Yield: 5 dozen rolls

*Ann W. Lowrey*

## Schaum Torte

| | |
|---|---|
| 6 egg whites | 3 pints raspberries or 3 10-ounce |
| ¼ teaspoon salt | packages frozen raspberries, |
| 1 tablespoon vinegar | drained |
| 2 cups superfine sugar | 1 pint heavy cream, whipped and |
| 1 teaspoon vanilla | sweetened to taste |

Beat egg whites in large bowl at high speed until foamy; add salt and vinegar. Reduce speed and add sugar slowly. Beat until sugar is dissolved and mixture is quite stiff. Add vanilla. Spread evenly in 2 greased 9-inch cake pans, lined with greased wax paper. Allow wax paper to come up above sides of pans for easier removal. Bake at 250° for 1 hour.

Remove from pans *immediately*. Mix half of the whipped cream with the raspberries; spread between layers. Frost torte with remaining whipped cream. The layers may be made the day before serving and torte may be assembled several hours in advance.

*Virginia B. Klock*

# WELCOME TO FALL         *(Serves 12)*

A hearty "do your own thing" buffet featuring a Louisiana standby, the "Po-Boy" sandwich. This meal on a six-inch loaf of French bread originated during Depression days when it sold for a nickel.

*Plantation Potage*

*Barbecued Brisket*
*Very Hot Mustard Sauce*      *Horseradish Sauce*
*Po-Boy Rolls or Buns*
*Salad Bar*
*Thousand Island Dressing*      *Roquefort Dressing*
*Avocado Dressing*

*Petite Cherry Cheese Cakes*   or   *Yam Cake*
*Coffee*

*Light Claret or Ruby Cabernet*

## Plantation Potage

| | |
|---|---|
| 2 cups chopped green onions | 2 cups milk |
| 2 onions, chopped | 6 cups chicken stock |
| 12 turnips, sliced | 2 13-ounce cans evaporated milk |
| 2 potatoes, peeled and sliced | ½ cup chopped parsley |
| ¼ pound margarine | Salt, pepper and soy sauce to taste |

Steam vegetables in margarine in covered pan until tender. Purée with ¼ cup of the milk. Add remaining ingredients and stir until smooth. Serve hot or cold. Freezes well.

Yield: 3½ to 4 quarts

*Margaret D. Ratelle*

## Barbecued Brisket

| | |
|---|---|
| 6 pounds beef brisket | Pepper to taste |
| 4 ounces liquid smoke | 2 tablespoons Worcestershire sauce |
| 1 teaspoon seasoned salt | 1 cup Heinz Barbecue Sauce with Onions |
| ½ teaspoon celery salt | |
| ½ teaspoon garlic salt | |
| ½ teaspoon onion salt | |

Coat the brisket with salts, pepper, and liquid smoke. Wrap in foil and refrigerate overnight. Before baking, sprinkle both sides of meat with Worcestershire sauce. Bake at 250° in tight foil covering for 5 hours. Uncover, add barbecue sauce, and continue baking 1 hour longer. Cool, refrigerate, and remove congealed fat. Slice thinly, replace in foil, and refrigerate until ready to reheat and serve. Freezes well.

*Billie B. Tibbets*

## Very Hot Mustard Sauce

1 cup sugar
1 cup vinegar
½ teaspoon salt

4 ounces Coleman's dry mustard
3 eggs

Blend all ingredients until smooth in the top of a double boiler. Cook, stirring often, over simmering water until thick and the consistency of mayonnaise. Keeps for months in the refrigerator.

*Margaret D. Ratelle*

## Horseradish Sauce

1 pint sour cream
1 5-ounce jar prepared
horseradish

Milk

Mix together sour cream and horseradish. Thin to desired consistency with milk.

*Norrine B. Caplan*

## Salad Bar

2 heads lettuce
6 tomatoes, sliced, or 2 pints
cherry tomatoes, halved
2 cucumbers, sliced
3 avocados, peeled, cut in
wedges, sprinkled with lemon
juice
3 carrots, peeled and sliced
1 bunch radishes, sliced
1 cup chopped green onions

1 1-pound jar sliced pickled beets,
drained
2 14-ounce cans green asparagus
spears, drained
2 14-ounce cans artichoke hearts,
drained and quartered
2 green peppers, sliced in rings
2 yellow squash, sliced
2 zucchini, sliced

Chill all ingredients. Arrange large outer lettuce leaves on a tray and top each with a different vegetable. Tear remaining lettuce into a bowl. Surround the tray and bowl with small dishes containing the following condiments and dressings.

Croutons                                Capers, drained
Grated Parmesan cheese                  Marinated kidney beans, drained
Bean sprouts, drained                   Bacon crumbles

### Avocado Dressing

1   egg                                 ½   teaspoon white pepper
½   cup salad oil                       2   avocados, peeled and sliced
½   teaspoon dry mustard                ½   cup chopped green onion tops
¼   teaspoon Tabasco                    1   clove garlic, pressed
4   tablespoons lemon juice             1   ounce anchovy fillets, drained
1   teaspoon Worcestershire             4   ounces mayonnaise
½   teaspoon salt                       ½   teaspoon saffron

Purée the first 12 ingredients until smooth. Add mayonnaise and saffron and mix thoroughly. Chill for at least 2 hours.
Variation: May be used as a dip.
Yield: 1½ pints

*Mike Totah*

### Roquefort Cheese Dressing

4   ounces Roquefort cheese             2   tablespoons grated onion
1   pint mayonnaise                     ½   teaspoon dry mustard
2   cloves garlic, pressed              ½   cup vinegar
1   cup sour cream                      2   tablespoons lemon juice

Mash cheese and blend into mayonnaise. Add all other ingredients and mix well. Refrigerate.
Variation: For a milder flavor, substitute blue cheese.

*Carol M. Hensel*

### Thousand Island Dressing

½   cup pimiento-stuffed green          ½   cup chili sauce
    olives, chopped                     1   tablespoon prepared mustard
1   hard-boiled egg, chopped            2   cups mayonnaise
2   sprigs parsley

Blend all ingredients. Refrigerate.

*Mary Frances L. James*

## Petite Cherry Cheese Cakes

16  ounces cream cheese, softened
¾  cup sugar
2  eggs
1  tablespoon lemon juice
1  teaspoon vanilla
24  vanilla wafers
1  21-ounce can cherry pie filling

Beat first 5 ingredients until light and fluffy. Line small muffin tins with paper baking cups and place a vanilla wafer in the bottom of each. Fill cups ⅔ full with cream cheese mixture. Bake at 375° for 15 to 20 minutes until set. Top each with 1 tablespoon cherry pie filling. Chill.
   Yield: 24 cakes

*Frances H. Dean*

## Yam Cake

2  cups sifted flour
1½ teaspoon baking soda
1  teaspoon salt
1  teaspoon baking powder
1  teaspoon ground cloves
1½ teaspoons cinnamon
1  teaspoon nutmeg
1¼ cups salad oil
2  cups sugar
4  eggs
3  teaspoons vanilla
2  cups mashed yams
1  cup chopped pecans
3  ounces cream cheese
4  tablespoons margarine or butter
½  pound confectioners' sugar

Yams are a special variety of Louisiana sweet potatoes.
   Sift together the first 7 ingredients. In large mixer bowl beat oil and sugar; add eggs, 1 at a time, beating well after each addition. Gradually blend in dry ingredients; add yams, 2 teaspoons vanilla and ½ cup pecans. Bake in a well-greased 10½-inch tube or bundt pan at 350° for 1 hour and 15 minutes. Invert on rack until cool. Remove cake from pan and wrap in foil. Refrigerate for several hours or overnight.
   Beat together cream cheese, margarine and confectioners' sugar. Stir in 1 teaspoon vanilla and remaining pecans. Split cake crosswise; spread filling between layers. Return to refrigerator until ready to serve.

*Bobbie S. McCampbell*

# A MEMORABLE REPAST                    *(Serves 24)*

A special shrimp and eggplant casserole for an important event.

***Champagne***
***\*Onion-Parsley Sandwiches***

***\*Shrimp-Eggplant Casserole***
***\*Apricot Mold   or   \*Cantaloupe-Nut Mold***
***\*Mixed Green Salad***
***Toasted French Bread Slices***

***\*Lemon Tarts***
***Coffee***

*Vouvray or Pouilly-Fumé*

## Onion-Parsley Sandwiches

| | |
|---|---|
| 20  very thin slices white bread | 3   onions, thinly sliced |
| ⅔  cup mayonnaise | Salt |
| 1   tablespoon lemon juice | ½  cup finely chopped parsley |
| ½  teaspoon curry powder | |

Cut bread into 1-inch rounds. Blend half the mayonnaise with lemon juice and curry powder. Spread this mixture lightly on the bread rounds. Arrange onion slices on half the rounds. Season with salt and cover with remaining rounds. Roll the edges of each sandwich lightly through remaining mayonnaise and then parsley. Cover and chill.

*Izy R. Steinschulte*

## Shrimp-Eggplant Casserole

| | |
|---|---|
| 10  eggplants, peeled and diced | 2   cups Italian-seasoned bread |
| 4   cups chopped celery | crumbs |
| 2   cups chopped white onion | 4   tablespoons chicken bouillon |
| 2   cups chopped green pepper | granules |
| 2   cups chopped green onions | 4   cups peeled raw shrimp |
| 2   tablespoons chopped garlic | 2   tablespoons MSG |
| 2   cups peeled chopped tomatoes | 2   teaspoons Tabasco |
| 1   cup olive oil | Salt to taste |
| ½  pound butter | |

Soak eggplant in salted ice water for 10 to 15 minutes. Sauté chopped vegetables in oil until soft; add butter. Stir in drained eggplant, bread crumbs and bouillon granules. Cover and cook until eggplant is tender. Add shrimp and cook until they are pink, stirring constantly. Add seasonings. Bake in 2 3-quart casserole dishes at 350° for 30 minutes.

Variation: Crawfish tails or crabmeat may be substituted for shrimp.

*Dorothy I. Stuckey*

## Apricot Mold

3   3-ounce packages apricot
gelatin dessert
2   cups hot water
2   cups cold water
8   ounces cream cheese, softened
1   cup chopped pecans

1   16-ounce can crushed
pineapple
1   cup chopped celery
2   1½-ounce envelopes non-dairy
topping, whipped

Dissolve gelatin in hot water; add cold water and chill until thickened. Take 1 cup chilled gelatin and whip with cream cheese until fluffy. Add remaining gelatin and whip until well blended. Stir in nuts, celery and pineapple. Fold in whipped topping. Pour into a 3-quart mold or 24 ½-cup molds and chill.

*Mary Ann K. Brame*

## Cantaloupe-Nut Mold

3   3-ounce packages gelatin
dessert (orange, lemon or
lemon-lime)
¼   teaspoon salt
3   cups boiling water
2¼ cups cold water

3   teaspoons lemon juice
3   cups diced cantaloupe
¾   cup diced celery
¾   cup slivered almonds
9   ounces cream cheese
6   tablespoons mayonnaise

Dissolve gelatin and salt in boiling water. Add cold water and lemon juice. Chill ½ of the gelatin mixture until thick. Fold in cantaloupe, celery and almonds. Pour into shallow 3-quart mold or 24 ½-cup molds. Chill until set, but not firm. Mix cream cheese and mayonnaise until smooth. Gradually add remaining gelatin. Pour over cantaloupe layer and chill until firm.

*Laura F. Waring*

## Mixed Green Salad

10  ounces spinach
2   heads red tip lettuce
1   head Romaine lettuce
1   head iceberg or Bibb lettuce
3   cucumbers, sliced
1   pint cherry tomatoes
6   hard-boiled eggs, sliced
1   14-ounce jar pimiento-stuffed
    olives, drained and sliced

1   pound bacon, cooked and
    crumbled
3   6-ounce jars marinated
    artichoke hearts, drained and
    quartered
1   cup chopped green onions
2   cups croutons (optional)

Tear greens into bite-sized pieces. Place all ingredients in large bowl and chill. When ready to serve, toss with Vermouth Dressing on page 103, doubling the amount.

## Lemon Tarts

4   eggs
4   egg yolks
½   pound butter (may use half
    margarine)

2 cups sugar
8   tablespoons lemon juice
Grated peel of 4 lemons

Place eggs and yolks in top of double boiler and mix gently; add remaining ingredients. Cook over simmering water stirring with a wooden spoon until thickened. Store covered in refrigerator.

Prepare tart shells by recipe below. Spoon filling into shells. Refrigerate until serving time.

### Tart Shells

2¼ cups flour
½ pound butter (may use half
    margarine), softened

½  teaspoon salt
2   eggs, beaten

Mix ingredients; turn out on lightly floured surface and work for a few seconds until dough is formed. Chill for several hours. Pinch off small pieces of dough and place in miniature muffin cups or small tart shell tins. With thumb, press dough on bottom and sides of form. Bake at 450° for 5 minutes. Reduce heat to 400° and continue to bake for approximately 8 to 10 minutes. Cool and store, tightly covered.
    Yield:  60 tart shells

*Jacque S. Caplan*

# SUMPTUOUS  SIDEBOARD    *(Serves 50)*

A menu for a momentous occasion featuring advance preparation and ease of service.

*Chablis Cassis*      *Apricot Punch*

*Company Chicken*
*and *Cold Dill Beans*
or
*Chicken and Asparagus Casserole*
*and Sliced Tomatoes*

*Watermelon Fruit Basket with *Poppy Seed Dressing*
*Parkerhouse Rolls*

*Pralines*
*Coffee*

*Sylvaner or German Mosel*

## Chablis Cassis

2   gallons Chablis                    2   cups Cassis

Mix and chill. Pour over ice in punch bowl.

## Apricot Punch

4   46-ounce cans apricot nectar,      4   32-ounce bottles lemon-lime
chilled                                    soda, chilled
4   32-ounce bottles ginger ale,
chilled

Combine ingredients in punch bowl.

*Leta'dele B. Defee*

## Company Chicken

7 to 9 fryers (about 20 to 25
   pounds chicken)
10 6-ounce cans whole
   mushrooms, drained
10 14-ounce cans artichoke hearts,
   drained and halved
2½ pounds margarine
2½ cups flour

4½ quarts milk
2  tablespoons white pepper
1  tablespoon cayenne
4  cloves garlic, pressed
10 ounces medium sharp Cheddar
   cheese, cubed
15 ounces Gruyère cheese, cubed

Boil chickens in water to cover until tender (about 1 hour). Cool and drain; reserve stock for other use. Remove meat from bones; skin and chop. Combine with mushrooms and artichokes in 4 3-quart casseroles. Melt margarine and stir in flour. Blend in milk and seasonings, stirring constantly until thickened. Add cheese and continue to cook, stirring until sauce is bubbling and cheese is melted. Pour sauce over chicken mixture. Bake 30 to 45 minutes at 350°.

*Norrine B. Caplan*

## Chicken and Asparagus Casserole

16 cups cubed cooked chicken
6  14½-ounce cans green
   asparagus, drained
3  cups chopped onion
2  6-ounce cans mushrooms,
   drained
½  pound margarine
4  10-ounce cans cream of
   mushroom soup
2  10-ounce cans cream of
   chicken soup

1½ pounds sharp Cheddar cheese,
   grated
1  teaspoon Tabasco
3  teaspoons salt
1  teaspoon pepper
2  tablespoons soy sauce
6  tablespoons chopped pimiento
2  teaspoons MSG
1½ cups slivered almonds

In each of 4 flat 3-quart casserole dishes place a layer of asparagus. Cover with chicken. Sauté onions and mushrooms in margarine; stir in all other ingredients except almonds. Simmer until cheese melts. Pour sauce over chicken and asparagus in casseroles and sprinkle with almonds. Bake at 350° for 20 minutes or until bubbly.

*Mary Frances L. James*

## Cold Dill Beans

| | | | |
|---|---|---|---|
| 1 | quart salad oil | 1 | tablespoon dill weed |
| 1 | quart white vinegar | 1 | teaspoon salt |
| 1 | cup water | 1 | teaspoon pepper |
| 2 | cloves garlic, pressed | 3 | 6-pound 9-ounce cans of green |
| ¼ | cup sugar | | beans, rinsed and drained |
| 2 | tablespoons dry mustard | 5 | white onions, thinly sliced |
| 1 | tablespoon celery seed | | |

Mix first 10 ingredients together in a saucepan. Add the beans and heat to boiling; cool. Layer beans with onions in shallow pans and pour marinade over them. Cover and refrigerate at least 24 hours. Serve cold with a slotted spoon.

## Watermelon Fruit Basket

| | | | |
|---|---|---|---|
| 1 | large watermelon, halved | 1 | quart strawberries |
| 1 | cantaloupe, peeled and cut into wedges | 4 | pounds peaches, peeled, sliced, and sprinkled with lemon juice |
| 1 | honeydew melon, peeled and cut into wedges | 2 | pounds seedless grapes |
| 1 | pineapple, peeled, cored, and cut into chunks | ½ | cup sugar |

Scoop meat from watermelon and cut into balls or wedges. Mix with other fruit and sugar; chill. (Any assortment of fresh fruit in season may be used, allowing enough to have 5 quarts of fruit.)

Pile fruit in watermelon shells and serve with poppy seed dressing.

### Poppy Seed Dressing

| | | | |
|---|---|---|---|
| 1½ | cups sugar | ⅔ | cup white vinegar |
| 2 | teaspoons salt | 2 | cups salad oil |
| 2 | teaspoons dry mustard | 4 | tablespoons poppy seed |
| 5 | tablespoons grated onion | | |

Combine first 6 ingredients in blender. Add oil slowly while blender is running. Stir in poppy seed by hand.

Yield: 1 quart

## Parkerhouse Rolls

| | |
|---|---|
| 1   cup boiling water | 2   eggs, beaten |
| 1   cup shortening | 2   packages yeast |
| 1   cup sugar | 1   cup lukewarm water |
| 1½ teaspoons salt | 6   cups flour |

Pour boiling water over shortening; add sugar and salt. Blend with wire whisk and cool. Add eggs. Let yeast stand in lukewarm water 5 minutes or until dissolved; add to mixture. Sift and add flour, blending well. Put dough into greased bowl; cover and let rise until doubled in bulk. Knead dough on floured board several times and roll out to about ⅜-inch thick. Cut small circles, crease each slightly off center and fold to form rolls. Put in greased pan, cover and let rise again until doubled in bulk. Bake at 375° until nicely browned (about 10 minutes). When cool, these rolls can be stored in plastic bag in freezer.
Yield: 5 to 6 dozen

*Bess L. Foster*

## Pralines

| | |
|---|---|
| 3   cups sugar | 2   tablespoons butter |
| ¾ cup milk | 2½ cups pecans |
| ¾ teaspoon vanilla | |

Place 2 cups of sugar and milk in a large saucepan. Cook slowly. At the same time put other cup of sugar in another saucepan on low heat; stir until melted. Pour melted sugar slowly into the milk and sugar that should be ready to boil, mixing while adding. Cook slowly until a firm ball will form when dropped into cold water. Remove from heat. Add vanilla and butter and beat until mixture begins to thicken. Stir in pecans. Grease counter top with cooking oil and cover with wax paper. Drop batter by small spoonfuls onto wax paper. Pralines will set immediately and will come up easily without breaking.
Yield: 2½ dozen. To serve 50, make 2 or 3 batches.

*Carrie F. Cade*

# Evening

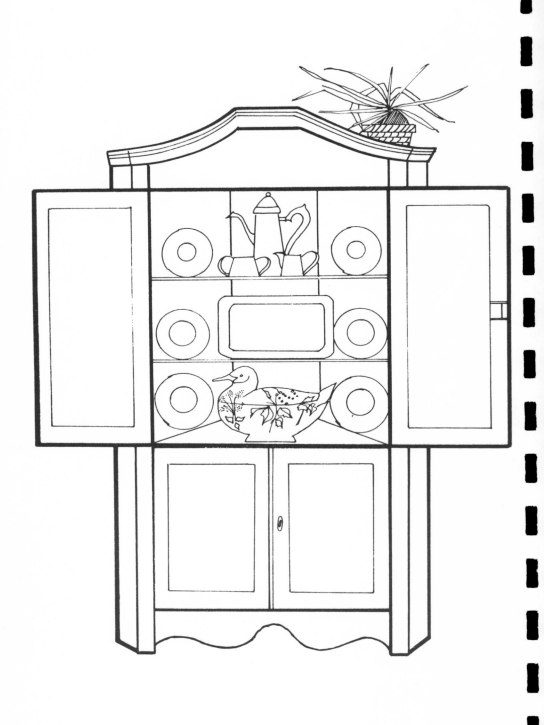

A Party of Two
Entre Nous
Cajun Catch
Haute Cuisine
Encore Supper
Plantation Memories
Steak Dinner
Dinner at Eight
Wild Geese
Tailgate Picnic
Midsummer Dinner
Creoles and Company
Guests on the Gallery
Winter Dinner
Sunday Night Supper
Fish Fry
Five Courses
Al Fresco Evening
Gumbo Supper
Bienvenue! (Welcome!)
Italian Dinner
Christmas Eve
Louisiana Bounty
Veranda Supper
Fare Extraordinaire
Bayou Specialties
Crêpe Supper
Buffet
Mexican Fiesta
After the Rehearsal

# A PARTY OF TWO

*(Serves 2)*

For a memorable twosome.

### *Oysters River Road*

**\*Hard Times
Plantation Quail**      or      **\*Filet Mignon with
Herbed Mushrooms**

### *Steamed Asparagus*

**\*Oranges à la Louisiane**   or   **\*Green Grape Custard**

### *Brandy Snaps*

### Coffee

*Red Burgundy*

## Oysters River Road

| | |
|---|---|
| 2  artichokes, boiled in salted water | ¾  teaspoon salt |
| 2  tablespoons butter | ⅛  teaspoon white pepper |
| 1  tablespoon flour | ⅛  teaspoon cayenne |
| ¼  cup minced green onions and tops | ¼  teaspoon Tabasco |
| 2  tablespoons minced parsley | ½  teaspoon Worcestershire sauce |
| ¼  cup white wine | ⅓  cup bread crumbs |
| ½  cup oyster liquor | ¼  cup grated Parmesan cheese |
| 12  oysters, drained | Paprika and minced parsley for garnish |
| | 1  teaspoon butter |

Scrape artichoke leaves, chop bottoms and hearts, and combine, making about 1 cup of artichoke pulp.

In a saucepan, melt the 2 tablespoons of butter and stir in flour. Add onions and parsley and cook, stirring occasionally, over low heat for 3 minutes, or until vegetables are soft. Stir in the wine and oyster liquor and continue to cook for 5 minutes over low heat. Add the artichoke pulp, oysters and seasonings, cover, and simmer 10 minutes. Pour into 2 buttered ramekins, top with the bread crumbs and cheese, sprinkle with the garnish, and dot with remaining butter. May be refrigerated at this point.

When ready to serve, bake at 375° for 10 minutes or until hot and bubbly.

*Hope J. Norman*

## Hard Times Plantation Quail

4   quail
Salt and pepper to taste
3 to 4 tablespoons butter
½ cup water
¼ cup dry sherry or ½ cup white
    wine

2   tablespoons lemon juice
Tabasco to taste
2   teaspoons Worcestershire sauce
1   tablespoon flour
½ to 1 cup cream

Season birds with salt and pepper and brown lightly in butter. Add the water, wine, juice and other seasonings. Cover and cook over low heat until tender (1 to 1½ hours). Blend flour into cream and stir into sauce in pan; cook until slightly thickened.

May be cooked ahead, refrigerated, and reheated in a chafing dish or slow oven.

Variation: Doves may be substituted for quail.

*Caroline K. Gilliland*

## Filet Mignon with Herbed Mushrooms

¼   pound mushroom caps
5   tablespoons butter
¼   lemon
Salt and freshly ground pepper
    to taste
⅛ teaspoon sugar
½ teaspoon tarragon
1   teaspoon chopped green
    onions

1   teaspoon chopped parsley
2   tablespoons sherry
2   1¼-inch thick filet mignon
    steaks
⅓ cup cognac, warmed
2   slices toast

Heat 3 tablespoons of the butter in skillet; add mushroom caps and sprinkle with drops of lemon juice, salt and pepper. Sauté about 3 to 4 minutes; add sugar, herbs and sherry and simmer about 3 more minutes. Remove from skillet and set aside.

Add remaining butter to skillet over moderate to high heat; brown meat lightly on one side and turn; season browned side and cook to desired doneness. Pour in the mushrooms and cognac. Ignite; stir to blend flavors and heat mushrooms. Serve on toast.

*Bertie M. Deming*

## Steamed Asparagus

1   pound asparagus
Salt and pepper to taste
2   tablespoons butter, melted

Lemon juice to taste
(optional)

Tie asparagus loosely with string. Stand upright in a deep pan. Add boiling water up to 1-inch depth. Cook, covered, over medium heat about 15 minutes. Drain and season.

Asparagus may be boiled flat in a skillet with water to cover, 10 to 12 minutes.

*Gloria W. Hearn*

## Oranges à la Louisiane

2   navel oranges, peeled
¼   cup sugar

⅛   cup water
⅛   cup warm water

Mix sugar and ⅛ cup water in a heavy saucepan and heat very slowly until dissolved. *Do not stir.* Continue to cook to a rich caramel color. The water will evaporate and the color will change quickly after about 30 to 45 minutes. Remove from heat and quickly and carefully (there will be a lot of steam) pour in warm water. Return to heat and bring mixture back to a boil, stirring until caramel is completely dissolved. Cool.

Slice each orange crosswise into 4 to 6 parts and reshape, using toothpicks to fasten the slices back together. Pour caramel syrup on top and chill.

For an extra special touch, pare thin strips of orange peel, cook for 5 minutes in boiling water, drain, dry and sprinkle over oranges.

*Judy M. Heyman*

## Green Grape Custard

3   egg yolks
¼   cup sugar
⅔   cup milk
⅔   cup half and half

1   teaspoon vanilla
½ to ¾ cup green seedless grapes,
    peeled

Beat egg yolks until thick, then gradually add sugar. Heat milk and cream in top of double boiler over simmering water, then pour gradually over egg mixture. Return to double boiler and cook, stirring constantly, until thick. Add vanilla and grapes. Refrigerate and serve cold.

*Mary W. Black*

## Brandy Snaps

4 tablespoons butter
¼ cup sugar
2 tablespoons molasses
½ cup flour
Pinch of salt

½ teaspoon ground ginger
½ teaspoon lemon juice
1 teaspoon brandy
½ cup heavy cream, whipped

Melt butter, sugar and molasses; cool. Sift in flour, salt and ginger. Mix in lemon juice and brandy. Drop a tablespoonful at a time 4 inches apart on a well-greased baking sheet. Bake at 325° for 7 to 8 minutes or until brown. Remove pan from oven and, after waiting about 1 minute, roll each cookie carefully around the handle of a wooden spoon, forming a cylinder. Remove to a plate and allow to cool completely. Fill with whipped cream just before serving.

*Judy M. Heyman*

# ENTRE NOUS                              *(Serves 4)*

An evening with favorite friends.

### *Oysters Rockefeller*

### *Cornish Hens with Cherry Sauce*
### *Sautéed Green Beans*      *Rice*

### *Chocolate Soufflé*

### *Coffee*

*German Riesling or California White Riesling*

## Oysters Rockefeller

| | |
|---|---|
| 2  dozen oyster half-shells | 2  dozen oysters |
| 2  quarts boiling water | 2  cups Rockefeller sauce (recipe |
| 4  tablespoons salt | page 96) |
| 4  tablespoons baking soda | Rock salt |

Scrub shells in soapy water; rinse and drain. Add salt and soda to boiling water and simmer shells for 30 minutes. Drain and spread outside in sunny weather for several days. Rinse shells and boil again in plain water for 30 minutes. Drain and store until needed. After each use, scrub shells in soapy water, rinse, and boil in plain water.

Spread rock salt in 4 ovenproof plates; place 6 shells on each and top each shell with 1 oyster. Bake at 450° until edges of oysters curl, 5 to 10 minutes. Drain off excess juice; cover each oyster with sauce, return to oven and bake 5 to 10 minutes longer or until bubbly. Serve immediately.

*Frances A. Morris*

## Cornish Hens with Cherry Sauce

| | |
|---|---|
| 2  Rock Cornish hens | 1  1-pound can pitted sour red |
| 4  tablespoons cornstarch | cherries |
| 4  tablespoons sugar | ½  cup dry sherry |
| ¾  teaspoon salt | 1  tablespoon slivered orange peel |
| ¾  teaspoon dry mustard | ½  cup orange juice |
| ¾  teaspoon ground ginger | ¼  cup red currant jelly |

Roast hens at 425° for 1 hour.

In saucepan, combine next 5 ingredients. Drain cherries, reserving juice. Pour sherry over cherries and set aside. Add cherry juice to cornstarch mixture. Stir in orange peel, juice and jelly, cooking over medium heat until mixture thickens. Add cherries and sherry just before serving and pour over hens.

*Nancy C. Weems*

## Sautéed Green Beans

| | |
|---|---|
| 1 pound green beans, ends removed | 3 tablespoons butter |
| 2 quarts boiling water | Salt and pepper to taste |

Parboil beans for 5 minutes in water. Drain and plunge immediately into cold water. Drain again and cut lengthwise in French style. Refrigerate if desired until serving time. Melt butter over moderately high heat, add beans and toss lightly for about 4 minutes with seasonings. Serve immediately.

## Chocolate Soufflé

| | |
|---|---|
| 1½ ounces semi-sweet chocolate | 2 eggs, separated |
| 1 tablespoon strong black coffee | ⅛ teaspoon salt |
| 4 teaspoons cornstarch | ⅛ teaspoon cream of tartar |
| 6 tablespoons milk | 1 cup heavy cream, whipped with |
| 2½ tablespoons sugar | 1 tablespoon vanilla (optional) |
| ¾ tablespoon butter, softened | |

Melt chocolate in coffee; cool. Blend cornstarch with 2 tablespoons milk to a smooth paste; add remaining milk and 2 tablespoons sugar. Bring to a boil, stirring constantly. Spread butter on top, remove from heat, and beat in chocolate mixture and egg yolks. Beat egg whites by hand until foamy, add salt and cream of tartar and continue beating until peaks form. Gradually beat in remaining ½ tablespoon sugar until mixture is stiff. Fold the mixtures together and pour into 4 greased and sugared 4-ounce soufflé dishes. Bake about 35 minutes at 375°. Do not open oven door for at least 30 minutes. If a sauce is desired, serve with whipped cream flavored with vanilla.

*Louise A. Simon*

# CAJUN CATCH                                      *(Serves 6)*

Louisiana's highly prized frog legs are a delectable local treat. The native bullfrog is the largest true frog in the eastern hemisphere. Frogging is a popular nighttime sport for two persons—one holds the strong light while the other reaches out and grabs the catch.

Speckled trout are a favorite saltwater species because they prefer inland coastal waters, which are more easily accessible to amateur anglers than the open gulf. Catching trout by surf fishing as well as from boats is gaining popularity with Louisiana anglers.

## *Potato Soup

## *Sautéed Frog Legs   or   *Trout Amandine
## *Rapides Rice
## *Tomatoes Florentine

## *Peaches Melba   or   *Richland Figs
## Coffee

*Graves or White Burgundy*

## Potato Soup

4   potatoes, peeled and thinly
    sliced
1   onion, quartered
2 to 3 cups chicken broth

4   tablespoons butter
2   cups milk or cream
1   tablespoon chopped parsley
Salt, pepper and Tabasco to taste

Cook potatoes and onion in chicken broth about 30 minutes, or until tender. Add butter. Cool slightly and purée. Stir in seasonings, milk and parsley. Serve hot or cold. Freezes well.

*Joann T. Ayres*

## Sautéed Frog Legs

2   eggs
3   cups milk
2   dozen frog legs, washed and
    drained
2   cups flour
Salt and pepper to taste

½   pound butter
4   tablespoons onion juice
4   tablespoons garlic juice
4   tablespoons lemon juice
4   tablespoons Worcestershire
    sauce

Beat eggs into milk. Dip frog legs in mixture, then dredge in seasoned flour. Melt 12 tablespoons of the butter over medium heat in a heavy skillet. Add the remaining ingredients, stirring constantly. Sauté frog legs until golden brown, about 8 minutes. Remove to a warm platter. Add the remaining butter to the skillet, stir, and pour sauce over the frog legs.

*Barbara S. Downs*

## Trout Amandine

3 pounds trout or bass fillets
1½ cups milk
1 cup flour
Salt and pepper to taste
12 tablespoons butter

½ cup slivered almonds
3 to 4 tablespoons lemon juice
1 to 2 tablespoons Worcestershire
   sauce
1½ tablespoons chopped parsley

Cover fish with milk and refrigerate several hours. Drain. Salt and pepper fillets, dredge in flour and sauté in butter until golden brown. Remove fish to warm platter. Add almonds to skillet and brown lightly, stirring constantly. Add remaining ingredients. Heat thoroughly and pour over fish.

*Nancy C. Weems*

## Rapides Rice

¾ cup chopped onion
6 tablespoons butter or margarine
1 10¾-ounce can chicken broth
1 tablespoon grated orange peel
¾ cup orange juice
1 cup water
¾ teaspoon poultry seasoning

½ teaspoon salt
½ teaspoon pepper
1½ cups rice
½ cup ripe olives, drained and
   chopped
1 cup sliced celery

Sauté onion lightly in butter; add broth, orange peel, juice, water and seasonings and bring to a boil. Stir in rice and olives, return to boil, lower heat, cover tightly and cook 10 minutes. Add celery and continue cooking about 10 minutes more or until rice is tender and water absorbed. Fluff with a fork.

*Frances B. Davis*

## Tomatoes Florentine

2   10-ounce packages frozen
    chopped spinach, cooked and
    well-drained
½   green pepper, chopped
¼   cup chopped onion
2   ribs celery, chopped

2   hard-boiled eggs, chopped
Salt and pepper to taste
¼   cup mayonnaise
6   tomatoes, hollowed and
    drained
1   teaspoon lemon juice

Mix spinach with pepper, onion, celery and eggs. Season; stir in mayonnaise and lemon juice. Spoon into tomato shells. Serve warm or cold.

*Nancy C. Weems*

## Peaches Melba

3   peaches
3   cups boiling water
½   cup sugar
1   cup water

½   lemon
6   scoops vanilla ice cream
3   cups Melba sauce
    (recipe page 67)

Immerse each peach in the boiling water for 10 seconds. Slip skin off and halve, removing seed. Mix sugar with 1 cup water and boil 2 minutes. Add peach halves and poach until barely tender (10 to 15 minutes). Drain, sprinkle with lemon juice and refrigerate.

To serve, place 1 scoop of vanilla ice cream in each half and top with Melba sauce.

## Richland Figs

1   quart peeled figs, sugared
¼   cup crème de cacao

1   cup sour cream

Mix figs with liqueur and refrigerate several hours. Serve topped with sour cream.

*Innes E. Green*

# HAUTE CUISINE

*(Serves 6)*

Dining elegantly with a dramatic conclusion.

### *Soupe à L'Ail*
### *or*
### *Chilled Consommé with Caviar*

### *Veal Cordon Bleu*
### *Noodles Bravo*
### *Baked Zucchini*

### *Crêpes Fitzgerald*
### *Coffee*

*Dolcetto or Barbera*
*Asti Spumante with dessert*

## Soupe à L'Ail

| | |
|---|---|
| 2 tablespoons butter | ½ teaspoon salt |
| 4 tablespoons olive oil | ½ teaspoon Tabasco |
| ½ cup peeled, cut garlic cloves (4 to 5 whole pods) | ½ teaspoon nutmeg |
| | 6 slices French bread, lightly toasted |
| 4 cups chicken stock | |
| 3 egg yolks | 1 tablespoon minced parsley |

Melt butter with 1 tablespoon of the oil. Add garlic and cook over low heat 15 minutes (do not brown garlic). Pour in stock, bring to a boil, partially cover, and simmer 20 minutes. Beat egg yolks until thick; add remaining oil a drop at a time, beating constantly. Stir a little soup into yolk mixture, then pour into soup. Heat thoroughly without boiling. Pour through a sieve into a heated tureen. Mash garlic pieces through sieve. Season and serve over bread rounds sprinkled with parsley.

*Hope E. O'Quin*

## Chilled Consommé with Caviar

| | |
|---|---|
| 3 10½-ounce cans consommé | 6 lemon slices |
| ½ pint sour cream | Chopped parsley |
| 1 3-ounce jar red caviar | |

Pour consommé into individual serving dishes. Refrigerate until firm. When ready to serve, top with a dollop of sour cream and a sprinkle of caviar. Garnish with parsley and a lemon slice.

*Marguerite D. Jacobson*

## Veal Cordon Bleu

12 pieces thinly sliced veal,
   pounded as thin as possible
   (about 1½ pounds)
1 tablespoon anchovy paste
3 tablespoons butter, softened
6 thin slices boiled ham
6 thin slices Gruyère or baby
   Swiss cheese

1 egg, beaten with 1 tablespoon
   water
½ cup flour
½ cup dry bread crumbs
4 tablespoons butter
Paprika
6 lemon wedges
6 parsley sprigs

Blend anchovy paste with softened butter. Spread mixture on veal slices. Cover with 1 slice of ham and 1 slice of cheese. Top with remaining veal, sandwich style. Secure edges with toothpicks. Dip each veal "sandwich" into beaten egg mixture, then flour, then bread crumbs. In large skillet, melt remaining butter; sauté the veal pieces about 4 or 5 minutes to a side until golden brown. Sprinkle with paprika and garnish with lemon and parsley. Serve hot.

Variation: Chicken breasts may be substituted for veal.

*Jo Timmerman*

## Noodles Bravo

8 ounces medium egg noodles
Salt

4 tablespoons butter
4 ounces fine egg noodles

Boil medium egg noodles in 2 quarts of salted water until tender. Drain, rinse with hot water, drain again and toss with 2 tablespoons butter. Place in 2-quart flat casserole dish. Melt remaining butter in a large skillet and sauté the fine egg noodles until they turn a rich golden brown, stirring occasionally. Cover top of casserole with these and reheat, if necessary, at 300°.

Variation: For a less bland dish, sauté ½ cup minced onions and 1 clove minced garlic with the topping and/or toss medium noodles with 1 cup grated cheese.

*Thelma W. Green*

## Baked Zucchini

6 zucchini
1 clove garlic, halved
Salt, black pepper and cayenne
   to taste

4 tablespoons butter

Slice zucchini in half lengthwise and score cut surface. Rub with garlic and season; dot with butter. Bake at 325° for 40 minutes.

*Betty S. Gaiennie*

## Crêpes Fitzgerald

¾ cup plus 3 tablespoons flour
1 tablespoon sugar
⅛ teaspoon salt
3 eggs
2 tablespoons cognac
1 teaspoon grated lemon peel
3 tablespoons melted butter
1½ cups milk
4 ounces cream cheese

¾ cup sour cream
3 to 4 tablespoons sugar
⅛ teaspoon vanilla
⅛ teaspoon almond extract
2 tablespoons butter
2 cups strawberries
6 tablespoons Kirsch
3 tablespoons strawberry liqueur

Sift flour, sugar, and salt into mixing bowl. Add 1 egg at a time, beating well after each addition. Mix until there are no lumps. Stir in cognac, lemon peel, 2 tablespoons melted butter and milk. The batter should have the consistency of thin cream. Let stand in refrigerator at least 1 hour.

To make crêpes, heat a crêpe pan and brush with remaining melted butter. Add about 2 tablespoons of the batter and swirl around to cover bottom of pan. Pour any excess back into bowl. Cook until brown on one side, just a few seconds. Turn and cook other side. May be prepared several hours ahead and reheated in oven, covered with a damp cloth to prevent drying. Also may be separated with wax paper and frozen in a plastic bag. Makes about 24 crêpes.

Combine cream cheese and sour cream. Add 1 tablespoon sugar, vanilla and almond extract. Spread cream cheese mixture on warm crêpes and roll. Combine remaining ingredients in a chafing dish. Heat and stir until strawberries are well-cooked, like preserves, then ignite. When flame dies, pour over crêpes and serve.

*John Bennet Waters*

# ENCORE SUPPER
*(Serves 6)*

After the concert for the best critics.

### *Onion-Potato Soup*

### *Cabbage Rolls*   or   *Steak and Oyster Pie*
### *Brown Bread*
### Green Salad

### *Coffee Freeze*

Côte d'or-Villages (red) or California Pinot Noir

## Onion-Potato Soup

3   onions, chopped
2   tablespoons butter
3   tablespoons flour
2   cups boiling water

3   potatoes, peeled, cooked, and
     mashed
1   quart milk, scalded
Salt and white pepper to taste

Sauté onions in butter; stir in flour. Add water gradually. Combine potatoes with milk and add to onion mixture. Season and purée. Reheat gently when ready to serve.

*Zelda C. Kaplan*

## Cabbage Rolls

2 or 3 cabbages
1   pound ground chuck
1   egg
2   tablespoons long grain rice
1   onion, chopped
1   slice stale bread, soaked in
     water and squeezed dry
1   teaspoon salt

½   pound brisket, sliced
3   tablespoons brown sugar
1½ teaspoons salt
½   cup raisins
1   8-ounce package dried mixed
     fruit
1   10¾-ounce can tomato soup
1   cup sour cream

Core cabbages and immerse in boiling water until leaves are tender and separate easily but are not cooked, about 5 minutes. It may be necessary to cut away part of the spine if it is too thick and hard.

Mix together ground meat, egg, rice, onion, bread and 1 teaspoon salt. Place about 1 tablespoon of this mixture on each cabbage leaf. Fold (or roll) and tuck in ends, securing with a toothpick if necessary.

In a large heavy pot which can be used both on top of the stove and in the oven, place the brisket slices. Stack cabbage rolls on top. Cover pot tightly and cook very slowly for 30 minutes.

Add remaining ingredients, except sour cream, recover and cook very slowly for 2 hours. It may be necessary to add a little water. At this point the whole pot may be refrigerated overnight to allow the flavors to marry.

Bake uncovered 1 hour at 300°. Serve accompanied by sour cream.

*Sylvia D. Kushner*

## Steak and Oyster Pie

| | |
|---|---|
| 1   double pie crust | 1   egg, beaten |
| 1   pound sirloin or round steak, cubed and floured | ¼   cup port |
| | 1   tablespoon catsup |
| 1¼ pints oysters, drained, liquor reserved | 1   tablespoon lemon juice |
| | Mace, garlic powder, and Tabasco to taste |
| Salt and pepper to taste | |

Line a deep pie pan with one of the pie crusts. Place a layer of meat and a layer of oysters in pie shell. Repeat, seasoning each layer with salt and pepper. Add 2 tablespoons oyster liquor. Cover with remaining pastry. Brush top with egg. Cut hole to allow steam to escape. Bake at 400° for 10 minutes. Mix ¼ cup oyster liquor with remaining ingredients; heat and pour through hole in pastry. Bake another 40 minutes at 350°.

*Katie S. O'Neal*

## Brown Bread

| | |
|---|---|
| 3   cups whole wheat flour, stirred | ½   cup brown sugar |
| 1   package yeast | 3   teaspoons salt |
| 5   cups white flour | ¼   cup shortening |
| 2¾ cups hot water (about 120°) | |

In large bowl, thoroughly combine the whole wheat flour, yeast and 1 cup white flour. Mix water, sugar, salt and shortening; gradually add to dry ingredients, beating well. Add white flour 1 cup at a time, beating until the dough is moderately stiff. Knead on floured board until smooth and satiny (10 to 12 minutes). Shape into ball and place in greased bowl, turning to grease top side. Let rise, covered, until doubled in bulk—about 1½ hours. Punch down, divide in half and let rest 10 minutes. Shape into loaves and place in 2 greased 8½×4½×2½-inch loaf pans. Let rise until doubled. Bake 45 minutes at 375°. To prevent overbrowning, cover with foil the last 20 minutes.

*Carol B. Alley*

## Coffee Freeze

| | |
|---|---|
| 1   quart chocolate chip (or vanilla) ice cream | 4   ounces bourbon |
| | 4   ounces strong coffee, chilled |

Blend to the consistency of a milk shake. Serve in champagne glasses.

# PLANTATION MEMORIES                          *(Serves 6)*

Gracious dining rooms of the past provide inspiration for distinctive South-ern hospitality today.

### *Kent House Oysters*

### *Chicken Hollandaise*      *Buttered Spinach*
### *Homemade Bread*

### *Angel Pie*
### *Coffee*

*White Burgundy or California Chardonnay*

## Kent House Oysters

2   pints oysters, drained, rinsed,
    liquor reserved
¼   pound butter or margarine
4   tablespoons flour
2   tablespoons finely chopped
    celery
2   tablespoons finely chopped
    green pepper

2   tablespoons minced parsley
1   onion, grated
Salt and pepper to taste
2   tablespoons Worcestershire
    sauce
1   cup coarsely crushed cracker
    crumbs

In a 10-inch black iron skillet melt the butter over medium heat. Sprinkle in the flour and stir constantly until flour turns a golden brown. Add vegetables and stir until transparent. Stir in ¼ to ½ cup oyster liquor and simmer to make a smooth gravy. Add oysters, salt and pepper to taste. Cook, stirring occa-sionally, until edges of oysters curl. Remove from heat and add Worcester-shire sauce. Divide oysters into small individual ramekins. May be prepared to this point and stored in refrigerator for several hours or overnight.

Just before serving, top with cracker crumbs and bake at 350° for 10 to 15 minutes.

*Peggy McL. Bolton*

## Chicken Hollandaise

8   halves chicken breasts
2   cups water
1   tablespoon chopped onion
1   tablespoon chopped celery
1   tablespoon chopped green
    pepper
1   tablespoon minced parsley

½   teaspoon salt
½   teaspoon garlic salt
¼   pound butter
¾   cup brandy
1¼  cups mushrooms
¾   cup white wine
Salt and pepper to taste

Place chicken and water in saucepan; add onion, celery, green pepper, parsley, salt and garlic salt. Cover and simmer until chicken is tender (about 30 minutes). Remove chicken; strain stock, boil rapidly to reduce to 1 cup, and reserve.

Skin and debone chicken. In a heavy skillet, melt butter and brown meat evenly. Heat brandy, pour over chicken and ignite. When flame subsides, add mushrooms, stock and wine. Simmer 5 minutes. Season with salt and pepper.

Transfer to a shallow ovenproof dish, cover, and bake 1 hour at 325°. Before serving, top chicken with the following sauce.

### Blender Hollandaise Sauce

| | |
|---|---|
| 6 egg yolks | ⅛ teaspoon cayenne |
| 2 tablespoons lemon juice | ½ pound butter |

Combine first 3 ingredients in blender just until mixed. Melt butter; while still hot, slowly add to mixture, blending 30 seconds, waiting 30 seconds. Repeat until desired consistency is reached.

*Tricia W. Henderson*

## Buttered Spinach

| | |
|---|---|
| 20 ounces spinach, rinsed | Salt, pepper, and nutmeg to taste |
| 3 tablespoons butter | |

Toss spinach in large skillet over moderate heat for 3 to 4 minutes. Add butter and seasonings.

## Angel Pie

| | |
|---|---|
| 6 egg whites, at room temperature | 1 teaspoon vanilla |
| ¼ teaspoon salt | ½ pint heavy cream |
| ¼ teaspoon cream of tartar | 1 tablespoon sugar |
| 1½ cups sugar | 2 cups raspberries (optional) |
| | 1 cup sugar (optional) |

Preheat oven to 450°. Beat egg whites with salt until stiff. Add cream of tartar and beat until bowl can be inverted and whites remain in bowl. Add 1½ cups sugar in small amounts, beating constantly. Add vanilla and beat 15 minutes (by the clock). Spoon into buttered 8-inch pie plate. Place in oven and turn heat off. Leave overnight.

Whip cream, adding 1 tablespoon sugar gradually. Spread over top of pie. If sauce is desired, purée berries in blender with 1 cup sugar. Serve over pie portions after cutting.

Variation: 2 or 3 tablespoons of crème de menthe may be added to whipping cream when sauce is not used.

*Ruth O. Prince*

# STEAK DINNER                                    (Serve 6)

Invite friends over for a choice steak, grilled to order, accompanied by piquant vegetables and a beautiful dessert.

*Fried Eggplant Appetizer*

**Grilled Steak**
*Venetian Potatoes*     **French Bread**

*Zucchini Vinaigrette*
*or*
*Red and Green Pepper Salad*

*Mocha Angel Pie*
**Coffee**

*Claret, California Cabernet Sauvignon or Zinfandel*

## Fried Eggplant Appetizer

2   eggplants                        3   cups cracker crumbs
2   eggs, beaten                     Salad oil
Salt and pepper to taste

Peel and cut eggplants lengthwise into strips ¼-inch thick. Spread on paper towel, sprinkle with salt and let set about 20 minutes to draw out any bitterness. Pat dry. Dip slices in eggs, beaten with salt and pepper, then in cracker crumbs. Fry in hot oil about a minute on each side. Serve immediately.

## Venetian Potatoes

9   red potatoes                     3   cups sour cream
6   tablespoons butter               ½   cup chopped green onions
3   cups grated sharp Cheddar        Salt and pepper to taste
    cheese

Boil potatoes; chill, peel and grate into large bowl. In medium saucepan over low heat, combine butter and cheese and stir until melted. Remove from heat and blend in sour cream, onions and seasonings. Pour over potatoes and mix well. Place mixture in buttered 3-quart casserole; dot with additional butter. Bake 45 minutes at 350°. Freezes well.

*Vinita S. Johnson*

## Zucchini Vinaigrette

1 to 2 red onions, sliced
1   tablespoon sugar
¼   cup Chablis
1   0.6-ounce envelope Italian
     salad dressing mix
¼   cup salad oil
¼   cup white wine vinegar
4   tablespoons finely chopped
     green onions

3   tablespoons sweet pickle relish,
     drained
2   tablespoons minced parsley
2 to 3 tablespoons minced green
     pepper
5 to 6 zucchini, cut in lengthwise
     strips
Salt to taste
4   tomatoes, chilled

Place onions in a flat dish and sprinkle with sugar. Cover with iced water and refrigerate. Combine wine and dressing mix. Add next 6 ingredients and blend well. Cook zucchini in salted water about 3 minutes or until barely tender. Drain well, place in a shallow dish and sprinkle lightly with salt. Drench with the wine dressing and refrigerate overnight.

When ready to serve, slice tomatoes and arrange with drained zucchini and onions on serving platter. Top with a little of the marinade. The zucchini in the marinade is practically immortal if kept refrigerated. The tomatoes and onions may be replenished if there is zucchini left to serve at a later date.

*Dorothy G. Portier*

## Red and Green Pepper Salad

2   sweet red peppers, seeded
2   green peppers, seeded
1   onion, thinly sliced
2   tablespoons vinegar

2   tablespoons water
2   tablespoons sugar
1   teaspoon salt

Cut peppers into thin slices and layer with onion. Combine vinegar, sugar, water and salt and pour over the pepper-onion mixture. Chill several hours or overnight. Drain and serve.

(Note: Red sweet peppers are seasonal, but this is worth the effort to find the peppers!)

*Dorothy I. Stuckey*

## Mocha Angel Pie

3   egg whites, at room
    temperature
⅛ teaspoon cream of tartar
Pinch of salt
¾ cup sifted sugar
¾ cup chopped pecans or walnuts
2   teaspoons vanilla

4   ounces sweet chocolate
3   tablespoons strong black coffee
1   cup heavy cream, whipped
½ cup heavy cream, whipped, for
    topping
Shaved chocolate

Beat egg whites until foamy. Add cream of tartar and salt; continue beating until egg whites stand in soft peaks. Gradually add sugar and continue beating until very stiff. Fold in nuts and 1 teaspoon vanilla. Turn into a buttered 9-inch pie pan and make a nestlike shell, building up the sides ½ inch above the edge of the plate. Bake at 300° for 50 to 55 minutes. Cool thoroughly.

Melt chocolate in saucepan over low heat with coffee, stirring until smooth. Cool; add 1 teaspoon vanilla. Fold 1 cup whipped cream into chocolate mixture and pour into meringue shell. Chill.

Garnish each serving with a dollop of remaining whipped cream and a sprinkling of shaved chocolate.

*Dorothy I. Stuckey*

# DINNER AT EIGHT

*(Serves 8)*

A special menu with a Southern accent.

### *Mint Juleps*

### *Mushrooms with Crabmeat*

### *Charcoaled Lamb*
### *Squash Bechamel*    *Hot Asparagus Vinaigrette*
### French Bread

### *Charlotte Russe*
### Coffee

*White Burgundy or Chardonnay with mushrooms*
*Rich Claret or California Cabernet with lamb*

## Mint Juleps

| | |
|---|---|
| 2 cups sugar | 8 1½-ounce jiggers bourbon |
| 1 cup water | Confectioners' sugar and mint |
| 16 sprigs mint | for garnish |
| 4 pounds finely crushed ice | |

Mix sugar and water; bring to a boil, stirring. Cool. Place 2 sprigs of mint in each glass; crush to release mint flavor. Add 2 ounces of the sugar syrup, stirring gently. Fill glass with ice. Add 1 jigger of whiskey. Stir until glass frosts. Top with sprig of mint and sprinkling of powdered sugar.

*Wilbert Martin*

## Mushrooms with Crabmeat

| | |
|---|---|
| 1 pound lump crabmeat | 1 teaspoon celery seed |
| 1 cup mayonnaise | 1 tablespoon grated onion |
| 1½ teaspoons salt | 2 pounds large mushrooms, |
| ⅛ teaspoon pepper | stems removed |
| ⅛ teaspoon paprika | ¼ pound butter |
| 1 teaspoon sugar | 1 tablespoon flour |
| 2 tablespoons lemon juice | Salt, pepper and garlic powder |
| 2 tablespoons milk | to taste |

Mix first 10 ingredients together; refrigerate.
Sauté mushroom caps in butter. Sprinkle lightly with flour and season to

taste. Cover and cook over low heat until tender—about 10 minutes, stirring occasionally. Cool.

To serve, stuff mushrooms with crabmeat mixture.

*Nancy C. Weems*


## Charcoaled Lamb

| | | |
|---|---|---|
| 1 | 6-pound leg of lamb, boned and butterflied | 1½ teaspoons thyme |
| 1 | cup olive oil | ½ cup beef stock |
| ⅔ | cup lemon juice | ¼ cup red wine |
| 3 | cloves garlic, pressed | 2 tablespoons chopped green onions |
| 2 | bay leaves | 1½ teaspoons sage |
| 6 | sprigs parsley | 1½ teaspoons rosemary |

1    6-pound leg of lamb, boned
     and butterflied
1    cup olive oil
⅔   cup lemon juice
3    cloves garlic, pressed
2    bay leaves
6    sprigs parsley
Salt to taste
½   teaspoon pepper
1½  teaspoons sage
1½  teaspoons rosemary

1½ teaspoons thyme
½ cup beef stock
¼ cup red wine
2    tablespoons chopped green
     onions
1½ teaspoons sage
1½ teaspoons rosemary
1½ teaspoons thyme
3    tablespoons butter, at room
     temperature
3    tablespoons minced parsley

Remove all fat and skin from lamb. Combine next 10 ingredients; pour over lamb. Cover and refrigerate for 24 hours, turning occasionally. Drain and reserve marinade.

Using outdoor charcoal grill, place lamb flat on hot grill; sear each side. Cover and cook 45 minutes to 1 hour over moderate fire, brushing with reserved marinade. Use meat thermometer to achieve desired doneness. Let rest at room temperature about 20 minutes.

Boil next 6 ingredients together until reduced to ½ cup. Remove from heat. Swirl butter into sauce a little at a time; add minced parsley. Pour over lamb.

Variation: Substitute 2  4-pound racks of lamb; cook approximately 30 minutes.

*Bertie M. Deming*


## Squash Béchamel

2    pounds yellow squash, sliced
1    onion, sliced
½   teaspoon thyme
½   bay leaf
3    sprigs parsley
2    tablespoons butter
2    tablespoons flour
1    cup milk

2    egg yolks, beaten
¼   teaspoon nutmeg
¾   cup grated Swiss or Gruyère
     cheese
Salt, white pepper, and cayenne
     to taste
¼   cup bread crumbs

In water to cover, boil squash with next 4 ingredients until just tender; drain. Remove bay leaf and parsley. Place squash and onion in greased 2-quart casserole. Melt butter; blend in flour and add milk. Add ¼ cup sauce to eggs, mixing well. Stir egg mixture back into sauce. Add ½ cup cheese and stir in remaining seasonings. Pour sauce over squash; cover with mixture of remaining cheese and bread crumbs. Bake, uncovered, for 25 minutes at 350°.

*Caroline K. Gilliland*

## Hot Asparagus Vinaigrette

½ cup vegetable oil
1½ tablespoons white wine vinegar
1 tablespoon finely chopped sweet pickle
½ teaspoon dry mustard
½ teaspoon salt
⅛ teaspoon pepper
1 teaspoon minced parsley
1 teaspoon minced chives
2 pounds asparagus, cooked and drained
2 teaspoons capers

Heat first 6 ingredients just to boiling. Stir in parsley and chives. Pour over hot asparagus. Top with capers.

*Gloria W. Heam*

## Charlotte Russe

2 tablespoons gelatin
¼ cup cold water
8 egg yolks
1 cup sugar
2 cups milk
1 teaspoon vanilla
½ cup strawberry liqueur
2 cups heavy cream, whipped
12 ladyfingers, split
1 pint strawberries, sugared

Soften gelatin in cold water. In the top of a double boiler blend egg yolks and sugar with wooden spoon until smooth. Bring milk and vanilla to a boil; add gradually to egg yolk mixture, stirring rapidly with whisk. Cook over boiling water until mixture thickens, stirring constantly. Add softened gelatin and cook at least 1 more minute. Cool custard; add liqueur and fold in whipped cream. Line a spring-form pan with ladyfingers, standing them upright around sides. Pour custard into pan and chill 24 hours. Unmold and garnish with strawberries.

*JoAnn W. Kellogg*

# WILD GEESE                                    *(Serves 8)*

Coastal marshlands of Louisiana abound in ducks and geese in the winter-time. The white-fronted goose, or "specklebelly", is the most uncommon variety of wild goose in Louisiana but also the most highly esteemed for its taste.

Mirlitons, or vegetable pears, are Louisiana cousins of the gourd and are harvested abundantly in late summer and fall. Refrigerated, they will keep well throughout the winter. Squash or eggplant may be substituted in mirliton recipes but will lack the delicate flavor of the chayote.

### *Oysters en Brochette*

### *Coastal Geese*     *Mirliton Dressing*
### *Cornbread Sticks*

### *Brandied Flan*
### or
### *Brandy Ice*

### Coffee

*Red Burgundy, Barolo or Rioja*

## Oysters en brochette

24  oysters, drained            12  slices of bacon, halved
Salt and pepper to taste        8   lemon wedges
Tabasco

Salt and pepper oysters; sprinkle one drop Tabasco on each oyster. Wrap each oyster with bacon, securing with toothpick. Broil 6 inches from heat for 10 to 15 minutes. Serve with lemon wedges.

## Coastal Geese

2   wild geese                  8   turnips, peeled and quartered
Salt and pepper to taste        1   fifth dry red wine
1   bunch mustard greens

Salt and pepper cavities and outsides of geese. Mix half of the greens with turnips, which have been lightly salted and peppered, and stuff geese. Place remaining greens over geese, pressing tightly to tops and sides. Place birds in roasting pan and pour the wine over them. Cover and cook at 350° for 2 to 2½ hours, basting occasionally with pan juices.

*Felix Broussard*

## Mirliton Dressing

4   mirlitons, scalded, peeled, and
    cubed
⅔   cup bacon drippings
1   onion, chopped
½   pound ground meat (beef, pork,
    or mixed)
1   cup cooked rice (or cornbread,
    crumbled)

¼   cup minced parsley
Worcestershire sauce, salt, and
    pepper to taste

Using a heavy 10-inch skillet, sauté vegetables in fat until mirlitons are soft. Add meat and continue cooking until meat is done. Add rice or cornbread and seasonings and cook until well-heated. May be prepared the day before serving, refrigerated and reheated. Freezes well.

*Amy R. Gremillion*

## Cornbread Sticks

2   cups buttermilk
½   teaspoon baking soda
1½  cups corn meal
¾   cup flour
3   tablespoons sugar

1½  teaspoons salt
2   teaspoons baking powder
2   eggs, beaten
8   tablespoons vegetable oil

Mix buttermilk and soda and let stand 30 minutes. Combine remaining dry ingredients; make a well in the center and add eggs and buttermilk mixture, blending well. Let stand 30 minutes.

Grease iron breadstick pans and heat in 450° oven until oil sizzles. Heat remaining oil, pour into batter and stir well.

Fill pans half full with batter. Bake at 450° for 17 minutes in top third of oven.

Yield: 22 sticks

*Grady A. McDuff*

## Brandied Flan

¾  cup sugar
2   cups milk
2   cups cream
6   eggs
½  cup sugar

½  teaspoon salt
1½ teaspoons vanilla
⅓  cup brandy
1   tablespoon brandy for
     flaming custard

Place ¾ cup sugar in an iron skillet and cook over medium heat until sugar melts and forms a light brown syrup. Stir to blend. Immediately pour syrup into a heated 8¼-inch round, shallow baking dish. Quickly rotate dish to cover bottom and sides completely. Set aside.

In medium saucepan, heat milk and cream just until bubbles form around edge of pan. In large bowl, beat eggs slightly. Add sugar, salt and vanilla. Gradually stir in hot milk mixture and brandy. Pour into prepared caramel-lined dish. Set dish in shallow pan; pour boiling water to ½ inch level around dish. Bake at 325° for 35 to 40 minutes or until silver knife inserted in center comes out clean. Let custard cool; refrigerate 4 hours or overnight.

To serve, run small knife around edge to loosen and invert on heatproof serving platter. Warm the tablespoon of brandy, pour over flan, and ignite. When brought flaming to the table, an impressive finale.

*Virginia B. Klock*

## Brandy Ice

8   servings vanilla ice cream
2   ounces crème de cacao

3   ounces brandy

Place half of ingredients in blender. Blend one minute. Pour into 4 champagne glasses. Repeat. May be prepared ahead and stored in the freezer. Remove from freezer 30 minutes before serving.

# TAILGATE PICNIC *(Serves 8)*

Pack this meal into your ice chest and head for the stadium.

***Gazpacho***
***Cheese Straws***

***Cold Tenderloin***
***Rice Salad***    ***Dijon Mustard***
***LSU Rolls***    ***Mayonnaise***

***Golden Cake***

*California red jug Burgundy*

## Gazpacho

| | |
|---|---|
| 2   14½-ounce cans Contadina round peeled tomatoes with juice | ½   teaspoon Tabasco |
| 2   cloves garlic, chopped | ½   cup tomato paste |
| 1   cup quartered green peppers | ½   teaspoon white pepper |
| ½   cup sliced cucumbers | 4   teaspoons salt |
| ⅔   cup quartered white onions | 4   tablespoons olive oil |
| | 2   teaspoons Worcestershire sauce |
| | 4   tablespoons lemon juice |

Place half the ingredients in blender or food processor and purée. Repeat. Chill, covered, overnight.
Yield: 48 ounces

*Richard B. Crowell*

## Cold Tenderloin

3 to 4 pounds beef tenderloin      Freshly ground pepper

Rub meat with pepper and place on rack in pan. Roast at 425° for 15 to 20 minutes or until meat thermometer registers desired degree of doneness. Cool. Slice thinly and refrigerate.

## Rice Salad

1  6-ounce box chicken-flavored rice
1  6-ounce jar marinated artichoke bottoms
2 to 3 tablespoons minced green onions

12  ripe or pimiento-stuffed olives, drained and sliced
¼  cup mayonnaise
½ to 1 teaspoon curry powder
Salt and pepper to taste

Cook rice according to directions on box. Drain and chop artichokes, reserving liquid. Add onions, olives and artichokes to rice. Combine mayonnaise with curry powder; add to rice mixture. Slowly add artichoke marinade until salad is desired consistency; season. Serve immediately or refrigerate and serve chilled.

*Toni V. Foote*

## LSU Rolls

6  tablespoons shortening
4  tablespoons sugar
1  package yeast, dissolved in ½ cup lukewarm water

1  cup lukewarm milk
3½ cups flour

In large mixing bowl, cream sugar and shortening. Add yeast, milk and flour; mix well. Let rise 2 hours. Roll out on floured board to thickness of about ½ inch. Cut with biscuit cutter and place on greased baking sheet. Let rise for 2 more hours. Bake at 400° for 20 minutes or until golden brown.
    Yield: 16 rolls

*Blanche G. Lee*

## Golden Cake

¾  pound butter
3  cups sugar
7  eggs
3  cups sifted flour

1  teaspoon vanilla
1  tablespoon lemon juice
1  cup chopped almonds or pecans

Cream butter and sugar; add eggs 1 at a time, beating well after each addition. Blend in flour ½ cup at a time. Add flavorings. Pour batter into greased 8-inch tube pan lined with wax paper. Sprinkle batter with nuts. Bake at 325° for 1½ to 1¾ hours. Cool 10 minutes before removing from pan.

*Mary Frances P. Ewing*

# MIDSUMMER DINNER
*(Serves 8)*

The charisma of a summer setting and the taste of Louisiana food combine to create an enchanting evening.

***Stuffed Mushrooms**

***Barbecued Lamb**
***Baked New Potatoes**    ***Petit Pois**
***Chickamaw Plantation Tomatoes**
**Rolls**

***Buttermilk Pie*   or   *Old-time Lemon Pie**
**Coffee**

*Claret or California Cabernet Sauvignon*

## Stuffed Mushrooms

| | |
|---|---|
| 1  pound mushrooms | 1  tablespoon sherry |
| 2  tablespoons minced onion | ½  teaspoon salt |
| 1  tablespoon butter | ⅛  teaspoon white pepper |
| ½  cup heavy cream | ¼  teaspoon nutmeg |

Remove mushroom stems and mince; sauté stems with onions in butter until limp. Add cream, sherry and seasonings and cook slowly until thick, stirring constantly, 10 to 15 minutes. Fill mushroom caps with mixture and place on greased baking sheet. At this point, mushrooms may be refrigerated or frozen. When ready to serve, broil until brown and bubbling.

*Louise A. Simon*

## Barbecued Lamb

| | |
|---|---|
| 2  tablespoons barbecue spice | 2  tablespoons Worcestershire |
| 1  teaspoon hickory smoked salt |      sauce |
| ½  teaspoon garlic powder | ¼  cup soy sauce |
| ⅛  teaspoon celery salt | 1  cup corn oil |
| 1  tablespoon cayenne | Salt and pepper to taste |
| ¼  cup lemon juice | 6-pound leg of lamb |

Blend ingredients and marinate lamb several hours. Smoke, covered, over low coals about 25 minutes per pound or until meat thermometer registers desired degree of doneness. Baste frequently. Let rest 20 minutes at room tempeature before carving.

*Willie E. Braxton*

## Baked New Potatoes

12  new potatoes, unpeeled, boiled
1   cup grated sharp Cheddar
    cheese

2   slices crisp bacon, crumbled
4 to 8 tablespoons butter, melted
Salt and pepper to taste

Slice potatoes and place half in a shallow greased casserole. Sprinkle with salt, pepper and half the cheese, bacon and butter. Repeat. Bake at 350° until cheese melts (about 10 minutes).

*Lisa L. Norman*

## Petit Pois

½  cup mayonnaise
1   onion, chopped
½  pound mushrooms (optional)
2   15-ounce cans petit pois,
    drained

2   ounces sliced pimientos
Rosemary to taste
Parsley

Sauté onions and mushrooms in mayonnaise. Add other ingredients and heat thoroughly.

*Marc Dupuy*

## Chickamaw Plantation Tomatoes

8   tomatoes, at their peak
2   fresh green hot peppers,
    minced, or ½ teaspoon
    cayenne

1 to 2 tablespoons minced green
    or red onions
Salt and pepper to taste

Peel and cut tomatoes into wedges, removing every woody part. Toss with remaining ingredients. Chill several hours. The secret of this dish is to select perfectly ripened tomatoes and to use only the best sections.

*Betty S. Gaiennie*

## Buttermilk Pie

3   eggs, beaten
2   cups sugar
¼   pound butter
1   cup buttermilk
3   tablespoons flour

½   teaspoon vanilla
1   tablespoon lemon juice
Grated peel of ½ lemon
½   teaspoon nutmeg
1   9-inch unbaked pie shell

Mix first 8 ingredients and pour into pie shell. Bake at 350° for 45 minutes to 1 hour. (Pie is done when middle is firm.) Freezes well before or after baking.

*Geraldine P. Brian*

## Old-time Lemon Pie

1   9-inch pie shell
2   eggs, separated
4   tablespoons lemon juice
Grated peel of 2 lemons
1   cup sugar

⅛   teaspoon salt
4   tablespoons flour
1   tablespoon melted butter
1   cup milk

Wrap foil around edges of pastry shell and bake 5 minutes at 400°. Remove foil.

Beat egg yolks until thick. Add lemon juice and peel. Mix salt with sugar and stir in. Blend in flour, then milk and butter. Beat egg whites until stiff and fold into mixture. Pour into pie shell and bake 10 minutes at 400°. Reduce heat to 325° and continue baking for 20 minutes longer or until center is firm.

*Bootsie P. Voelker*

# CREOLES AND COMPANY          *(Serves 8)*

Redfish (Poisson Rouge) is easily distinguished from the more familiar red snapper by the single dark spot on the tail. It is a member of the bass family and has very firm flesh which flakes in large pieces. The flavor is worth the trouble to find this fish.

Making this very thick soup is a festive event where all take part in assembling and preparing the ingredients, stirring the pot, sipping and tasting until it's just right. (Of course, courtbouillon may also be prepared ahead.)

### *Cheeses*

### *\*Redfish Courtbouillon*
### *\*Chapon Salad     French Bread*

### *\*Bananas Foster*
### *or*
### *\*Oranges Jubilee*

### *Coffee*

*Chenin Blanc or Muscadet*

## *Redfish Courtbouillon*

| | |
|---|---|
| ¼ pound butter | ½ teaspoon thyme |
| ½ cup olive oil | 2 bay leaves |
| 1 cup flour | ½ lemon, thinly sliced |
| ½ cup chopped green onion tops | ½ to 1 cup claret |
| 4 onions, finely chopped | ½ teaspoon cayenne |
| 3 ribs celery, finely chopped | ¼ teaspoon Tabasco |
| 1 green pepper, finely chopped | 1 teaspoon Worcestershire |
| 1 cup minced parsley | Green pepper sauce to taste |
| 4 cloves garlic, minced | Salt to taste |
| 1 8-ounce can tomato sauce | 1 6 to 8 pound redfish, filleted |
| 1 6-ounce can tomato paste | and cut into chunks. |
| 1½ pints hot water (approximate) | |

In a heavy pot, melt butter with olive oil. Add flour and cook over low heat until golden brown to make a roux. Add vegetables and cook until tender. Add tomato sauce and paste. Cook slowly, then add enough water to achieve desired thickness. Add remaining ingredients and cook slowly for 20 minutes. More hot water may be added to correct consistency.

Serve in gumbo bowls over hot fluffy rice.

*Miriam W. Wilkins*

## Chapon Salad

| | | | |
|---|---|---|---|
| 4 | tablespoons wine vinegar | | Freshly ground black pepper |
| 12 | tablespoons salad oil | |    to taste |
| 1 | teaspoon salt | 1 | head red tip lettuce |
| 3 | small cloves garlic, minced | 1 | head Romaine lettuce |

Combine dressing ingredients in glass jar with tightly fitting lid and shake well. Tear salad greens into bite-sized pieces and chill. When ready to serve, toss greens with dressing.

*Beck McL. Crowell*


## Bananas Foster

| | | | |
|---|---|---|---|
| 12 | tablespoons butter | 2 | ounces banana liqueur |
| 1½ | cups dark brown sugar | 1 | cup dark rum, warmed |
| 1½ | teaspoons cinnamon | 1 | quart French vanilla ice cream |
| 6 | bananas, halved lengthwise, then quartered | | |

In a flat skillet or flambé pan, melt and stir together the butter, sugar and cinnamon over low heat. When blended, add bananas and liqueur. Cook just to coat bananas, stirring gently. Add rum and ignite. Baste fruit with sauce until flame dies. Serve over ice cream.

*Hope E. Norman*


## Oranges Jubilee

| | | | |
|---|---|---|---|
| 2 | cups orange juice | 4 | oranges, peeled and sectioned |
| 2 | cups water | ⅓ | cup chopped almonds |
| 1½ | cups sugar | 1 | cup brandy, warmed |
| 3 | tablespoons cornstarch | 8 | servings vanilla ice cream |

Mix 1½ cups orange juice with water and sugar and bring to a boil. Simmer 5 minutes. Blend remaining juice with cornstarch and add to hot mixture, stirring constantly. Cook and stir until slightly thickened and glossy (about 10 minutes). Place orange sections in a chafing dish, sprinkle with almonds, pour in hot syrup, add brandy and ignite. When flame dies, spoon over ice cream.

*Julie D. Simon*

# GUESTS ON THE GALLERY                    *(Serves 10)*

For summertime—or any time—when the "livin' is easy."

### *Daiquiris     *Cheese Puffs

### *Bar-B-Q Shrimp
### *Olive Coleslaw     French Bread

### *Chess Pie
### Coffee

*California white jug wine*

## Daiquiris

1   quart light rum
1   6-ounce can frozen limeade

1   quart water
Mint sprigs and lime slices

Mix first 3 ingredients in large pitcher and freeze overnight. Serve in frosted cocktail glasses. Garnish with mint and lime.
    Yield: 14   5-ounce drinks

## Cheese Puffs

¼   pound butter or margarine
2   cups grated very sharp Cheddar
    cheese
1   cup flour

¼   teaspoon thyme
⅛   teaspoon salt
¼   teaspoon cayenne

Mix all ingredients and shape into small balls; freeze. When ready to serve, bake 15 minutes at 350°.

*Willie Lee McQ. Brook*

## Bar-B-Q Shrimp

3   cups Wishbone Italian salad
    dressing
4 to 6 tablespoons Worcestershire
    sauce
1 to 2 cloves garlic, pressed
1   lemon, thinly sliced

1   teaspoon salt
2 to 3 teaspoons cayenne
Tabasco to taste
6   pounds shrimp, unpeeled
¾   cup melted butter
½ to 1 cup dry white wine

Mix first 7 ingredients and pour over raw shrimp. Refrigerate 2 to 3 hours. Place shrimp with marinade in roaster; add butter and wine. Stir and bake at

400° for 20 minutes. If shrimp are very large, bake for 25 minutes, but don't overcook. Serve in soup bowls with sauce from pan, or remove shrimp to large platter and serve sauce in individual bowls for dunking bread.

*Gail C. Little*

## Olive Coleslaw

| | |
|---|---|
| 1 cup mayonnaise | 2 tablespoons milk |
| 1½ teaspoons salt | 1 teaspoon celery seed |
| ⅛ teaspoon pepper | 1 cup pimiento-stuffed olives, sliced |
| ⅛ teaspoon paprika | |
| 1 teaspoon sugar | 1 tablespoon grated onion |
| 2 tablespoons lemon juice | 1 head cabbage |

Mix all ingredients except cabbage and refrigerate overnight. Shred cabbage and toss well with dressing.

*Helen B. Weems*

## Chess Pie

| | |
|---|---|
| 8 egg yolks | 2 tablespoons flour |
| 2 cups sugar | 1 cup water |
| ½ pound butter at room temperature | 4 teaspoons vanilla |
| | 1 10-inch pie shell (see below) |

Cream egg yolks, sugar and butter. Add remaining ingredients. Pour into pie shell and bake at 350° until knife blade inserted in pie will come out clean (approximately 35 to 40 minutes). Pastry and filling should be golden brown. Mixture looks curdled, and bubbles during cooking, but end result is perfect and beautiful.

*Anne M. Welch*

### No-roll Pastry

| | |
|---|---|
| 3 ounces cream cheese | 1 cup flour |
| ¼ pound butter | |

Blend cream cheese and butter; add flour. Press into ungreased 10-inch pie plate.

*Marie E. Polk*

# WINTER DINNER                              *(Serves 10)*

A menu for the hearty appetite that frosty weather brings.

## *Devilled Oysters*
## *Roast Pork*
## *Baked Butternut Squash*
### or
## *Butternut Squash Soufflé*
## *Marinated Vegetables*
## *Biscuits*
## *Baked Fudge Pudding*
## *Coffee*

*Light Claret or Charbono*

## Devilled Oysters

| | |
|---|---|
| 3 pints oysters, drained, rinsed, liquor reserved | 2 tablespoons Worcestershire sauce |
| 1 cup finely chopped celery | 2 tablespoons catsup |
| 1 cup finely chopped green onion | 2 tablespoons white wine |
| 1 green pepper, finely chopped | ½ teaspoon Tabasco |
| ½ cup minced parsley | ½ teaspoon black pepper |
| 20 saltine crackers | Salt to taste |
| 2 eggs, beaten | ¼ cup bread crumbs |
| 3 tablespoons butter or margarine | ¼ cup grated Parmesan cheese |

Dry oysters on paper towels. Place celery, onion, green pepper and parsley in a saucepan with oyster liquor (add water to liquor to make 1 cup, if necessary) and simmer until liquid is gone. Coarsely chop oysters and saltines together; add to vegetables along with eggs, and sauté mixture in melted butter, stirring constantly until very dry (10 to 15 minutes). Season with next 6 ingredients. Divide into 10 buttered 4-ounce ramekins and refrigerate for 12 hours.

About an hour before serving, remove from refrigerator and allow to come to room temperature. Top with mixture of bread crumbs and cheese; place ramekins in roasting pan containing ½-inch very hot water. Bake at 350° for 20 to 30 minutes. Serves 6 as a main dish; freezes well.

*Donnis N. Beckman*

## Roast Pork

| | |
|---|---|
| 1 5-pound boneless loin of pork | 3 sprigs parsley, minced |
| 1 clove garlic, halved | Salt and freshly ground pepper |
| ½ teaspoon paprika | to taste |
| 2 cups chopped onions | 1 fifth Burgundy |
| 1 cup chopped leeks (optional) | ¼ cup flour |
| 8 carrots, peeled and cut | ½ cup beef broth |
| 1 bay leaf, crushed | ¼ teaspoon nutmeg |
| ½ tablespoon rosemary | 2 tablespoons butter, softened |
| 1 teaspoon ground coriander | |

Rub the pork loin with the garlic and paprika; place in a deep bowl. Add the onions, leeks, carrots, bay leaf, rosemary, coriander, parsley, salt, pepper and wine; cover and refrigerate for 24 hours, turning occasionally.

Remove meat from marinade. Strain the liquid and reserve both the liquid and the vegetables. Sear the meat in a Dutch oven on moderate to high heat, browning on all sides. Roast, fat side down, uncovered at 400° for 30 minutes. Pour off the fat, turn the loin to fat side up, scatter the vegetables around it, sprinkle with flour and roast uncovered 15 minutes longer. Add the marinade and broth, cover, and roast an additional 60 minutes.

Remove meat to a warm platter and cover. Strain the liquid from the pot, skim off the fat, and pour into a saucepan. Cook over moderate heat 20 minutes. Add nutmeg and butter. Pour the sauce over the meat to serve.

*Bertie M. Deming*

## Baked Butternut Squash

| | |
|---|---|
| 3 pounds butternut squash, peeled and diced | 1½ tablespoons grated orange peel |
| ¾ cup sugar | 1½ tablespoons grated lemon peel |
| 1 teaspoon mace (optional) | ¾ cup orange juice |
| | 6 tablespoons margarine |

Place squash in a 9×12×2-inch greased baking dish. Combine sugar and mace with grated peels and sprinkle over squash. Pour juice over all and dot with margarine. Cover and bake at 350° for 1 to 1½ hours. Uncover to brown for the last 10 minutes.

May be prepared the day before and browned just before serving; freezes well.

*Hope J. Norman*

## Butternut Squash Soufflé

| | |
|---|---|
| 2 cups cooked, mashed butternut squash | ½ cup milk |
| 3 eggs, beaten | ¾ to 1 cup sugar |
| ⅓ cup melted butter | ½ teaspoon ground ginger |
| | ½ teaspoon coconut extract |

Mix all ingredients together. Pour into lightly greased 1½ quart casserole and bake 1 hour at 350°.

*Diane H. Barber*

## Marinated Vegetables

| | |
|---|---|
| 1 cup cider vinegar | 1 head cauliflower, cut into bite-sized pieces |
| 1½ cups olive or salad oil | 1 bunch of broccoli, cut into bite-sized pieces |
| 1 tablespoon dill weed | 1 green pepper, thinly sliced in rings |
| 1 tablespoon sugar | 1 red onion, thinly sliced in rings |
| 1 tablespoon MSG | 1 6-ounce can pitted ripe olives, drained and sliced |
| 1 teaspoon salt | 2 zucchini, thinly sliced |
| 1 teaspoon pepper | |
| 1 teaspoon seasoning salt (Jane's Krazy Mixed-Up Salt, if available) | |

Combine first 8 ingredients and pour over vegetables in a shallow container. Refrigerate overnight, stirring occasionally.

To serve, drain vegetables. Reserve the marinade, which will keep several days under refrigeration.

*Martha M. Grasty*

## Baked Fudge Pudding

| | |
|---|---|
| ½ pound butter or margarine, melted and cooled | 4 tablespoons cocoa |
| 4 eggs, beaten | 2 teaspoons vanilla |
| 2 cups sugar | 1 cup chopped nuts |
| 4 tablespoons flour | ½ pint heavy cream, whipped (optional) |
| ½ teaspoon salt | |

Combine eggs and sugar. Sift flour, salt and cocoa together and add to egg mixture alternately with melted butter. Stir in vanilla and nuts. Bake in a greased 7×11-inch pan set in a larger pan of hot water for 1 hour at 300°. Cool.

To serve, cut into individual squares. Top with whipped cream.

*Linnie S. Wilkinson*

# SUNDAY NIGHT SUPPER *(Serves 10)*

Supper is a Southern term for the evening meal, traditionally informal on Sunday.

***\*Black Beans with Rice***
*or*
***\*Chicken and Cornbread Casserole***

***\*Beet and Onion Salad***
***French Bread***

***\*Apple Pie***
*or*
***\*Mayhaw Pie***

*California Barbera or the Black Wine of Cahors*

## *Black Beans with Rice*

| | |
|---|---|
| 2 quarts water | 3 cloves garlic, minced |
| 1 pound black beans | ¼ pound salt pork, chopped |
| 1 teaspoon baking soda | ¼ pound bacon, chopped |
| ¾ cup dry white wine | 2 bay leaves |
| 1 cup olive oil | Salt and pepper |
| 4 yellow onions, chopped | 5 cups cooked rice (1½ cups raw) |
| 1½ green peppers, chopped | 3 red onions, sliced |

Bring water to a boil. Dribble beans by handfuls into water. Let boil 5 minutes. Remove from heat and cool 1 hour. Add baking soda; let stand overnight.

Rinse beans and place in a 3-quart pot. Add wine and enough water to cover beans. Place in 350° oven. Heat oil in skillet until very hot. Fry chopped vegetables until tender, add meats, and cook until brown. Remove beans from oven. Add contents of skillet, bay leaves, salt and pepper; replace in oven and adjust heat until contents of pot barely boil. Cook 3 to 5 hours (ready in 3 hours, better in 5). Serve beans over rice. Top with red onions.

*Ned Sciortino*

## Chicken and Cornbread Casserole

| | |
|---|---|
| 2 fryers | Tabasco and Worcestershire sauce |
| 2 teaspoons salt | to taste (optional) |
| 1 teaspoon pepper | ¾ cup flour |
| 1 bay leaf | 3 teaspoons baking powder |
| 1 rib celery, chopped | 2 tablespoons sugar |
| ½ cup chopped onion | ¾ tablespoon salt |
| 6 tablespoons margarine | ¾ cup corn meal |
| ⅓ cup flour | 1 egg |
| 2 cups chicken broth | 2 tablespoons vegetable oil |
| 1 cup evaporated milk | ¾ cup milk |

Boil chicken, salt, pepper, bay leaf, celery and onion in water to cover until chicken is tender. Drain. Save stock. Debone and chop chicken.

Melt margarine; blend in ⅓ cup flour. Add broth and evaporated milk slowly, stirring until smooth and thickened. Add chicken; season. Sift next 5 ingredients together. Blend in egg, oil and milk. Pour hot creamed chicken into flat 3-quart greased casserole and cover evenly with batter. Bake at 450° for about 25 minutes, or until top is golden brown.

*Marjorie K. McBride*

## Beet and Onion Salad

| | |
|---|---|
| 2 quarts beets | 2 cups white vinegar |
| 2 teaspoons salt | 1 red onion, sliced |
| ½ cup sugar | 2 hard-boiled eggs, sliced |
| 2 teaspoons coarsely ground | (optional) |
| black pepper | Lettuce |

Boil beets and salt in water to cover until tender, approximately 30 minutes. Cool, drain, and slip off peelings. Slice beets into bowl; sprinkle with sugar and pepper. Pour vinegar over beets and chill several hours. To serve, drain and place on lettuce leaves; top with onion and egg.

## Apple Pie

1⅓ cups flour
½ teaspoon salt
½ cup shortening
¼ cup water
6 tart apples, such as Winesap, peeled and thinly sliced
2 tablespoons butter

1½ cups sugar
½ cup flour
½ teaspoon cinnamon
½ teaspoon nutmeg
¼ teaspoon cloves
¼ teaspoon allspice
½ lemon

To make crust, mix 1⅓ cups flour with salt. Blend in shortening. Add just enough water to make a stiff dough that does not stick to hands. Work dough together quickly. Roll out on floured wax paper to make a bottom crust and lattice top. Place bottom crust in a 9-inch deep-dish pie pan.

Place ½ the apple slices in the pie crust. Dot with 1 tablespoon butter. Mix next 6 ingredients together and sprinkle half of this over the apples. Squeeze a few drops of lemon juice on top. Repeat entire procedure with remaining apples, spice mixture and lemon. Cover with lattice pie crust. May be frozen at this stage.

Place the pie plate in a foil "boat" by wrapping foil around the bottom of the pie dish, leaving the top open, since this pie overflows with juices. Bake 10 minutes at 425°; reduce heat to 325° and bake 45 to 60 minutes longer.

*Lillie G. Sanders*

## Mayhaw Pie

3 cups mayhaw pulp, sieved (see page 7)
1 to 1½ cups sugar

2 tablespoons butter or margarine
Double crust for 9-inch pie
Ice cream (optional)

Heat pulp with sugar and butter, adjusting sweetness to taste (berries vary in tartness). Cool. Pour into pie shell and cover with top crust, piercing holes in top. Bake 45 minutes at 325°. Serve warm, topped with ice cream.

*Annie Lou S. McBride*

# FISH FRY                                              *(Serves 10)*

Freshwater fishing is one of the most popular forms of outdoor recreation for countless Louisianians. The catch varies from sac-au-lait (white perch) to goggle-eye bream as well as bass of diverse species. Anglers delight in serving fresh fish in a tasty outdoor fish fry. Hushpuppies—fried cornbread supposedly tossed to the hounds to quiet them—are a *must*. (One giant 12-quart black iron pot, half filled with hot oil, will serve for all the frying.)

***Keg of Beer***
***\*Onion Rings***

***\*Fried Fish***
***\*Hushpuppies        \*Riverbend Salad***

***\*Fig Ice Cream***
***\*Lace Cookies***
***Coffee***

## Onion Rings

1½ cups flour
1½ cups beer (12-ounce can)
6   onions, sliced and separated
     into rings

Cooking oil
Salt to taste

Combine flour and beer; let set 1 hour. Dip onion rings in batter and fry in oil heated to 375° until light brown. Drain, salt lightly, and serve.

*Barbara S. Domingos*

## Fried Fish

50 to 60 fish fillets, cut into
     1×2×½-inch strips
Salt and pepper to taste
1   cup prepared mustard
1   teaspoon Tabasco (optional)

2   tablespoons Worcestershire
     sauce (optional)
3   cups yellow corn meal
5 to 6 quarts cooking oil

Salt and pepper fillets. Combine mustard with Tabasco and Worcestershire; coat fillets with mixture and allow to set about 30 minutes.

Put corn meal in a bag and shake coated fillets in meal. Heat oil in heavy iron pot to about 380°. (If thermometer is not available, drop a lemon half into grease. Oil is ready when lemon floats to top.) Fry fish, one layer deep, in hot oil for 2½ minutes or until they rise to the top. Drain on paper towels.

*Tom Reedy*
*Noel T. Simmonds*

## Hushpuppies

| | | | |
|---|---|---|---|
| 4 | cups white corn meal | 4 | onions, grated |
| 6 | tablespoons flour | 2 | eggs, beaten |
| 3 | teaspoons salt | 2 | cups milk |
| 8 | teaspoons baking powder | | Cooking oil |

Combine dry ingredients; add onion. Combine eggs with milk and stir in. Heat oil to 350°; drop batter by teaspoonfuls into hot oil and fry until pock-marked (about 3 minutes). Turn and cook an additional 3 to 4 minutes or until done. Drain on paper towels.

*Nancy W. Cotton*

## Riverbend Salad

| | | | |
|---|---|---|---|
| 1 | 15½-ounce can French style green beans, rinsed and drained | 1 | red onion, thinly sliced |
| | | ¼ | cup diced green pepper |
| 1 | 15½-ounce can yellow wax beans, rinsed and drained | 1 | tablespoon soy sauce |
| | | 1 | teaspoon celery salt |
| 1 | 15½-ounce can red kidney beans, rinsed and drained | ½ | teaspoon MSG |
| | | ½ | teaspoon salt |
| ¾ | cup cider vinegar | ½ | teaspoon pepper |
| ¾ | cup sugar | ¼ | cup salad oil |

Combine all ingredients except oil. Refrigerate, covered, overnight, stirring occasionally. When ready to serve, drain and toss with oil.

*Nelda N. Laborde*

## Fig Ice Cream

1½ quarts peeled, mashed figs
2   tablespoons lemon juice
1¾ cups sugar
1½ tablespoons crème de cacao
      (optional)

2   eggs, beaten
2   cups milk
2   cups heavy cream, whipped
      slightly

Combine figs, lemon juice, 1 cup of the sugar, and the liqueur and let stand until sugar is dissolved. Add remaining sugar to eggs and beat continuously while adding milk. Combine fig mixture with milk mixture and fold in cream. Freeze in 4-quart freezer.
   Yield: 3 to 4 quarts

*Caroline K. Gilliland*

## Lace Cookies

1   cup flour
1   cup finely chopped pecans
½ cup light corn syrup

½ cup brown sugar
¼ pound butter
1   teaspoon vanilla

Mix flour and nuts and set aside. Combine syrup, brown sugar and butter in large, heavy saucepan. Bring to boil over medium heat, stirring constantly. Remove from heat and blend in flour-nut mixture and then vanilla. Drop onto foil-covered cookie sheets by teaspoonfuls, 3 inches apart. Bake at 350° for 8 to 10 minutes until golden. Cool 3 to 5 minutes until foil peels off easily. Remove to paper towels.
   Yield: 4 dozen

*Louise A. Simon*

# FIVE COURSES

(Serves 10)

The French order of menu arrangement, observed in the most elegant Creole homes, follows this traditional form: soup, fish, then the "coupe de milieu" or middle course (iced sherbet to cleanse the palate). The meat course follows, accompanied by the *entremet*, a side dish to enhance the entrée. The salad course precedes the dessert course. *Always* a *demitasse* of coffee is the finale.

### *Spinach Soup*

### *Fillets Priory*
Grand Cru/Premier Cru Chablis

### *Cranberry Sorbet*

### *Tenderloin Marchand de Vin*      Claret

### *Pêches au Gratin*      *Wild Rice*

### *French Bread*
### *Watercress Salad*

### *Crème Brulée*      Sauterne

### *Coffee*


## Spinach Soup

| | |
|---|---|
| 1  onion, finely chopped | 1  cup consommé |
| 2  tablespoons butter | Salt and pepper to taste |
| 3  tablespoons flour | 2  cups cream |
| 2  cups milk | ½ cup sherry |
| 2  cups cooked spinach, drained | 1  cup chopped toasted almonds |

Sauté onion in butter until tender but not brown; remove from skillet with slotted spoon. Stir in flour and milk. Purée spinach with consommé and add to sauce with seasonings. Add cream and mix well. Refrigerate at this point if desired.

Before serving, heat carefully without boiling; stir in sherry and pour into soup bowls or cups. Sprinkle with almonds.

*Sally F. McSween*

## Fillets Priory

10  fillets of trout, seasoned with        ½  cup bread crumbs
    salt, pepper and cayenne            ½  cup chopped parsley
2   cups grated sharp Cheddar            4  tablespoons butter
    cheese (preferably white
    English or Canadian)

Place fillets in shallow buttered baking dish. Sprinkle with mixture of cheese, bread crumbs and parsley. Dot with butter. Place about 5 inches under broiler and cook 10 to 15 minutes, until fish becomes opaque and top is browned.

*Caroline K. Gilliland*

## Cranberry Sorbet

1   pound cranberries                     2   cups sugar
3   cups boiling water                    ⅛  teaspoon salt
1   tablespoon gelatin                    1¼ cups orange juice
½   cup cold water                        1   tablespoon lemon juice

Cook berries in boiling water until soft. Purée. Soak gelatin in cold water 5 minutes. Combine berry purée with sugar, salt and juices in a heavy saucepan and bring to a boil. Stir in gelatin, blending until thoroughly dissolved. Cool. Freeze until almost firm. Beat until light and flutfy. Freeze until firm.

*Thelma W. Green*

## Tenderloin Marchand de Vin

5 to 6 pound filet of beef               ½  cup chopped green onions
    at room temperature               4  ounces sliced mushrooms
Olive oil                                 1  cup claret
Salt, pepper, and garlic powder          1  cup consommé
    to taste                          3  teaspoons cornstarch
4   tablespoons butter                    1  tablespoon lemon juice

Rub meat with oil and seasonings. Bake in shallow pan at 350° for about 45 minutes or until meat thermometer registers desired degree of doneness.

Sauté onions and mushrooms in butter until wilted. Add claret and simmer until reduced by half, about 1 hour. Mix consommé and cornstarch and stir into mixture; simmer until thickened. Add lemon juice and pan drippings from meat. Sauce may be made ahead except for the addition of meat juices.

*Helen B. Weems*

## Pêches au Gratin

10  Elberta peach halves
2 to 3 tablespoons butter

2 to 3 tablespoons sugar
10 to 12 macaroons, crumbled

Place peaches in baking dish, cut sides up. Into each hollow, put a dab of butter and sprinkle lightly with sugar. Cover with macaroon crumbs, pressing them lightly into butter. Bake at 350° for 30 minutes. Serve bubbling hot with ice cold sherry sauce.

### Sherry Sauce

6  egg yolks
3  tablespoons sugar

⅔ cup dry sherry

Beat egg yolks and sugar in top of double boiler until light and fluffy. Gradually add sherry. Cook over simmering, not boiling, water, stirring constantly with whisk until smooth and thickened. Place in a serving dish, cover, and refrigerate. Sauce thickens as it cools. Chill thoroughly.

*Louise A. Simon*

## Watercress Salad

4  teaspoons salt
1  teaspoon pepper
2  tablespoons prepared mustard
1  tablespoon Worcestershire
   sauce

4  tablespoons catsup
¼  cup lemon juice
1  cup salad oil
5  bunches watercress, washed,
   drained, stems removed

Shake first 7 ingredients in a jar until well blended. To serve, pour over watercress and toss gently so as not to bruise the tender greens.

*Fanny K. Alcus*

## *Crème Brulée*

1½ pints heavy cream
4½ tablespoons brown sugar
6  egg yolks, beaten

10  tablespoons cream sherry
5   tablespoons brown sugar,
    sifted, for topping

Scald cream in double boiler with sugar. Add to egg yolks very slowly. Return to double boiler. Stir constantly while cooking over boiling water just until mixture thickens and coats spoon. Cool. Pour into individual custard cups and add 1 tablespoon sherry to each. Chill thoroughly.

About 2 hours before serving, sprinkle sifted brown sugar on top of each custard. Place under broiler until sugar caramelizes, 1 to 2 minutes. (If custard cups aren't ovenproof, place them on a wooden board.) Chill again before serving.

*Polly M. Keller*

# AL FRESCO EVENING       *(Serves 10)*

On a sultry summer night serve this unusual vegetable dish, Maque Choux, said to have been handed down from the Indians.

## *Eggplant-Shrimp Appetizer*

### *Cold Pork Loin*
### *Pepper Jelly*
### *Maque Choux     Sliced Cucumbers*

### *Caramel Cup Custard*
### *Coffee*

*Zinfandel or Gattinara*

### Eggplant-Shrimp Appetizer

5   small eggplants, halved
½   cup olive oil
¼   pound butter
1   cup chopped green onions
1   cup chopped celery
½   cup chopped onion
1   cup chopped green pepper
2   cloves garlic, pressed
1   cup peeled chopped tomatoes

1½ cups Italian-seasoned bread crumbs
2   cups peeled raw shrimp
1   tablespoon MSG
1   teaspoon Tabasco
2   tablespoons chicken bouillon granules
Salt to taste

Scoop the meat out of the eggplant halves and dice. Wash and lightly salt shells; drain. Steam the eggplant pulp and other vegetables in the oil and butter until tender (about 30 minutes). Stir in 1 cup of the crumbs and the other ingredients. Cook until shrimp are pink, stirring constantly (about 5 minutes). Stuff lightly into the eggplant shells and sprinkle with remaining crumbs. Bake at 350° for 30 minutes.

Variation: Crabmeat or ham may be substituted for shrimp.

*Dorothy I. Stuckey*

## Cold Pork Loin

1   6-pound pork loin roast rubbed
    generously with thyme and dry
    mustard
½   cup dry sherry
½   cup soy sauce
2   tablespoons ground ginger

3   cloves garlic, pressed
8   ounces currant or apple jelly
1   tablespoon soy sauce
2   tablespoons dry sherry
Orange slices (optional)

Combine the ½ cup sherry, soy sauce, ginger and garlic and pour over roast. Marinate overnight.

Remove meat from marinade, which should be reserved. Bake at 325° for 25 minutes per pound or until meat thermometer reaches 175°, basting often with marinade. Melt jelly over medium heat. Add soy sauce and the 2 tablespoons of sherry, mixing well. Cool.

Place roast on a rack in a shallow pan. Spoon glaze over roast. As mixture runs off into pan, repeat to build up a coating. Slice and serve cold, garnished with orange slices.

*Margaret D. Ratelle*

## Pepper Jelly

¾   cup seeded, ground green
    peppers
½   cup seeded, ground hot peppers

5   cups sugar
1¾  cups cider vinegar
6   ounces liquid pectin

Mix peppers with sugar and vinegar; bring to a boil and cook for 10 minutes. Remove from heat; stir in pectin and pour into jelly jars.

Yield: 7 ½-pint jars

*SueEllen G. Butler*

## Maque Choux

18 ears corn
2   tablespoons cooking oil
1   onion, chopped
1   green pepper, chopped
Salt and pepper to taste
¼   teaspoon thyme

¼   teaspoon basil
3   tomatoes, peeled and chopped
2   tablespoons cream
2   tablespoons tomato paste
    (optional)
1   tablespoon minced parsley

Cut corn from cob by cutting down through kernels, then scraping pulp. Sauté onion and pepper in oil. Add the corn and seasonings. Stir and add remaining ingredients. Simmer, covered, over low heat 5 to 10 minutes.

Variation: 3   10-ounce cans corn kernels may be substituted for fresh corn.

*Peggy E. Brian*

## Caramel Cup Custard

2   cups sugar
6   egg yolks
Pinch of salt

4   cups half and half, scalded
2   teaspoons vanilla

In a flat baking dish, melt 1½ cups sugar in oven at 350° for about 30 to 45 minutes until caramel colored, or, caramelize sugar in heavy skillet on top of stove. Lightly butter 10  6-ounce custard cups. Pour caramel syrup into cups and let set. Beat egg yolks with remaining sugar and salt. Pour hot cream into egg mixture very slowly, beating constantly with a wire whisk. Add vanilla. Pour into cups set in hot water 1 inch deep. Bake in bottom third of oven at 325° for 40 minutes or until silver knife blade inserted in center comes out clean. For smoothest texture, do not allow water to boil. Invert on dessert plates and serve warm or chilled. Custards are easier to remove when chilled and may be kept 2 to 3 days in refrigerator.

*Martha B. Walker*

# GUMBO SUPPER                                 *(Serves 10)*

Good gumbos are like good sunsets: no two are exactly alike, and their delight lies in their variety. An exciting gumbo combines seafood or game with pungent Creole seasonings to become a uniquely flavored soup, thickened with either okra—a vegetable lent by Africa to Louisiana—or filé, powdered sassafras leaves introduced by the Choctaw Indians. Whatever your own innovations may be, serve your gumbo over steamed rice.

### *Seafood, *Chicken, *Wild Duck, or *Dove Gumbo
### Green Salad
### French Bread

#### *Tourte de Gelée
#### Coffee

*Côte de Beaune Red, Hermitage,*
*Côte Rôtie or California Burgundy*

## Seafood Gumbo

½  cup cooking oil or bacon
   drippings
½  cup flour
1  onion, chopped
2  ribs celery, chopped
2 to 3 quarts boiling water
Salt and pepper
1  teaspoon liquid crab and shrimp
   boil seasoning (optional)

1 to 1½ pounds peeled shrimp
1  pound crabmeat
⅓ to ½ cup chopped green onions
1  pint oysters
2  tablespoons minced parsley
Filé to taste

Heat oil in heavy iron skillet and add flour. Stir constantly until dark brown in color, being careful not to burn it. Reduce heat and add chopped onion and celery. Sauté until soft. Gradually add 2 to 3 quarts of water and seasonings, stirring to a smooth consistency. Simmer gently for 10 minutes. Add shrimp, crabmeat and green onions and cook over low heat until shrimp are tender. Just before serving add oysters and parsley. Heat until oysters curl. Add filé to taste and serve over rice.

*Frank G. Fletcher*

## Chicken Gumbo

1 large (4 to 5 pounds) hen, cut up
Salt, cayenne and black pepper to taste
1 to 2 cups corn oil
½ cup flour
2 onions, chopped
8 ribs celery, chopped
1 green pepper, chopped
1 teaspoon ground bay leaf
½ teaspoon thyme
1 teaspoon garlic powder
¼ teaspoon oregano
1 teaspoon celery seed
¼ teaspoon marjoram
1 pound chicken gizzards
2 gallons water
Tabasco to taste
1 pound smoked sausage, sliced (optional)
1 cup minced parsley
Filé to taste

Salt and pepper chicken; brown in large cast iron pot in oil over medium heat. When well browned, remove chicken and set aside. Pour off all but ½ cup oil and add flour, browning well to make dark roux. Reduce heat to low and add onion, celery and green pepper. Sauté until soft, stirring regularly. Gradually add enough water to make a smooth sauce, stirring constantly. Add remaining water, chicken, and all other ingredients, except parsley and sausage. Cook over medium heat until chicken is very tender, 1½ to 2 hours. Sausage may be added during last 45 minutes of cooking time. Remove chicken, debone and return meat to gumbo mixture. Remove from heat, add parsley and let set for 15 minutes. Sprinkle with filé and serve over rice.

*Frank G. Fletcher*

## Wild Duck Gumbo

5 wild ducks, cut into pieces
1½ to 2 cups cooking oil
Salt and pepper to taste
½ cup flour
2 white onions, chopped
2 cloves garlic, chopped
4 quarts water
12 green onions, chopped
1 cup minced parsley
4 pounds shrimp, peeled
1 pound smoked sausage, sliced (optional)
Filé to taste

In a large black kettle, brown ducks in 1 to 1½ cups of cooking oil; sprinkle with salt and pepper and set aside. Discard oil remaining in pot. Using ½ cup fresh oil and the flour, make a dark roux, browning flour in oil and stirring constantly. Add onion and garlic and sauté until soft. Gradually stir in enough water to make a smooth sauce. Add ducks and remaining water. Bring to a boil, reduce heat and simmer 2 to 3 hours. About 45 minutes before end of cooking time, add green onions, parsley, shrimp and sausage. Serve over rice, with filé to taste.

*Maude Allen F. Bossier*

## Dove Gumbo

5   cups chopped onions
5   cups chopped celery
2   cups chopped green pepper
1½ cups vegetable oil
20 dove breasts
1   cup flour
4   quarts water
1½ tablespoons Kitchen Bouquet
1   teaspoon garlic powder
½   teaspoon chili powder

¼   teaspoon dry mustard
1   tablespoon salt
¼   teaspoon black pepper
¼   teaspoon cayenne
¼   teaspoon MSG
2   chicken bouillon cubes
2   beef bouillon cubes
1   can onion soup
1   pint okra, sliced
1   pint stewed tomatoes

Sauté chopped vegetables in ½ cup oil until wilted; set aside. Brown dove breasts in 1 cup oil; remove doves and add 1 cup flour, stirring and cooking until roux is brown. Add vegetables, doves and remaining ingredients. Simmer slowly until doves are tender. Remove meat from bones and return to gumbo. Serve steaming hot over rice.

*Betty Fay W. Lipsey*

## Tourte de Gelée

1   pound margarine
2   cups sugar
2   cups tart jelly (mayhaw, plum or
    currant)

8   eggs
2   8-inch pie shells

Cream margarine and sugar together. Add jelly and mix until smooth. Beat in eggs, 1 at a time. Pour into unbaked pie shells and bake at 300° for 45 to 60 minutes.

*Annie S. Johnson*

# BIENVENUE! (WELCOME!) *(Serves 10)*

Louisiana's wetlands furnish an abundance of wild ducks for its avid hunters. The coastal marshes are recognized worldwide as a duck paradise. Winter hospitality often features these fine waterfowl.

The cushaw, a mammoth crooked-neck green-striped white squash, is a sweet and versatile vegetable closely related to gourds and pumpkins.

### *Lemon-Thyme Oysters*

### *Duck Breasts à l'Orange*
### *Baked Cushaw   or   *Tipsy Sweet Potatoes*
### *Wilted Lettuce Salad*
### French Bread

### *Profiteroles   or   *Floating Island*
### Coffee

*Chablis and Côte de Nuits Red Burgundy*

## Lemon-Thyme Oysters

| | |
|---|---|
| 1 quart oysters, drained and halved, liquor reserved | ½ teaspoon thyme |
| 2 cups soft bread crumbs | ¼ cup white wine (optional) |
| 4 ribs celery, finely chopped | ½ teaspoon salt |
| 2 onions, finely chopped or 1 bunch green onions, chopped | Dash of Tabasco |
| 2 tablespoons butter | Dash of Worcestershire sauce |
| 2 slices lemon, finely chopped | Black pepper and cayenne to taste |
| 1 clove garlic, minced | 1 egg, slightly beaten |
| 1 bay leaf, crushed | ¾ cup buttered bread crumbs |
| | 2 tablespoons minced parsley |
| | Paprika |

Pour oyster liquor over soft bread crumbs and squeeze out excess. Sauté celery and onions in butter until soft. Add lemon, garlic, bay leaf, thyme and bread crumbs. Simmer 30 minutes, adding wine or oyster liquor if too dry. Add oysters, salt, Tabasco, Worcestershire and pepper. Cook until oysters curl (about 2 minutes). Quickly stir in egg and cook 2 minutes more. Pour into buttered ramekins and top with mixture of buttered bread crumbs and parsley; sprinkle with paprika. Bake at 350° until bubbly, about 20 minutes.

*Frances B. Davis*

## Duck Breasts à l'Orange

8　large wild ducks
Salt and pepper to taste
4　onions, quartered
4 or 5 apples, quartered
4　oranges, quartered
8　ribs celery
8　garlic cloves, chopped
　　(optional)
½ to ¾ cup vegetable oil
1　quart orange wine or 1 quart
　　Chablis mixed with 12-ounces
　　frozen orange juice concentrate

1　cup water
4　oranges, halved
3　ounces orange brandy, Triple
　　Sec or other orange liqueur
6　ounces frozen orange juice
　　concentrate
3　tablespoons Worcestershire
　　sauce
1　orange, sliced
12　sprigs parsley, minced

Salt and pepper inside and outside of each duck well. Stuff each with pieces of onion, apple, orange, celery and garlic. Brown ducks in vegetable oil and place them close together in a large heavy roaster. Pour wine and water over ducks and squeeze remaining oranges, adding juice and squeezed pieces to the pan. Cover tightly and roast at 350° for 4½ to 5 hours, basting every half hour until tender. (If roaster is tightly sealed, basting may not be necessary.) Remove ducks and cool. Strain and refrigerate pan juices. Skin and debone ducks; breast meat should come off in 2 large pieces per duck. Place breasts in a shallow casserole. May be prepared to this point, tightly covered and refrigerated overnight.

Mix brandy with orange juice concentrate and Worcestershire and pour over duck breasts. Add reserved juices, fat removed. Garnish with orange slices; sprinkle with parsley. Cover and heat at 350° until piping hot, about 45 minutes.

*Van O. Farnsworth*

## Baked Cushaw

1　8-pound cushaw, peeled and
　　diced
½　cup water
2　cups sugar
½　pound margarine or butter
1　teaspoon allspice
½　cup brown sugar

Bring the cushaw and water to a boil in a large pot. Cover, turn heat to low and continue to cook until fork tender (30 to 45 minutes). Mash well and stir in sugar and butter. Cook, stirring occasionally, on low heat for 5 to 10 minutes more, being careful not to scorch. Stir in allspice. Pour into buttered 3-quart casserole, sprinkle top with brown sugar and bake at 400° for 15 minutes or until hot and bubbly. Freezes well before or after baking. Good also at breakfast or brunch.

*Betty B. Ingrish*

## Tipsy Sweet Potatoes

| | |
|---|---|
| 8 sweet potatoes, cooked, peeled and mashed | 1 teaspoon cinnamon |
| ¼ pound butter, softened | ½ cup bourbon |
| 2 cups brown sugar | ½ cup flour |
| 1 teaspoon allspice | 2 tablespoons butter |
| 1 teaspoon nutmeg | 1 cup chopped pecans |

Combine sweet potatoes with softened butter, 1 cup brown sugar, spices and bourbon; mix well. Pour into a buttered 2-quart casserole.

Cut the 2 tablespoons butter into flour with a pastry blender until crumbly. Add remaining cup of brown sugar and pecans and blend well. Sprinkle on top of potatoes and bake at 350° for 20 to 25 minutes.

*SueEllen G. Butler*

## Wilted Lettuce Salad

| | |
|---|---|
| 2 heads of Boston lettuce | 2½ teaspoons sugar |
| 10 slices cooked bacon | 2¼ teaspoons salt |
| 5 tablespoons warm bacon drippings | ⅔ cup cider vinegar |

Tear lettuce into a large bowl. Crumble bacon over lettuce. Stir salt and sugar into hot bacon grease; add vinegar and pour hot mixture over lettuce. Toss lightly and serve.

## *Profiteroles*

1   cup water
¼  pound butter
1   teaspoon sugar
¼  teaspoon salt

1   cup flour
4   eggs
Ice cream

In large saucepan, heat water, butter, sugar and salt to full boil. Add flour all at once. Stir with wooden spoon until mixture forms a thick, smooth ball that leaves sides of pan clean (approximately 1 minute). Remove from heat. Add eggs, 1 at a time, beating well after each addition until paste is shiny and smooth. Shape by dropping slightly rounded tablespoonfuls 1½ inches apart on ungreased cookie sheet. Bake at 400° for 35 minutes. Remove to wire rack; cool completely.

Cut a slice from top of each puff and fill with ice cream. Replace top; freeze until serving time. Remove from freezer 10 minutes before serving.

Yield: 20

### *Espresso Sauce*

1¼ cups light brown sugar
1   tablespoon instant espresso
    coffee or 1½ tablespoons
    regular instant coffee powder
¼  cup light corn syrup

½  cup water
2   tablespoons butter
1 or 2 tablespoons brandy
    or whiskey

Heat sugar, coffee, corn syrup and water to boiling, stirring constantly. Cook over low heat 5 minutes, stirring often. Remove from heat; stir in butter and brandy and cool, stirring several times. Spoon sauce over profiteroles; serve immediately.

*Sylvia D. Kushner*

## Floating Island

9   egg yolks, slightly beaten
1⅔ cups sugar
4   cups milk

4   tablespoons rum
6   egg whites, at room
      temperature

Combine egg yolks and 1 cup sugar. Scald 3 cups milk in a double boiler. Stir a little hot milk into the yolks, then stir this mixture back into the rest of the milk. Cook and stir in the double boiler until custard thickens and will coat a silver spoon. Cool. Stir in rum. Refrigerate.

Whip whites until stiff. Bring remaining 1 cup milk to simmer in a large skillet. Drop large spoonfuls of egg white into the milk. Poach for about 1 minute (longer and it will be leathery). Lift out with a slotted spoon, drain, and, when ready to serve, place on custard. Meringues should be made no more than 2 hours before serving. Never add meringues to the custard until time to serve.

Caramelize remaining ⅔ cup of sugar in a black iron skillet and drizzle on top of "floating islands."

*Hélène K. Kahn*

# ITALIAN DINNER                    *(Serves 10)*

Louisiana variations of old favorites.

*Antipasto Tray*
*Lasagna Marinara*
or
*Braciolini*
or
*Veal Parmigiana with Spinach Noodles*

*Italian Bread*        *Caesar Salad*

*Bisquit Tortoni   or   *Chocolate Gelato*
Coffee*

*Barbaresco, Chianti Classico or California Barbera*

## Antipasto Tray

| | |
|---|---|
| 20  slices prosciutto | 8  ounces spiced olives, drained |
| 20  wedges honeydew melon | 6  ounces pickled mushrooms |
| 20  slices Provolone cheese | |

## Lasagna Marinara

| | |
|---|---|
| ½  cup olive oil | ½  pound mushrooms, chopped |
| 4  cups chopped onions | 1  teaspoon chopped garlic |
| 2  carrots, cut into rounds | 3  tablespoons butter |
| 4  cloves garlic, minced | 3  tablespoons flour |
| 4  1-pound cans Italian plum tomatoes (8 cups), puréed | 1  cup milk |
| | 1¼ cups heavy cream |
| Salt and pepper to taste | ¼  teaspoon nutmeg |
| ¼  pound butter | 1  pound green or white lasagna noodles |
| 3  teaspoons oregano | |
| 3  tablespoons chopped fresh basil or 3 teaspoons dried basil | 2  pounds Mozzarella cheese, cubed |
| 1  pound sweet Italian sausage | 2  cups freshly grated Parmesan cheese |
| 1  pound ground chuck | |

To prepare marinara sauce, heat the oil in a large heavy pan. Add onions, carrots and minced garlic and sauté until golden, stirring frequently. Add tomatoes, salt and pepper; partially cover and simmer 15 minutes. Strain solids from sauce and purée in blender. Return to sauce; add ¼ pound butter, oregano, and basil. Partially cover and simmer 30 minutes longer.

Brown sausage, remove skin, slice thinly, and set aside. Pour off almost all the fat and add beef; salt and pepper to taste. Break up lumps in meat, add mushrooms and chopped garlic and cook, stirring frequently, until meat browns. Drain excess fat; add sausage. Mix in the sauce, partly cover and simmer 45 minutes, stirring occasionally.

Melt the 3 tablespoons butter in a saucepan; stir in flour. Add milk, stirring rapidly until thickened. Stir in cream and season with salt, pepper and nutmeg. Stir this sauce into the meat sauce.

Cook the noodles *al dente*. Drain and rinse immediately in cold water.

To assemble, cover the bottoms of 2 8×14-inch baking dishes with sauce. Layer noodles, sauce and Mozzarella until all ingredients are used. Top with Parmesan and bake at 375° for 45 minutes or until bubbling. Freezes well.

*Murel B. Trimble*

## Braciolini

| | |
|---|---|
| 2 cups chopped onion | 1 10-ounce can tomato sauce |
| 4 cloves garlic, minced | 3 cups Italian-style bread crumbs |
| 1 teaspoon olive oil | 2 cups grated Romano cheese |
| 10 6-ounce cans tomato paste | 1 teaspoon basil |
| 30 6-ounce cans water | ¾ cup olive oil |
| Salt to taste | ½ bunch parsley, minced |
| 1 tablespoon sugar | 2 teaspoons salt |
| 2 bay leaves | 4 eggs, beaten |
| ¼ teaspoon oregano | 2 2½ to 3-pound round steaks, tenderized |
| 1 teaspoon basil | |
| 1 tablespoon dried celery | 4 hard-boiled eggs, sliced |
| 1 tablespoon dried onions | 1 pound ground chuck |
| 1 tablespoon dried parsley | |

To prepare tomato sauce, sauté 1 cup onion and half of the garlic in olive oil. Add the next 11 ingredients and simmer at least 4 hours.

Combine bread crumbs, 1 cup cheese, basil, ¼ cup olive oil, remaining onion and garlic, parsley and salt. Add beaten eggs and a small amount of water and blend well. Generously coat tops of steaks with remaining olive oil, spread with crumb mixture and top with sliced eggs. Sprinkle with remaining cheese and ground meat. Roll up jelly-roll style; tie securely with string. Place in deep baking dish and cover with sauce; seal with foil and bake 2 hours at 350°.

To serve, remove strings, slice, and serve with sauce. Freezes well.

*Father Earl Provenza*

## Veal Parmigiana

3   cups Italian-style bread crumbs
2   cups grated Parmesan cheese
5   pounds veal round steaks, cut
     into serving pieces and
     pounded thin
Salt and pepper to taste
4   eggs, beaten
8   tablespoons olive oil
4   tablespoons butter
2   cups chopped onions

2   cloves garlic, pressed
2   1-pound cans tomatoes
32   ounces tomato sauce
4   teaspoons basil
2   teaspoons salt
1   teaspoon black pepper
1   teaspoon garlic powder
Cayenne and Tabasco to taste
2   pounds Mozzarella cheese,
     sliced

Combine bread crumbs and 1 cup Parmesan cheese. Salt and pepper veal pieces; dip in beaten eggs, then in crumb mixture. In large heavy skillet, heat 4 tablespoons of the olive oil and the butter; sauté veal until golden brown. Set aside.

In separate pan, heat the remaining oil and sauté onions and garlic until golden. Add rest of ingredients except cheeses. Cover and simmer 15 minutes. Put a film of sauce in 2  9×13-inch casseroles. Cover with a layer of veal, then Mozzarella cheese and sauce in that order. Repeat. Top with remaining Parmesan cheese and bake uncovered for 30 minutes at 350°. Freezes well.

*Nancy C. Weems*

## Italian Bread

2   cups lukewarm water
1   package yeast
1½ tablespoons sugar
1   teaspoon salt
1   tablespoon vegetable oil
1   egg

5 to 6 cups flour
Yellow corn meal
Egg white mixed with a few drops
     water, for glaze
Sesame or poppy seeds, for
     topping

In a heated bowl, dissolve yeast in water. Add next 4 ingredients and beat with a rotary beater until frothy. Gradually add flour, blending in well. Turn out onto a pastry cloth and knead well. Place dough in a large greased bowl, turning dough to grease outside completely. Cover with a damp cloth and let rise 2 hours or until doubled. Knead again. Divide dough into thirds and shape or braid into loaves. Place loaves on cookie sheet which has been sprinkled with corn meal. Brush tops with egg white mixture and sprinkle with seeds. Let rise for 1 hour. Cook at 400° for 35 minutes or until golden brown. When lightly browned (about 25 minutes), reglaze. If desired, loaves may be cooked only 20 minutes and saved to "brown and serve" at mealtime.

*Teska Moreau*

## Caesar Salad

| | |
|---|---|
| 1 clove garlic, halved | 6 tablespoons olive oil |
| 1 egg | 4 tablespoons lemon juice |
| ¼ teaspoon dry mustard | Garlic salt and Worcestershire |
| ¼ teaspoon freshly ground black | sauce to taste |
| pepper | 2 to 3 heads Romaine lettuce, |
| ½ teaspoon salt | torn and chilled |
| ½ cup grated Parmesan cheese | 2 cups croutons |

Rub salad bowl generously with garlic. Break egg into bowl and stir briskly with a fork until egg is no longer stringy. Add the mustard, pepper, salt, ¼ cup Parmesan, and oil and mix well. Stir in the lemon juice. Sprinkle with garlic salt and Worcestershire. Add lettuce and toss. Sprinkle with 1 cup of croutons and ⅛ cup Parmesan and toss again. Repeat.

Caesar salad is always a delight to prepare at the table. To prepare the dressing ahead place mustard, pepper, salt, ¼ cup Parmesan and olive oil in a jar and shake well. Refrigerate until serving time. Then proceed with recipe, adding contents of jar after stirring the egg. Do not add lemon juice until ready to assemble the salad in order to retain the fresh lemon flavor.

*John Bennet Waters*


## Bisquit Tortoni

| | |
|---|---|
| ¾ cup macaroon crumbs | 1 quart vanilla ice cream, |
| ½ cup diced almonds | softened |
| 20 Maraschino cherries, drained | |
| and diced | |

Place all ingredients in a large bowl and mix well. Spoon into paper muffin cups and freeze.

*Persis J. Crawford*


## Gelato Chocolato

| | |
|---|---|
| 10 balls of chocolate fudge ice | 1½ cups grated semi-sweet |
| cream, slightly softened | chocolate |
| 10 Maraschino cherries | |

Insert cherry in center of ice cream ball; roll in chocolate and freeze.

*Tita O. Stafford*

# CHRISTMAS EVE                    *(Serves 12)*

A landmark family evening—simple enough to allow time and appetite for other demands, but festive enough to be a celebration. Oyster stew is the tradition for many Southern households on this holiday eve. Two superlative cakes wait on the sideboard for tonight and later.

### *Wassail Bowl      *Old Fashioneds
### *Pâté en Terrine

### *Oyster Stew
### French Bread or Crackers      Green Salad
### *Jam Cake      *Date Cake
### Coffee

*White Burgundy*

## Wassail Bowl

20  whole cloves
2   oranges
½   gallon apple cider
6   ounces frozen orange juice
    concentrate

6   ounces frozen lemon juice
    concentrate
3   cups water
1   stick cinnamon
1   cup sugar

Stud oranges with cloves. Bake at 350° for 20 minutes. Combine with remaining ingredients in large pot and simmer on low heat 1½ hours. Cool and refrigerate overnight or longer. Serve hot or cold.
    Yield: 20   5-ounce drinks

*Geraldine P. Brian*


## Old Fashioneds

12  tablespoons sugar
1   quart club soda
Angostura bitters
12  1½-ounce jiggers bourbon or
    rum

Ice cubes
Orange slices
Cherries
12  teaspoons rum

For each drink: Place 1 tablespoon sugar into a 6-ounce glass. Add 1 to 2 teaspoons soda and stir until sugar is dissolved. Splash in 4 to 5 drops of bitters. Add a jigger of whiskey and several ice cubes. Fill glass with soda; garnish with fruit and float a teaspoon of rum on top.

*Harry M. Brian*

## Pâté en Terrine

1   yellow onion, chopped
1 to 2 cloves garlic, minced
1   tablespoon corn oil
1   pound chicken livers
1   pound smoked pork sausage,
    removed from casing
¾   teaspoon salt
1   teaspoon oregano

1   teaspoon thyme
⅛   teaspoon cayenne
⅛   teaspoon nutmeg
3   tablespoons chopped parsley
1   egg
2   tablespooons brandy
1   hard-boiled egg yolk, sieved
Minced parsley

Sauté onion and garlic in oil until tender. Add chicken livers and cook until they are light in color. Mix in sausage and cook 15 minutes longer, stirring occasionally. Add dry seasonings, parsley and egg. Remove from heat and grind to the consistency of lumpy corn meal. Blend in brandy and pack mixture into earthenware terrine. Garnish with egg yolk and minced parsley. Refrigerate until firm.

*Sally F. McSween*

## Oyster Stew

2   quarts oysters, drained, liquor
    reserved
½   pound butter
2   bunches green onions, minced
2   cups minced celery
3 to 4 cups water

4   quarts milk
4   teaspoons salt
½   teaspoon pepper
1   cup minced parsley
Worcestershire sauce

Steam onions, celery, butter, oyster liquor and 2 cups water in tigntly covered Dutch oven over low heat until vegetables are completely tender. Add additional water as needed to keep mixture from drying. Stir in milk slowly. Simmer until very hot, being careful not to allow milk to boil. Add oysters and cook until their edges begin to curl (about 4 minutes). Maintain heat as high as possible without bringing mixture to a boil, as boiling will curdle the soup and toughen the oysters. Just before removing from fire, add seasonings.

*Ione B. Hopkins*

## *Jam Cake*

3   cups flour
½   teaspoon baking powder
1   teaspoon cloves
1   teaspoon allspice
1   teaspoon cinnamon
½   teaspoon salt
1   cup buttermilk
1   teaspoon baking soda
½   pound corn oil margarine, at
    room temperature

3   cups sugar
4   eggs
1   cup chopped nuts
1   cup jam (strawberry or
    blackberry)
1   20-ounce can crushed
    pineapple, drained (juice
    reserved)
3   tablespoons cornstarch
2   tablespoons margarine

Sift flour 3 times; measure 3 cups and resift with baking powder and dry seasonings; set aside. Whip together soda and buttermilk until foamy; set aside. Beat margarine until creamy and continue beating while adding 2 cups sugar. Add eggs 1 at a time, beating after each addition. Add flour mixture alternately with milk mixture, beginning and ending with flour. Stir in jam and nuts. Divide batter evenly among 3 greased and floured 9-inch cake pans and smooth top of batter. Bake at 300° for about 40 minutes or until cake tester comes out clean. (Cake pans should not touch each other or side of oven while baking. Distribute pans on racks so one is not directly over the other.) Cool on wire rack.

Mix remaining sugar, cornstarch and reserved juice; cook until thick (about 5 minutes). Add pineapple and 2 tablespoons margarine. Cool and spread between cooled cake layers. Frost with the following icing.

### *Caramel Icing*

2½ cups sugar
1   5.33-ounce can evaporated
    milk with enough water added
    to make 1 cup

4   tablespoons butter or margarine
    Kettle of simmering water

Place ½ cup of the sugar in a small heavy skillet and melt over high heat, watching carefully and stirring constantly. When the sugar starts to brown, lower heat. At the same time (keep stirring) combine the remaining sugar and milk and bring to a boil in a large heavy saucepan, stirring with other hand. Add butter to milk-sugar mixture. When the sugar in the skillet is melted and a light brown, and as the other mixture is boiling, pour sugar into milk mixture, continuing to stir constantly. Pour a little water from the kettle into the skillet and leave on a burner set at simmer. (This will be added to the icing later.) Continue boiling milk mixture, mashing lumps as they appear, until syrup reaches the soft ball stage (235° on candy thermometer). Remove from heat and beat until smooth, thick, and creamy. Frost cake layers, adding a little of the warm water in the skillet if the icing gets too thick to spread. Add water several times if needed before cake is assembled and frosted on top and sides. Iced cake freezes well.

*Nena M. Love*

## Date Cake

| | |
|---|---|
| 1 pound pitted dates, chopped | 1 cup sugar |
| 2½ teaspoons baking soda | 1 egg |
| 1 cup boiling water | 2 cups flour |
| 2 tablespoons butter | 1 cup chopped nuts |

Pour boiling water over dates which have been sprinkled with 2 teaspoons soda. Cool. Cream butter and sugar; beat in egg. Combine nuts with date mixture and add flour which has been sifted with remaining soda. Stir fruit mixture into butter and egg mixture. Pour into 2 greased and floured 9-inch pans. Bake at 325° for 40 minutes. Let cool in pan 5 minutes, then turn onto rack to cool completely. Spread with the following frosting.

### Butter Frosting

| | |
|---|---|
| 1½ cups sugar | ½ cup flour |
| ⅓ cup boiling water | 1 teaspoon vanilla |
| ⅓ pound butter | |

Cook sugar and water to firm ball stage (about 255° on candy thermometer). Cream butter and mix in flour. Pour sugar mixture over butter mixture, beating to creamy, spreadable consistency. Add vanilla. Spread between cake layers and on top. (If icing hardens too quickly, add small amount of boiling water to soften).

*Nena M. Love*

# LOUISIANA BOUNTY                              *(Serves 12)*

The bayou state offers an affluence of produce in and around its water-ways. Diamondback terrapin and snapping turtles are trapped in the marsh, numerous varieties of ducks are brought home by avid hunters, oysters flourish in bays and bayous, and the lengthy growing season yields plentiful harvests of semitropical fruits and vegetables from fertile soil. Succulent rec-ipes utilizing these native foods attest to their abundance and popularity.

### *Turtle Soup

### *Wild Duck Burgundy
### *Eggplant-Oyster Dressing   or   *Stuffed Mirliton
### Grapefruit and Avocado Salad
### French Bread

### *Bread Pudding with *Whiskey Sauce
### Coffee

*Red Burgundy or California Pinot Noir*

## Turtle Soup

| | |
|---|---|
| 3   pounds turtle meat with bones, 2 pounds without bones | 8   cloves garlic |
| 4   quarts water | 1   green pepper |
| 2   onions, quartered | 2   tablespoons lemon juice |
| 4   ribs celery | ¼   cup Worcestershire sauce |
| 8   cloves unpeeled garlic, halved | ¼   teaspoon cayenne |
| 2   tablespoons salt | 2   tablespoons pickling spice, tied in bag |
| 12  peppercorns, crushed | 4   hard-boiled egg yolks, grated |
| ½   cup oil | 12  tablespoons sherry |
| 1   cup flour | 12  slices lemon dipped in finely cut parsley |
| 3   yellow onions | |
| 4   ribs celery | |

Bring meat to a boil in water; skim. Add next 5 ingredients and simmer until meat is tender—about 3 hours. Strain stock and reserve. Chop and set aside turtle meat.

Brown flour in oil over low heat in a heavy saucepan, stirring constantly until mixture is a rich dark brown (about 30 to 45 minutes). Purée vegetables and add to roux. Heat reserved stock and add slowly, a little at a time, until completely blended into roux. Add seasonings, turtle meat, and egg yolks. Simmer 2 hours.

Spoon 1 tablespoon sherry into each serving bowl. Fill with soup and garnish with lemon slices.

*Dorothy I. Stuckey*

## Wild Duck Burgundy

| | |
|---|---|
| 6 wild ducks, halved | 3 cups water |
| Salt and pepper | 4 cups Burgundy |
| 6 teaspoons Worcestershire sauce | 1½ pounds mushrooms, sliced and |
| 18 drops Tabasco | sautéed |
| 3 tablespoons butter | |

Season ducks with salt, pepper, Worcestershire and Tabasco and brown in melted butter. Add water and 3 cups Burgundy. Cover and cook slowly until fork tender, 2 to 3 hours, depending on size and age of ducks. Turn and baste frequently. When tender, remove to warm platter; add remaining wine to pot liquor; increase heat to high and boil rapidly until sauce is reduced to gravy. Add mushrooms and pour over ducks.

*Harry M. Brian*

## Eggplant-Oyster Dressing

| | |
|---|---|
| 1 green pepper, seeded and chopped | 1½ teaspoons salt |
| | ½ teaspoon black pepper |
| 2 onions, chopped | ¼ teaspoon cayenne |
| 1 eggplant, peeled and diced | 2 teaspoons thyme |
| 3 ribs celery, chopped | 1 tablespoon poultry seasoning |
| ¼ cup salad oil | 2 pints oysters, drained |
| ¼ cup ground pork or pork sausage, sautéed and drained | 1½ cups milk |
| | 6 cups cubed French bread |
| 1 cup chopped cooked chicken | ½ cup bread crumbs |
| 3 cups chicken stock | Paprika and minced parsley |

Sauté vegetables in oil until tender. Add pork and chicken; cook 5 minutes. Add stock and seasonings; cook 30 minutes longer. Remove from heat; stir in oysters, bread cubes and milk. Pour into 3-quart casserole. Sprinkle with bread crumbs; garnish with paprika and parsley. Bake 30 minutes at 350°.

*Teska Moreau*

### Stuffed Mirliton *(see page 146 for mirliton description)*

6   mirlitons
½  cup chopped green onions
½  cup chopped celery
4   sprigs parsley, minced
½  cup chopped onion
¼  pound margarine

1   pound shrimp, peeled
3   slices stale bread, soaked in
      water and squeezed out
Salt and pepper to taste
1   pound crabmeat
½ to 1 cup bread crumbs

Boil mirlitons in water to cover until tender. Cool. Cut each in half, remove seed, and scoop pulp from shell very carefully (shells are extremely delicate). Mash mirliton pulp; reserve shells.

Sauté vegetables in margarine until wilted. Add shrimp and cook 5 minutes stirring. Add mirliton pulp, bread, and crabmeat and cook slowly 5 minutes more, stirring occasionally.

Fill reserved shells with mixture and top with bread crumbs. Bake at 350° until crumbs brown (about 10 minutes).

Variation: Substitute diced cooked ham for seafood.

*Mosetta Collins*

### Bread Pudding

1   loaf stale French bread, cubed
1   quart milk
4   eggs, beaten
2   cups sugar
1   cup raisins

1   tablespoon vanilla
1   tablespoon nutmeg
1   tablespoon cinnamon
4   tablespoons butter

Mix all ingredients and pour into buttered 2-quart casserole. Bake 1 hour at 350°. Serve with the following sauce.

### Whiskey Sauce

¼  pound butter
1   cup sugar

2   eggs, beaten
½  cup bourbon

Heat butter and sugar together until sugar is dissolved and liquid is clear. Remove from heat and cool. Add eggs and beat for about 1 minute; add whiskey while continuing to beat.

*Terry H. Easterling*

# VERANDA SUPPER       *(Serves 12)*

A potpourri of tantalizing fragrances—from the magnolia blossoms outside to the highly seasoned foods on the porch.

### *Shrimp Remoulade   or   *Hot Shrimp Cocktail
### *Barbecued Ribeye
### *White Squash Casserole   or   *Zucchini-Corn Pudding
### *Mushroom and Tomato Salad
### French Bread
### *Pineapple Flambé   or   *Chocolate Pots de Crème
### Coffee

*Chenin Blanc or Muscadet with shrimp*
*Claret or California Cabernet with beef*

## Shrimp Remoulade

| | |
|---|---|
| 2   eggs | 2   tablespoons horseradish |
| 4   tablespoons paprika | 3   cloves garlic, minced |
| 2   teaspoons salt | ½   cup minced green onions |
| ½   cup Creole mustard | ½   cup minced celery |
| 1½   pints salad oil | ¼ to ½ cup minced parsley |
| ½   cup vinegar | 3 to 4 pounds cooked, peeled |
| 1   lemon, quartered |    shrimp |
| ½   cup catsup | Lettuce |
| 3   bay leaves | |

Put eggs, paprika, salt and mustard into mixing bowl. *Slowly* beat in oil. When thickened add vinegar; squeeze in lemon juice and drop in lemon pieces. Add remaining ingredients. Refrigerate 6 hours or more.

Remove lemon pieces from sauce. Arrange shrimp on bed of lettuce and top with sauce.

Yield: 1½ quarts of sauce

*Irving Goldstein*

## Hot Shrimp Cocktail

12  tablespoons lemon juice
2   tablespoons vinegar
2   tablespoons Worcestershire
    sauce
4   tablespoons soy sauce
½ to ¾ teaspoon Tabasco

1   pound butter, melted
1 to 2 teaspoons cornstarch
    (optional)
3 to 4 pounds cooked, peeled
    shrimp

Mix first 5 ingredients together. Add to butter and heat thoroughly but do not boil. Add cornstarch dissolved in a small amount of water if a thicker sauce is desired. Serve over shrimp.

*Dorothy G. Portier*

## Barbecued Ribeye

6   pound ribeye roast
2   tablespoons barbecue spice
1   teaspoon hickory smoked salt
½   teaspoon garlic powder
⅛   teaspoon celery salt
1   tablespoon cayenne

¼   cup lemon juice
2   tablespoons Worcestershire
    sauce
¼   cup soy sauce
1   cup vegetable oil
Salt and pepper

Marinate roast in combined remaining ingredients at least 1 hour. Cook over low coals in smoker type barbecue pit 1½ hours or until desired temperature is reached on meat thermometer, turning and basting occasionally with marinade. Allow to rest 20 minutes before carving.

*Willie E. Braxton*

## White Squash Casserole

6 to 8 white squash, grated
Salt and pepper
1   teaspoon basil
1   teaspoon MSG
1   teaspoon garlic salt

2   onions, chopped
¾   cup cream
2   cups Ritz crackers,
    crushed
Butter

Mix squash, seasonings, onions and cream. In a 3-quart buttered casserole, make layers of squash mixture and crushed crackers until all are used. Dot with butter. Bake 45 minutes at 350°.

*Annie Lou S. McBride*

## Zucchini-Corn Pudding

| | |
|---|---|
| 2 tablespoons butter | 1 teaspoon salt |
| 2 tablespoons olive oil | ½ teaspoon pepper |
| ½ cup minced onion | 1 teaspoon cayenne |
| ¼ cup chopped green pepper | 3 eggs, separated |
| 1 clove garlic, minced | 1 cup grated Cheddar cheese |
| 2 pounds zucchini, thinly sliced or chopped | ¼ pound butter, melted |
| 2 cups corn | 2 tablespoons sugar |

Sauté onion, pepper and garlic in butter and oil until tender. Add zucchini and cook slowly for 10 to 15 minutes. Stir in corn and seasonings. Cool. Add beaten egg yolks, cheese, melted butter and sugar. Beat egg whites until stiff and fold into vegetable mixture. Pour into greased 2½-quart casserole and set in pan of hot water. Bake 1 hour at 350°. May be baked ahead and reheated.

*Adona P. Cain*


## Mushroom and Tomato Salad

| | |
|---|---|
| 1½ pounds mushrooms, sliced | ½ cup chopped parsley |
| 6 tomatoes, chopped | 2 teaspoons salt |
| 2 onions, thinly sliced | 2 teaspoons sugar |
| 1 cup olive oil | 1 teaspoon garlic powder |
| ½ cup red wine vinegar | ½ teaspoon pepper |

Mix vegetables and refrigerate, covered. Combine remaining ingredients. An hour before serving, mix vegetables and dressing; refrigerate. Serve with slotted spoon.

*Nancy K. Young*


## Pineapple Flambé

| | |
|---|---|
| 4 tablespoons butter | 6 cups fresh pineapple chunks |
| ½ cup brown sugar | ½ cup Kirsch, warmed |
| 2 tablespoons lemon juice | ½ gallon vanilla ice cream |
| ½ cup Curaçao or Cointreau | |

Heat first 5 ingredients in chafing dish. Stir in Kirsch and ignite. Serve over ice cream.

*Dorothy I. Stuckey*

## Chocolate Pots de Crème

12  ounces semi-sweet chocolate      2  cups cream
      morsels                                    4  tablespoons Kahlua
5  tablespoons sugar                   2  tablespoons brandy
¼  teaspoon salt                        Whipped cream and grated
2  eggs                                          chocolate (optional)
2  teaspoons vanilla

Put chocolate, sugar, salt, eggs and vanilla into blender. Blend 10 seconds; stop, blend 10 more seconds. Heat cream to boiling point and add to chocolate mixture. Blend 10 more seconds. Add Kahlua and brandy and blend again for 10 seconds.

Pour into demitasse or pot de crème cups. Chill several hours; top with whipped cream and grated chocolate.

*Van O. Famsworth*

# FARE EXTRAORDINAIRE (Serves 12)

"Lagniappe" is a common Louisiana word which means "something extra". This dinner offers that extra something in food; guests will be eager for just one more taste.

***\*Oyster Bisque***        *Montrachet*

***\*Standing Rib Roast***        *Red Wine*
***with \*Bearnaise Sauce***        *Extraordinaire*

***\*Spinach-Stuffed Squash*        *\*Browned Rice***
***French Bread***

***\*Torte Lilli***        *Sauternes or Barsac*

***\*Café Brûlot***

## Oyster Bisque

| | |
|---|---|
| 1½ pints oysters | 1   teaspoon salt |
| 1   cup water | 3   tablespoons butter |
| 1   onion, sliced | 3   tablespoons flour |
| ⅓   cup chopped celery | Salt and pepper to taste |
| 1   sprig parsley, minced | 2   cups milk |
| 1   bay leaf | 1   cup heavy cream |
| ⅛   teaspoon mace | Dash of Tabasco |

Drain oysters, reserving liquor. Separate soft portion from hard muscles; chop and refrigerate soft portions. Grind or chop muscles and combine with oyster liquor and the next 6 ingredients; bring to boil. Reduce heat; cover and simmer 30 minutes. Press through sieve; add 1 teaspoon salt.

Melt butter over low heat; add flour, salt and pepper and stir until blended. Gradually add oyster stock and 1 cup milk; cook and stir until thick. Refrigerate 24 hours to aid in thickening.

Before serving, add soft oyster portions, cream and Tabasco. Heat carefully and remove from fire. Gradually stir in remaining cup of milk and return to heat, stirring constantly until thick and smooth.

Yield: 48 ounces

*Nancy W. Cotton*

## Standing Rib Roast

12 pound rib roast, at room            Salt, pepper, and garlic powder
    temperature                        to taste

Rub meat with salt, pepper and garlic powder. Place fat side up in shallow pan; bake uncovered at 325° 18 to 20 minutes per pound for rare roast, 22 to 25 minutes for medium, and 35 minutes for a well-done roast.

## Bearnaise Sauce

4  tablespoons white wine             4  tablespoons lemon juice
4  tablespoons tarragon vinegar       ½  teaspoon salt
4  teaspoons tarragon                 ½  teaspoon freshly ground black
4  teaspoons minced green onions         pepper
   and tops                           Cayenne to taste
6  egg yolks                          ½  pound butter, melted

Combine first 4 ingredients and heat in a saucepan until liquid is almost gone. In blender, mix egg yolks, lemon juice and seasonings. Pour in butter, a little at a time, turning blender off and on between additions. Add the herbs and blend 4 seconds.
   Yield:  4 cups

*Nancy C. Weems*

## Spinach-Stuffed Squash

6  yellow squash                      1  cup milk, at room temperature
2  cups cooked, chopped spinach,      Salt, pepper and cayenne to taste
   well-drained                       Dash of nutmeg
4  tablespoons butter                 ⅔  cup shredded Cheddar cheese
4  tablespoons minced green           8  slices bacon, cooked and
   onions                                crumbled
4  tablespoons flour

Trim ends off squash. Cook whole in salted boiling water about 10 minutes or until barely tender; drain well. Halve lengthwise and scoop out centers. Chop pulp and combine with spinach. In heavy saucepan, melt butter; sauté onions until wilted and blend in flour. Add milk, stirring constantly, and cook until thick. Add seasonings to spinach mixture and stir into sauce. Spoon into squash shells; top with cheese and bacon. Bake at 350° for 15 to 20 minutes. Freezes well.

## Browned Rice

¼  pound margarine                    5   cups chicken bouillon
3   cups rice

Melt margarine in Dutch oven; add rice slowly and stir over medium heat until rice is dark brown. Pour in bouillon carefully, reduce heat to low, cover and cook 20 to 25 minutes. Turn off heat and fluff up rice with a fork. Serve immediately or reheat over hot water.

*H. Leroy Johns*


## Torte Lilli

1   cup strong cold coffee            40  vanilla wafers
1½ tablespoons sugar                  1   cup heavy cream, whipped
2   tablespoons Grand Marnier         Candied cherries and colored sugar
½  pound butter                           (optional)
2   eggs
12 ounces semi-sweet chocolate,
    melted

Combine coffee, sugar and Grand Marnier. Cream butter and beat in eggs and chocolate. Line a 9×5-inch bread pan with foil, allowing enough extra at edges to fold back over top of pan. Arrange layer of wafers on bottom, sprinkle generously with coffee mixture, then spread with chocolate cream. Continue in layers, about 3 or 4, until all of chocolate mixture is used, ending with wafers. Fold foil to cover. Set identical pan on top of cake, bottom side down, and weight in place (a brick will do nicely). Let season 24 hours in refrigerator. To serve, remove foil and turn onto serving platter. Frost with whipped cream and garnish. Slice thinly.

*Laura F. Waring*

## Café Brûlot

4  strips orange peel
8  strips lemon peel
4  whole cloves
4  whole allspice or ½ teaspoon
   ground allspice
6  sticks cinnamon or ½ teaspoon
   ground cinnamon

½  cup sugar
1½ cups brandy
½  cup Curaçao (optional)
5  cups strong coffee, very hot

Combine first 6 ingredients in brûlot bowl or chafing dish. Mash with ladle. Gently heat brandy and Curaçao to lukewarm and add, reserving one ladleful which is then ignited and lowered into the bowl, setting the whole mixture aflame. Add coffee *very gradually*, continuing to stir mixture until flame dies. Ladle into demitasse or brûlot cups.

*Carolyn H. Norman*

# BAYOU SPECIALTIES *(Serves 16)*

Each south Louisiana chef has an individual recipe for these two estimable Louisiana dishes—and each is "the best".

Crawfish bisque, a thick brown soup of incomparable taste, is made during the spring when the "mudbugs" are in season. Allegedly, Cajun families had to be large to provide enough help to make the bisque! Here is a somewhat shortened method—still time-consuming, but rewarding.

Jambalaya, a descendant of Spanish "paella", was brought to New Orleans in the late 1700's by the Spaniards. The name originated from "jamón" (ham), but is said to mean, colloquially, "clean up the kitchen". Ham and shrimp may be the major ingredients but various combinations of sausage, chicken, game, oysters, crabmeat, and other meats or fish may be used. One constant component: rice.

***Jambalaya***
*or*
***Crawfish Bisque***

**Green Salad**     **French Bread**

***Chocolate Cake***
*with*
***Chocolate Fudge Frosting***
**Coffee**

*Beaujolais, Morgon, Moulin-à-Vent or Gamay Beaujolais*

## Chicken Jambalaya

| | | | |
|---|---|---|---|
| 2 | 2½ pound fryers | 2 | bunches green onions, chopped |
| 2 | quarts water | ¼ | pound butter |
| 3 | pounds smoked sausage, sliced, browned, and drained | 4 | cups raw rice |
| | | 4 | chicken bouillon cubes |
| 2 | green peppers, chopped | 1 | teaspoon Tabasco |
| 2 | onions, chopped | 2 | teaspoons Worcestershire sauce |
| 2 | ribs celery, chopped | 1 | tablespoon Kitchen Bouquet |
| 4 to 5 cloves garlic, chopped | | | |

Boil chicken in water until tender (about 1 to 1½ hours); debone and reserve the stock. In large black iron Dutch oven, sauté the vegetables in the butter until soft. Add the chicken meat, sausage, 1 quart of the stock, and remaining ingredients, stirring to blend well. Cover and cook over low heat 1 to 1½ hours, adding more stock if necessary. Adjust seasonings.

*Norman J. Chenevert*

## *Shrimp Jambalaya*

1    pound ham, cubed
½   cup vegetable oil
2    onions, chopped
½   cup diced celery
½   cup chopped green peppers
       (optional)
2    cloves garlic, pressed (optional)
¼   teaspoon thyme
2    bay leaves

½   teaspoon salt
½   teaspoon cayenne
2    1-pound cans tomatoes
1    6-ounce can tomato paste
½   lemon, quartered
2    pounds peeled shrimp
15   cups cooked rice (2 pounds
       raw)

Cook ham in hot oil until lightly browned. Add next 8 ingredients and cook 3 minutes. Stir in tomatoes, tomato paste, lemon pieces and shrimp. Simmer slowly, uncovered, tossing often until shrimp are pink (10 to 15 minutes). Remove bay leaves and lemon. May be refrigerated at this point until ready to serve. Mix with freshly steamed rice, heat well and adjust seasonings.

*Grady A. McDuff*

## *Crawfish Bisque*

4    quarts water
1    onion, quartered
1    lemon, quartered
4 to 6 tablespoons salt
2 or 3  3-ounce bags Crab Boil
3 to 5 pounds live crawfish, purged
       (See page 236)
2    pounds cooked and peeled
       crawfish tails
2    onions, diced
4    green onions, chopped
2    cloves garlic, minced
3    ribs celery, diced
5    tablespoons margarine
½   cup catsup
3    teaspoons Worcestershire sauce

1    teaspoon Tabasco
6    sprigs parsley, minced
4 to 6 slices bread, soaked in stock
       and squeezed out
Paprika, salt and pepper to taste
1    pound margarine
2    cups flour
4    ribs celery, diced
2    onions, diced
4    green onions, diced
2    cloves garlic, pressed
1    6-ounce can tomato paste
1    14½-ounce can tomato sauce
1    14½-ounce can stewed
       tomatoes

Bring water and next 4 ingredients to a boil and cook about 15 minutes. Add live crawfish and let boil 10 minutes. Turn off heat, cover pot and let set another 10 minutes. Drain, saving stock. Cool and pick crawfish, saving the fat and the cleaned heads, as well as the meat.

Sauté the next 4 vegetables in the 5 tablespoons margarine until wilted. Mix with next 5 ingredients, all crawfish meat, and some of the crawfish fat. Reseason to taste. Stuff mixture into cleaned heads.

Melt the 1 pound margarine, blend in flour and cook slowly, stirring constantly until roux is a light brown. Add remaining vegetables and crawfish fat; continue to stir and cook to a dark brown. Mix in remaining ingredients. Add reserved stock slowly and cook 30 to 45 minutes. Adjust seasoning. Gently drop in stuffed heads and cook 15 minutes. Serve in large bowls over steamed rice.

*Louise A. Simon*

## Chocolate Cake

2   cups flour
2   cups sugar
1   teaspoon baking soda
1   teaspoon salt
½   teaspoon baking powder
2   eggs
¾   cup water

¾   cup buttermilk
1   teaspoon vanilla
¼   pound margarine, melted and cooled
4   ounces unsweetened chocolate, melted and cooled

Sift all dry ingredients together. Add remaining ingredients and beat 2 minutes at high speed. *Do not overbeat.* Pour into 2 greased and floured 9-inch cake pans and bake 30 to 35 minutes at 350° or until cake tester inserted in center comes out clean. Cool 10 minutes. Invert on wire racks and remove pans. Allow to cool completely before icing.

*W. Ellis Powell*

## Chocolate Fudge Frosting

4   ounces unsweetened chocolate
¼   pound butter or margarine
1   pound confectioners' sugar
½   cup milk

2   teaspoons vanilla
½ to ⅔ cup chopped pecans (optional)

Melt butter and chocolate in a heavy saucepan over low heat. Stir sugar, milk and vanilla together until smooth; add chocolate mixture. Set bowl in a pan of ice and water and beat frosting with a wooden spoon until it is thick enough to spread and hold. Fold in nuts; fill and frost cake.

*Barbara S. Domingos*

# CRÊPE SUPPER                                    *(Serves 16)*

*Savoir Faire* with a taste of Louisiana!

*\*Crawfish Crêpes*
*\*Spinach and Orange Salad*
**French Bread**

*\*Lemon Glacé   or   \*Peppermint Sundae*
**Coffee**

Muscadet or Chenin Blanc

## Crawfish Crêpes

| | |
|---|---|
| 1½ cups cold milk | 3   pounds cooked crawfish tails |
| 1½ cups cold water | Salt and pepper to taste |
| 6   eggs | ⅛ teaspoon garlic powder |
| 1½ teaspoons salt | 1¾ cups vermouth |
| 3   cups sifted flour | 6   tablespoons cornstarch |
| 6   tablespoons melted butter | 6   tablespoons milk |
| Salt pork or butter to grease pan | 6   cups heavy cream |
| 12  tablespoons butter | Salt and white pepper to taste |
| 1½ cups minced green onions, | 4½ cups grated Swiss cheese |
| finely chopped | ¼   pound butter |

To make crêpes, mix first 6 ingredients at low speed in blender. Store in refrigerator several hours. (Important!)

Heat a 6 to 7-inch skillet or crêpe pan. Grease well. Pour scant ¼ cup of batter into pan and swirl for each crêpe. Cook until just golden, only a few seconds; lift edges of crêpe and flip over. Cook only a few seconds more. Invert skillet to flip out crêpe. To keep skillet from getting too hot, remove from burner after each crêpe for a second or two. Stack crêpes between layers of waxed paper. May be refrigerated or frozen.

Sauté onions in butter; add crawfish and seasonings and toss lightly. Stir in ¾ cup vermouth and boil rapidly until liquid is almost evaporated. Remove and set aside.

Add remaining vermouth to skillet and boil rapidly until reduced to about 1½ tablespoons. Remove from heat and stir in cornstarch and milk which have been mixed together. Return to low heat and add cream slowly, then salt and pepper. Cook several minutes until slightly thickened. Stir in 2¼ cups cheese and cook until cheese is melted.

Blend ½ of the sauce with the crawfish mixture. Put a generous serving on each crêpe; roll crêpe and place seam down in a buttered casserole. Spoon remaining sauce over crêpes and sprinkle with remaining cheese. Dot with butter. Cook at 400° for 20 minutes or until hot and bubbly.

Variation: Crabmeat or shrimp may be substituted for crawfish.

Yield: 36 to 45 crêpes

*Judy J. McLure*

## Spinach and Orange Salad

½ cup sesame seeds
1 cup sugar
½ teaspoon paprika
½ teaspoon dry mustard
1 teaspoon salt
⅛ teaspoon Worcestershire sauce

2 tablespoons grated onion
2 cups salad oil
1 cup vinegar
2 pounds spinach, washed and drained
8 oranges, peeled and sectioned

Toast sesame seeds in 200° oven, stirring occasionally until lightly browned. Combine next 6 ingredients in blender; add oil and vinegar slowly. Pour into quart jar, add sesame seed and refrigerate. When ready to serve, toss spinach and orange sections with dressing.

*Mary Frances L. James*

## Peppermint Ice Cream

10 eggs, beaten
3 cups sugar
1½ pints heavy cream
3 pints half and half

1 tablespoon vanilla
6 ounces striped hard peppermint candy, crushed
2 or 3 drops red food coloring

Beat eggs with sugar and cream. Add vanilla, candy and food coloring. Freeze in 1½ gallon freezer until firm.

*Nina W. Long*

## Fudge Sauce

1 cup sugar
1 cup light corn syrup
½ cup cream
½ cup cocoa

3 tablespoons butter
¼ teaspoon salt
1 teaspoon vanilla

Boil all ingredients except vanilla in a heavy saucepan 5 minutes. Remove from heat and stir in vanilla. Keeps well in refrigerator.

*Darline H. Crossland*

## Chocolate Sauce·

| | |
|---|---|
| 1   cup sugar | Pinch of salt |
| 4   tablespoons chocolate flavored | ½  cup milk |
|      Nestle's Quik | 2   tablespoons butter |
| 1   tablespoon flour | 1   teaspoon vanilla |

Mix dry ingredients in a saucepan; add milk and butter. Mix and boil 2 minutes. Remove from heat and add vanilla. Best made right before serving.

*Kathryn P. Keller*

## Lemon Glacé

| | |
|---|---|
| 8   eggs | ¼  cup lemon juice |
| 4⅔ cups sugar | ½  cup Curaçao, Triple Sec or |
| 2⅔ cups sifted flour |      Grand Marnier |
| 12 tablespoons melted butter | 4   cups heavy cream |
| 12 egg yolks | ½  cup whipped cream, sweetened |
| 1   teaspoon grated lemon peel | |

Combine the eggs and 2⅔ cups sugar in a porcelainized enamel (or copper) bowl set in a saucepan containing about 2 inches of boiling water. (The water should not touch the bowl.) Beat mixture 10 minutes, or until it is thick and pale yellow. Remove from heat and sift in flour very gradually, blending in well. Add butter slowly. Pour into 2  9-inch cake pans which have been greased, lined with a circle of wax paper in the bottom of each, re-greased and floured. Bake at 350° for 30 to 40 minutes or until a cake tester comes out clean. While hot, invert onto racks and remove wax paper. When cool, split into ½-inch thick layers; trim to fit 2 5-cup (or 1 10-cup) soufflé dishes.

In a mixing bowl, combine the egg yolks, 1½ cups sugar, lemon peel and juice. Place over a saucepan of simmering water and beat 10 minutes or until mixture "forms the ribbon". Beat in ¼ cup liqueur. Cool; refrigerate until cold.

Whip the cream until stiff with the remaining ½ cup sugar. Fold into egg mixture. Chill soufflé dishes at least 15 minutes in the freezer. Remove and fit each with a wax paper collar extending 1 inch above the top of the dish. Place a cake layer in the bottom of each dish, sprinkle with liqueur, and top with filling mixture. Repeat until all ingredients are used. Freeze for at least 3 hours; keeps for weeks.

When ready to serve, remove paper collar and top with whipped cream.

*Caroline K. Gilliland*

# BUFFET

(Serves 24)

For a convivial gathering.

### *Hot Shrimp Canapés    *Artichoke Appetizer
### *Chicken Spaghetti
### *Mixed Salad with Blue Cheese Dressing
### Toasted Garlic Bread

### *Butterscotch Sundae   or   *Honey Ginger Sundae
### *Oatmeal Cookies

### Coffee

*Chianti Classico or Barbera*

## Hot Shrimp Canapés

| | |
|---|---|
| 1 cup chopped cooked shrimp | ½ teaspoon onion juice |
| 1 cup grated sharp Cheddar cheese | ½ teaspoon coarse black pepper |
| 2 large kosher dill pickles, grated | ¼ teaspoon salt |
| ½ cup mayonnaise | 1 clove garlic, pressed |
| ½ teaspoon Tabasco | 50 1½-inch rounds of bread, toasted on one side |

Combine first 9 ingredients and spread on toasted side of rounds. Bake 10 minutes at 350°. Freezes well.
Yield: 50

*Jane F. Walker*

## Artichoke Appetizer

| | |
|---|---|
| 2 14-ounce cans artichoke hearts, drained and mashed | ½ teaspoon garlic salt |
| 2 cups mayonnaise | 3 6-ounce boxes Melba toast rounds |
| 1 0.6 ounce package dry Italian salad dressing mix | |

Mix first 4 ingredients thoroughly and chill 24 hours. Serve on toast rounds.

*Virginia S. Hopper*

## Chicken Spaghetti

15  pounds fryers
¾  pound margarine
12  cups chopped celery
3  onions, chopped
3  green peppers, chopped
   (optional)
3  cloves garlic, minced
3  10¾-ounce cans tomato soup
3  10¾-ounce cans cream of
   mushroom soup

4  cups chicken broth
6  tablespoons chili powder
Salt and garlic salt to taste
2  pounds spaghetti
24  ounces pasteurized process
   cheese spread, cubed
Dash of cayenne (optional)

Boil chickens in water to cover for 5 minutes; reduce heat and simmer until tender—approximately 2 hours. Remove chickens; debone, skin, and chop meat. Reserve broth.

In large pan melt margarine and sauté chopped vegetables; add garlic. Stir in soups, broth and seasonings and simmer for 45 minutes. Add chicken.

Cook spaghetti; drain and mix with sauce and cheese. Season with cayenne. Bake in 3 3-quart casseroles at 350° for 45 minutes.

*Geraldine L. White*

## Mixed Salad with Blue Cheese Dressing

2  pounds spinach, torn
2  heads red tip lettuce, torn
12  green onions, minced
4  cucumbers, thinly sliced
1  pint cherry tomatoes, halved
4  6-ounce jars marinated
   artichoke hearts, drained
8  hard-boiled eggs, chopped
1½ cups green olives, sliced
8  ounces blue cheese, crumbled
4  cups mayonnaise

2  cups sour cream
1  cup buttermilk
2  teaspoons pepper
2  teaspoons garlic powder
1  teaspoon Worcestershire sauce
2  pounds bacon, cooked and
   crumbled
2  cups croutons
Salt and freshly ground black
   pepper

Mix and chill first 8 ingredients. Blend next 7 ingredients to make dressing; chill. When ready to serve, combine the 2 mixtures and toss well with bacon and croutons. Season to taste.

*Patricia B. Brierley*

## Butterscotch Sundae

3  eggs, beaten
12 tablespoons butter
¾  cup water
2  cups light brown sugar

1  cup light corn syrup
¾  cup pecans (optional)
1  gallon vanilla ice cream

In top of double boiler combine first 5 ingredients and mix well. Cook until thick, stirring frequently. Before serving, beat sauce; then add pecans. Spoon over ice cream.

*Kathryn P. Keller*

## Honey Ginger Sundae

4  cups honey
1  cup water
1½ to 2 cups candied ginger

2  cups pecans, finely chopped
1  gallon vanilla ice cream

Combine honey and water in saucepan and bring to a boil. Stir in ginger and pecans. Serve over ice cream. Sauce may be stored in jars without refrigeration.

*Annelle B. Lewis*

## Oatmeal Cookies

½  pound butter
1  cup light brown sugar
1  cup sugar
2  eggs
1½ cups flour

1  teaspoon salt
1  teaspoon baking soda
3  cups quick-cooking oats
1  teaspoon vanilla

Cream together butter and sugar. Add eggs and beat until fluffy. Gradually beat in the sifted dry ingredients, vanilla and oats. Place greased foil on cookie sheet. Drop dough by rounded teaspoonfuls about 2 inches apart. Bake at 350° for 8 to 10 minutes, until delicately browned. Do not overbake. Unbaked dough may be frozen.

Yield: 6 dozen cookies

*Darline H. Crossland*

# MEXICAN FIESTA                          *(Serves 24)*

A casual buffet with plenty of zest.

*Margaritas*
*Nachos*

*Tacos with *Tomato-Pepper Relish*
*Hot Tamales*
*Chicken Enchiladas*
*Pinto Beans        *Guacamole Salad*

*Caramel Nut Candy*
*and*
*Peanut Brittle*

*Iced Tea and Beer*

## Margaritas

2   fifths tequila
1   pint Triple Sec
3½ quarts water
8   6-ounce cans frozen limeade

8   ounces lime juice (optional)
½  cup lemon juice
Salt

The day before serving, combine first 5 ingredients and refrigerate until chilled. Stir well and freeze until 6 hours before serving. Return to refrigerator.

To serve, dip rims of champagne glasses in lemon juice, then in a plate of salt; fill.

Yield: 58   4-ounce drinks

*Conway E. Crossland*

## Nachos

2   12-ounce bags Doritos (plain flavor)

1   dozen jalapeño peppers, sliced
1   pound sharp cheese, grated

Arrange Doritos on cookie sheets, place ½ to 1 pepper ring on each and sprinkle with cheese. Broil 2 to 3 minutes until cheese melts and serve immediately.

*Thomas F. Norman*

## Tacos

2   pounds ground beef
2¼ cups minced onion
2   cloves garlic, pressed
5   cups chopped tomatoes
4   teaspoons salt
Black pepper and cayenne to taste
2   tablespoons chili powder
1½ teaspoons cumin
2   jalapeño or chili peppers,
       minced (optional)

2   dozen taco shells
3   cups shredded cheese
3   cups shredded lettuce
2 to 3 avocados, sliced
Homemade tomato-pepper relish
       (see recipe following)
Taco sauce (optional)

Sauté ground beef with 1½ cups of the onions and garlic until browned. Add 1½ cups tomatoes, salt, pepper, chili powder, cumin and jalapeños. Cover and simmer 10 minutes, adding a little water if mixture appears dry.

Combine remaining tomatoes and onions and refrigerate at least 30 minutes. At serving time, crisp the taco shells at 350° for 5 minutes. Serve accompanied by bowls of meat mixture, tomato-onion combination, cheese, lettuce, avocados, tomato-pepper relish and taco sauce.

## Tomato-Pepper Relish

20  cups (50 to 60) ripe tomatoes
4   cups juice from the tomatoes
5   cups peppers, jalapeño and/or
       chili
5   cups chopped onions
1   cup tarragon vinegar
2   cups white vinegar

1   cup thinly sliced garlic
1   cup sugar
5   tablespoons salt
½   teaspoon garlic powder
2   tablespoons Lawry's seasoned
       salt

Place tomatoes in boiling water until the skins split. Peel, chop and drain, reserving juice. Wearing rubber gloves, seed and chop peppers. Place all ingredients in a large pot and simmer 2 to 2½ hours, stirring occasionally. Pack in sterilized pint jars.

Yield:  12 pints

*Rebecca T. Hemenway*

## Hot Tamales

½  cup tomato sauce
2 to 3 tablespoons salt
2  tablespoons chili powder
2  tablespoons Gebhardt's Chili
   Quick or McCormick Chili Mix
1  10-ounce can Rotel tomatoes
   and green chilies, drained
   (reserve juice)
2½ to 3 cups white corn meal
1  tablespoon salt
2  onions, grated
1  tablespoon salt

4  cloves garlic, minced
6  tablespoons chili powder
2  tablespoons Gebhardt's Chili
   Quick or McCormick Chili Mix
½  cup water
1½ cups tomato sauce
1  teaspoon cayenne
2  pounds ground beef
½  cup white corn meal
50 to 75 corn shucks, boiled for
   1 hour

Place first 4 ingredients plus half the tomatoes and all reserved juice in a one quart measure and add enough water to fill. Pour into saucepan and boil a few minutes. Remove from heat and set aside. Mix corn meal and salt in shallow pan. Set aside.

Combine remaining ingredients except shucks. Drop one rounded table-spoon of this mixture into the reserved corn meal mixture and roll lightly, shaping into a roll about 2 inches long. Place on shuck, sprinkle with 1 teaspoon of the corn meal mixture and wrap securely. Repeat until meat mixture is used. Stack tamales on a rack in large roaster. Heat sauce mixture to boiling and pour over tamales; simmer 1 hour and 15 minutes.

Yield:  4 to 5 dozen

*Rosemary R. Waters*

## Chicken Enchiladas

16 halves chicken breasts
Salt
4  cups chopped onions
4  cloves garlic, minced
¼  pound butter
4  1-pound cans tomatoes,
   chopped
32 ounces tomato sauce
1  cup canned green chili peppers,
   chopped

4  teaspoons sugar
4  teaspoons cumin
2  teaspoons salt
2  teaspoons oregano
2  teaspoons basil
4  dozen tortillas
Vegetable oil
10 cups shredded Monterey Jack
   cheese
3  cups sour cream (optional)

Simmer chicken breasts in water until fork tender. Drain; remove skin and bones. Sprinkle with salt. Cut each piece into 3 strips and set aside.

In a large saucepan, sauté onion and garlic in the butter until tender. Add tomatoes, tomato sauce, chilies, sugar, cumin, salt, oregano and basil. Bring to a boil, reduce heat and simmer covered for 20 minutes.

While the sauce is simmering, soft fry the tortillas in hot oil; drain and set aside. Place one strip of chicken and about 2 tablespoons of cheese in each tortilla, roll up and place seam side down in 4 9×13-inch casseroles. Blend sour cream into sauce and pour over tortillas. Sprinkle with remaining cheese and bake uncovered for 20 minutes at 375°.

Yield: 48

*Nina W. Long*

## Pinto Beans

2 pounds dried pinto beans, rinsed and drained
1 10-ounce can Rotel tomatoes and green chilies, chopped
1 14½-ounce can tomatoes, chopped
1 onion, chopped
1 clove garlic, sliced in half and skewered with toothpicks

3 drops Tabasco sauce
½ pound salt pork or 2 ham hocks
Freshly ground black pepper to taste
Salt to taste, added 1 hour before serving

In a large heavy kettle, place 5 to 6 quarts of water and the beans; bring to a boil. Add remaining ingredients, reduce heat and simmer at least 6 hours. Remove garlic before serving.

*Pam J. Hodges*

## Guacamole Salad

9 avocados, peeled and mashed
3 tomatoes, peeled and coarsely chopped
1 onion, finely chopped
6 green chilies, seeded and chopped

3 tablespoons lemon juice (optional)
Salt and pepper to taste
12 cups shredded lettuce

Stir tomatoes, onion, chilies and seasonings into avocados by hand. Chill and serve on lettuce.

*Nina W. Long*

## Caramel Nut Candy

| 3 | cups sugar | 1 | teaspoon vanilla |
| 1 | cup milk | | Pinch of baking powder |
| 1 | teaspoon cornstarch | 1 | cup chopped pecans |
| 1 | tablespoon butter | | |

Over low heat, melt 1 cup of the sugar slowly in a heavy saucepan. Add milk, bring to a boil and stir in remaining 2 cups of sugar to which cornstarch has been added. Continue boiling until soft ball stage or 235° on a candy thermometer is reached. Remove from heat, add butter, vanilla and the baking powder. Beat with a wooden spoon until creamy. Stir in nuts and pour into buttered 9×13-inch casserole. When nearly cooled, cut into squares.
    Yield: 24 pieces

*Winona P. Yeager*
*Nona L. Pace*

## Peanut Brittle

| 6 | cups sugar | 4 | tablespoons softened butter |
| 1⅓ | cups water | 1 | teaspoon salt |
| 2 | cups light Karo syrup | 2 | tablespoons baking soda |
| 6 | cups raw peanuts | 2 | teaspoons vanilla |

In a deep heavy saucepan bring sugar, water and syrup to a rolling boil, stirring frequently. Continue cooking and stirring until mixture spins a thread or reaches 275° on a candy thermometer. Add peanuts and continue cooking until mixture turns a golden color or 295° is reached. Remove from heat and add other ingredients. Mix thoroughly and pour into heavily buttered cookie pans. Spread mixture thinly, cool and break into pieces.
    Yield: 5 pounds

*Greater First Pentecostal Church*

# AFTER THE REHEARSAL  (Dinner for 60)

A beautiful party for a milestone evening, where careful planning and advance preparation will assure success.

*Whiskey Sour Punch*    *Orange Fizz*
Cheese Board

*Curried Pea Soup*

*Eye of Round with *Herbed Mushrooms*
*Tian à la Lakeland*    *Molded Beet Salad
with*
Buttered French Bread    *Homemade Mayonnaise*

*Daiquiri Soufflé*
Coffee

*California Burgundy or Côtes du Rhône*

## Whiskey Sour Punch

| | |
|---|---|
| 2 quarts orange juice | 6 pints lemon juice (fresh or |
| 12 ounces maraschino cherries | frozen) |
| 4½ cups sugar | Dash of Angostura bitters |
| 2½ cups water | 6 oranges, sliced |
| 6 quarts bourbon | 6 lemons, sliced |

Pour orange juice into 2 ring molds, arrange half the cherries in each, and freeze. Make simple syrup by boiling water and sugar 5 minutes. Cool; combine with remaining ingredients in large containers and chill 24 hours or overnight. Pour over frozen mold in punch bowl. Serve in punch cups over crushed ice.
Yield: 120  4-ounce drinks

*W. Sidney Easterling*

## Orange Fizz

6 quarts orange juice, chilled
6 quarts ginger ale, chilled

Combine ingredients in large pitchers. Pour over crushed ice in tumblers.
Yield: 64  6-ounce drinks

## Curried Pea Soup

5   pounds frozen green peas
9   onions, chopped
6 to 8 cloves garlic, pressed
9   carrots, chopped
9   ribs celery, chopped
9   potatoes, peeled and diced

3   tablespoons curry powder
3   tablespoons salt
4½ quarts chicken broth
1   quart cream
1   quart milk

Simmer the vegetables and seasonings in 1 quart of the broth for 15 minutes or until tender. Purée; add remaining broth. Refrigerate. When ready to serve, stir in cream and milk and adjust seasoning. Serve hot or cold.
Yield: 5½ gallons

*Dorothy I. Stuckey*

## Eye of Round

18  pounds eye of round roasts
Salt and pepper to taste

Tony's Creole seasoning
Worcestershire sauce

Rub meat with seasonings. Place on racks in 500° oven. Bake 7 minutes per pound of largest roast. Turn off oven; leave door closed at least 1 more hour. Chill, slice, and serve hot or cold with the following sauce.

## Herbed Mushrooms

1   pound butter
5 to 6 pounds mushrooms, sliced
1   cup lemon juice
Salt and pepper to taste
2   tablespoons sugar

4   tablespoons fresh tarragon
4   tablespoons chopped chives
½   cup chopped parsley
3   cups sherry
1½ cups cognac, warmed

Melt butter in skillet; add mushrooms. Sprinkle immediately with lemon juice, salt and pepper. Cook, stirring, until mushrooms start to wilt, approximately 5 minutes. Add sugar, herbs, and sherry; cover. Simmer 3 to 5 minutes longer; uncover. Remove from heat. Add cognac and ignite. Serve from chafing dish over the sliced meat.

Variation: Serve from chafing dish with toothpicks as appetizer or over toast points as first course.

*Bertie M. Deming*

### Tian à la Lakeland

12 pounds zucchini
5 cups minced onions
1 cup salad oil
5 tablespoons butter
10 10-ounce packages frozen
   chopped spinach
10 cloves garlic, minced

10 tablespoons flour
1 to 1½ quarts milk
10 cups cooked rice (2½ cups raw)
2 pounds Parmesan cheese,
   grated
Salt and pepper to taste

Grate, salt, and thoroughly drain zucchini, reserving juice. Sauté onions in oil and butter. Add spinach and garlic and cook until tender; blend in flour. Add enough milk to zucchini juice to make 7½ cups and blend into mixture. Cook, stirring, until thickened. Mix in zucchini, rice and all but 3 cups of the cheese. Season to taste. Pour into 5 3-quart casseroles, top with remaining cheese, and bake at 325° for 25 to 30 minutes until bubbly and lightly browned.

*Madelyn R. Waters*

### Molded Beet Salad

6 tablespoons gelatin
2 cups cold water
8 16-ounce cans beets, drained,
   liquid reserved
6 teaspoons salt
2 cups sugar

2 cups vinegar
6 cups minced celery
½ cup minced onion
1 cup prepared horseradish
Lettuce leaves

Dissolve gelatin in water. Heat and stir in 6 cups of the beet liquid. Grate the beets and combine with remaining ingredients, then with gelatin mixture. Pour into 4 9×13-inch flat dishes and chill. Cut into squares and serve on lettuce; top with the following mayonnaise, making recipe twice.

Yield: 72 servings

*Vladimir Veclev*

### Homemade Mayonnaise

1 egg
2 egg yolks
¼ teaspoon dry mustard
½ teaspoon salt

⅛ teaspoon paprika
4 tablespoons lemon juice
2 cups salad oil
Cayenne to taste

To make in food processor, combine first 5 ingredients and whizz 1 minute. Add 1 teaspoon of the lemon juice and, with motor running, begin adding oil slowly in a steady stream. After using 1 cup of oil, stop machine and add 1 tablespoon lemon juice. Continue as before, adding lemon juice alternately with remaining oil until all is used and mayonnaise is thick. Season to taste.

To make in blender, combine first 6 ingredients and ¼ cup oil in blender. Mix 3 seconds, then add remaining oil slowly while blending, until mixture thickens. Season to taste.

Yield: 2 cups

## Daiquiri Soufflé

*Make this 3 times for 60 servings.*

10  eggs, separated, at room
    temperature
2  cups sugar
Grated peel of 2 lemons and
    2 limes
½  cup lemon juice
½  cup lime juice
¼  teaspoon salt

2  tablespoons gelatin
½  cup rum
Green food coloring (optional)
3  cups heavy cream
2  tablespoons confectioners'
    sugar
½  cup pistachio nuts (optional)
Candied violets or fresh berries

Grease a 2-quart soufflé dish with vegetable oil. Grease enough wax paper to wrap around the top of dish as a collar. Overlap paper and tie firmly with string.

Beat egg yolks until light and fluffy. Gradually add 1 cup of sugar and continue beating until the mixture will "form the ribbon". Add grated peels, juices and salt; beat thoroughly. In a heavy pan over very low heat, cook and stir constantly until mixture thickens slightly.

Sprinkle the gelatin over the rum, then stir this mixture into the egg batter. Stir until the gelatin is completely dissolved, remove from heat, pour into a large bowl and let cool, stirring occasionally. Add food coloring.

Beat egg whites until foamy. Gradually add the remaining 1 cup of sugar, beating until the mixture looks like marshmallow. Feel it between thumb and forefinger; when smooth, it is ready.

In a chilled bowl, beat 2 cups of the cream until it mounds. Fold the beaten egg whites into the egg yolk mixture, then fold in the whipped cream. Pour into soufflé dish and chill for at least 3 hours.

To serve, whip the remaining 1 cup of cream with the confectioners' sugar until very stiff. Remove collar from the soufflé and press nuts into the top and sides gently. Decorate with the whipped cream and garnish.

Yield: 20 servings

*Carolyn Flournoy*
*Marilee Harter*

# *Celebrations*

# CASUAL NEW YEAR'S DAY          (Buffet for 16)

Picture favorite friends, a fireplace blazing in welcome and the cheers of armchair football fans, winners all.

All of these recipes, which may be prepared several days in advance, produce ample quantities for return trips to the buffet. Black-eyed peas, traditional Southern symbol of prosperity and good luck, are a must.

### Popcorn and Roasted Peanuts
### Assorted Cheeses and Crackers
### Basket of Apples

### *Vegetable Soup

### *Smoked Beef                         Hot Mustard
### Crusty Buns                          Mayonnaise

### *Pickled Black-Eyed Peas
### *Carrot Cake
### Coffee

*Spanish Rioja, Zinfandel or Egri Bikaver*

## Vegetable Soup

4 to 5 pounds beef marrowbones
1   pound lean beef soup meat, diced
6   quarts water
2 to 3 celery ribs with leaves, coarsely chopped
1   bay leaf
2   onions, halved
3 to 4 carrots, quartered
1   green pepper, quartered
2   carrots, thinly sliced
Kernels from 1 ear corn
1   turnip, diced
1   green pepper, diced
1   onion, diced
2   potatoes, diced
6 to 8 string beans, cut in small pieces
3   zucchini, finely diced
3 to 4 okra pods, sliced (optional)
Salt and freshly-ground black pepper, to taste
3   ounces tomato paste
1   1-pound can whole Italian-style tomatoes
1   cup red wine

Simmer bones and soup meat in water with next 5 ingredients for 4 hours, partially covered. Avoid boiling in order to keep stock clear. Remove and discard bones, vegetables and beef fat. Reserve stock and lean meat. Cover and refrigerate stock until grease solidifies on top for easy removal.

Reheat stock and beef with remaining ingredients. Cook for approximately 30 minutes until vegetables are tender. If desired, purée. Serve in mugs.

Yield: 6 quarts

*Barbara S. Provosty*

## Smoked Beef

2   4-pound eye-of-round roasts
1   clove garlic, slivered
1   dried red pepper, slivered
      (optional)
Salt and cracked black pepper
1   cup salad oil

¼   cup red wine vinegar
2   tablespoons lemon juice
2   tablespoons chopped onion
2   tablespoons marjoram
1   tablespoon salt
1   bay leaf

Insert garlic and red pepper slivers into slits in meat. Season with salt. Sprinkle generously with cracked black pepper, pressing the pepper into the meat. Combine remaining ingredients and pour over the roasts in a shallow pan. Refrigerate overnight, turning meat several times.

Remove meat from marinade; smoke in barbecue pit for 3 or 4 hours, or until desired degree of doneness is reached, using meat thermometer. Refrigerate, covered, for several days. Serve at room temperature.

*Dorothy G. Portier*

## Pickled Black-Eyed Peas

5   15-ounce cans black-eyed peas,
      drained
3   2¼-ounce cans pitted black
      olives, drained and sliced
2½ cups sliced red onions
2   cloves garlic, pressed

2   cups salad oil
¾   cup red wine vinegar
1   tablespoon minced parsley
Salt and pepper to taste
⅛   teaspoon Tabasco

Combine the peas, olives, onions and garlic. Mix all other ingredients and pour over vegetable mixture. Refrigerate, covered, for at least 24 hours.

*Harry M. Brian*

## Carrot Cake

2   cups sugar
3   cups flour
1   teaspoon baking soda
2   teaspoons cinnamon
½   teaspoon salt
1½ cups vegetable oil

1   teaspoon vanilla
1   cup crushed pineapple,
      undrained
2   cups grated carrots
1   cup chopped pecans

Sift dry ingredients together. Add remaining ingredients in order, blending well. Bake in greased 10-inch tube pan for 50 minutes at 350°.

*W. Ellis Powell*

# ANNIVERSARY OPEN HOUSE     *(Reception for 100)*

A "once in a lifetime" event.

*Sherried Pecans*
*Cheese Straws*     *Mints*
*Fruit*

*Iced Sandwich Loaves*

*White Cake with *Divinity Icing*
*Chocolate Pound Cakes*
*Lemon Pound Cakes*

*Reception Punch*
*Inglewood Plantation Wine Cooler*
*Tea and/or Coffee*

Amounts needed will vary with the guest list and the season. Serve a watermelon basket filled with 2 gallons of melon balls or a bowl of 8 quarts of strawberries surrounded by dishes containing 1 pint of sour cream, 1 cup of confectioners' sugar and 1 cup of brown sugar. Liquid refreshments should total 8 gallons: 4 to 6 gallons of punch and 2 to 4 gallons of coffee and tea served with 2 pounds of sugar, 1 quart cream, 6 thinly sliced lemons and 2 cups finely chopped crystallized ginger. The amounts indicated in the various recipes are sufficient for 100 people except that 2 chocolate pound cakes and 3 batches of the sherried pecans should be made.

## Sherried Pecans

1½ cups sugar
½ cup golden sherry

1   teaspoon cinnamon
3   cups pecan halves

Cook sugar and sherry to soft boil stage or 225° on a candy thermometer. Add cinnamon and pecans and stir until cloudy. Drop by teaspoonfuls onto wax paper.

## Cheese Straws

¼   pound margarine, at room
    temperature
2   cups grated sharp Cheddar
    cheese (½ pound), at room
    temperature

1½ cups flour, sifted
½ to ¾ teaspoon cayenne

Mix margarine and cheese together. Add remaining ingredients, blending well. Force mixture through cookie press, using choice of plates. Bake on ungreased cookie sheets at 275° for 20 minutes.

Yield: 11 dozen

Thelma M. Farrar

## Mints

6   tablespoons margarine
½ cup light corn syrup
1   pound confectioners' sugar, sifted

1   teaspoon vanilla
Peppermint oil to taste
Food coloring

Stir margarine, syrup and half the sugar over low heat until bubbly. Quickly blend in remaining sugar, flavorings and coloring. Remove from heat and stir until mixture just holds shape. Pour into greased pan. Cool until candy can be handled; knead until smooth. Shape into small patties.

Yield: 8 dozen

## Iced Sandwich Loaves

6   10-inch loaves unsliced bread, chilled or frozen
1   pound butter, softened
Choice of 3 filling spreads (see following)
56 ounces cream cheese, softened

1   cup mayonnaise
2   tablespoons lemon juice
⅛ teaspoon cayenne
1   cup sour cream
1   tablespoon grated onion (optional)

Trim crusts from bread and slice lengthwise into 4 layers. Spread each layer with softened butter and then with a filling; wrap reassembled loaf with a damp cloth. Enclose in plastic wrap or foil, weight and refrigerate for 12 to 24 hours.

Several hours before serving, beat remaining ingredients until smooth. Frost sides and top of loaves. Decorate at least one loaf, to place in center of platter, surrounded by the others which are sliced at ½ inch intervals.

# Fillings:

## Cheese Spread

12 ounces blue cheese, at room
   temperature
10 ounces processed Cheddar
   cheese spread, at room
   temperature
24 ounces cream cheese, at room
   temperature

1 teaspoon MSG
4 tablespoons grated onion
4 teaspoons Worcestershire sauce
1 cup ground pecans (optional)
⅓ cup minced parsley
¼ to ½ cup mayonnaise

Mix first 6 ingredients until thoroughly blended. Fold in pecans and parsley. Add mayonnaise to desired consistency. Keeps indefinitely in refrigerator; freezes well.

Variation: For an appetizer, omit mayonnaise and form into a cheese ball. Roll in additional pecans and parsley.

*Aimée C. Whatley*

## Chicken Salad

8 halves chicken breasts
1 quart chicken broth
1 rib celery with leaves
1 carrot
1 onion, halved
⅛ teaspoon black pepper
⅛ teaspoon cayenne

1 to 2 cups mayonnaise
2 tablespoons lemon juice
¼ teaspoon cayenne
1½ cups minced celery
Salt to taste
4 hard-boiled eggs, grated
   (optional)

Poach chicken in broth with next 5 ingredients 30 to 40 minutes or until tender. Salt to taste; cool in broth; debone and chop fine.

Blend chicken with 1 cup mayonnaise. Add next 3 ingredients and season to taste. Fold in eggs and add additional mayonnaise until mixture reaches desired consistency. Refrigerate several hours or overnight.

*Wilma H. Uhrich*

## Egg Salad

24 hard-boiled eggs, chopped
3 teaspoons salt
4½ to 6 teaspoons red wine vinegar
Pepper to taste
3 ribs celery, finely chopped

24 pitted green or ripe olives, finely
   chopped
½ teaspoon Creole mustard
½ to ⅔ cup mayonnaise

Mix all ingredients thoroughly, adding mayonnaise to desired consistency. Refrigerate.

*Barbara S. Provosty*

### Ham Salad

2½ pounds boneless ham, ground
1 pound baby Swiss cheese, grated
2½ tablespoons prepared mustard
3 to 4 tablespoons India relish
⅔ to 1 cup mayonnaise
Salt, pepper and cayenne to taste

Mix ham and cheese together; blend in remaining ingredients, adding mayonnaise to desired consistency. Season to taste. Refrigerate.

*Virginia B. Klock*

### Tuna Salad

14 ounces white tuna, rinsed and drained
¼ teaspoon lemon juice
6 hard-boiled eggs, chopped
16 pimiento-stuffed green olives, chopped
8 green onions, minced
2 apples, chopped
1 cup chopped pecans
1 rib celery, chopped
¼ teaspoon sugar (optional)
Salt, pepper and paprika to taste
1½ to 2 cups mayonnaise

Sprinkle tuna with lemon juice and blend with remaining ingredients to desired consistency. Season to taste and refrigerate.

*Katie T. Theus*

## White Cake

12 tablespoons butter
2 cups sugar
3 cups sifted cake flour
1 cup milk
1 teaspoon vanilla
¼ teaspoon almond extract
6 egg whites, stiffly beaten
4 teaspoons baking powder

Cream butter and sugar. Alternately add the flour and ¾ cup milk. Fold in flavorings and egg whites. Combine baking powder with remaining milk and pour into a well in the batter; mix thoroughly. Bake in 2 10-inch square or 3 9-inch round pans at 350° for 25 to 35 minutes, until a cake tester comes out clean. Cool in pans 10 minutes and then invert onto racks to cool completely. Frost with Divinity Icing.

## Divinity Icing

3   cups sugar
½  cup light corn syrup
⅔  cup water
2   egg whites, stiffly beaten

1   teaspoon vanilla
⅓  cup drained, chopped
     maraschino cherries
1   cup chopped pecans, toasted

Boil sugar, syrup and water until mixture reaches the soft ball stage or 225° on a candy thermometer. Pour very slowly and steadily into egg whites, beating continually until icing is creamy. Return syrup mixture to heat from time to time to maintain proper temperature for adding to egg whites. Add remaining ingredients and blend thoroughly.

*Frances S. Bolton*

## Chocolate Pound Cake

½  pound butter
½  cup shortening
3   cups sugar
6   eggs, at room temperature
3   cups cake flour

½  teaspoon baking powder
4   tablespoons cocoa
1   cup milk, at room temperature
1   tablespoon vanilla

Cream butter and shortening together; blend in sugar. Add eggs 1 at a time, beating well after each. Sift dry ingredients together and slowly add to batter alternately with the milk and vanilla just until blended. Pour into a 10-inch tube pan which has been completely lined with wax paper. Bake 1½ hours at 325° or until cake loosens from sides of pan. Let cool 10 minutes in pan; turn out to cool completely before icing with the following frosting.

### Chocolate Frosting

4   tablespoons butter
1   pound confectioners' sugar
4   tablespoons milk

2 to 3 tablespoons cocoa
1   teaspoon vanilla

Beat all ingredients together until fluffy. Spread on cooled cake.

*Linnie S. Wilkinson*

## Lemon Pound Cakes

1   pound margarine
2   cups sugar
8   eggs
4   cups flour

4   teaspoons baking powder
½   teaspoon salt
2   ounces lemon extract

Cream margarine and sugar. Add eggs 1 at a time, beating well after each addition. Sift flour with baking powder and salt and add to batter alternately with lemon extract. Pour into 3 9½-inch greased and floured loaf pans (or 1 bundt pan plus 1 9½-inch loaf pan) and bake about 1 hour at 325° or until a cake tester comes out clean.

*Frances H. Allen*

## Reception Punch

2½ cups water
4   cups sugar
2   quarts unsweetened pineapple
    juice

2   quarts orange juice
1   pint lemon juice
2½ quarts Collins mix, chilled

Simmer water and sugar 5 minutes. Cool and add to juices. Chill. When ready to serve, combine with Collins mix.

Yield: 2 gallons or 51 5-ounce cups

*Dorothy I. Stuckey*

## Inglewood Plantation Wine Cooler

60 ounces frozen lemonade
    concentrate
4   quarts club soda, chilled
1   pint strawberries (or Bing
    cherries)

12 sprigs mint
1   pint 190 proof grain alcohol
2   gallons white Rhine wine
8   quarts lemon-lime soda or
    Collins mix, chilled

Make 3 or 4 ring molds (bundt pans may be used) of 36 ounces of lemonade concentrate mixed with 2 quarts of the club soda. Float the fruit and mint sprigs in the molds and freeze. Make a concentrate of the alcohol, remaining lemonade concentrate and the wine. Chill.

When ready to serve, place frozen mold in punch bowl and add equal parts of the wine concentrate and lemon-lime soda plus a little club soda. Refill punch bowl as needed. With the last filling, the lemon-lime soda may be omitted because the melting lemonade mold may have sweetened the punch sufficiently.

Yield: 5½ gallons or 140 5-ounce cups

*Polly M. Keller*

# EASTER SUNDAY                          *(Dinner for 8)*

Celebrate Spring's renaissance with these tasteful delicacies.

## *Artichokes Mornay*

## *Leg of Lamb*
## *Herbed Green Beans*       *New Potatoes*
## Rolls

## *Strawberry Molds*   or   *Lemon Meringue Pie*
## Coffee

*French or California Claret*

## Artichokes Mornay

| | |
|---|---|
| 5   tablespoons butter | 1   egg yolk |
| 4½ tablespoons flour | ½   pound mushrooms, thinly sliced |
| 1¾ cups milk | 3   pounds spinach, cooked, |
| Salt and freshly ground pepper |     drained, and chopped |
|    to taste | 8   artichoke bottoms |
| 1   teaspoon grated nutmeg | 3   tablespoons grated Parmesan |
| ⅛   teaspoon cayenne |    cheese |
| ⅜   cup grated Gruyère (or Swiss) | |
|    cheese | |

Melt 3 tablespoons butter in a saucepan and add the flour. When blended, add the milk, stirring rapidly with a whisk. Add salt, pepper, ½ teaspoon nutmeg, and cayenne. Stir in the Gruyère cheese and heat until cheese is melted and blended. Remove from heat and add the yolk, stirring vigorously. Set aside. Sauté mushrooms in remaining butter; sprinkle with salt and pepper. Add the spinach and ½ teaspoon nutmeg. Toss to blend and heat thoroughly.

Spoon a little of the cheese sauce into a flat dish or individual ramekins. Place the artichoke bottoms on top of the sauce and cover with the spinach filling. Spoon the remaining cheese sauce over all and top with the Parmesan cheese. Bake at 400° until hot throughout and bubbling on top. To glaze further, run briefly under the broiler.

*Bertie M. Deming*

## Leg of Lamb

6-pound leg of lamb, boned and
    rolled
1  clove garlic, cut into thin slivers
2  tablespoons salad oil
2  tablespoons flour
1  teaspoon chopped fresh
    rosemary (or half the amount
    dried)

1  teaspoon thyme
¼  teaspoon mace
1  teaspoon marjoram
Salt and freshly ground pepper
    to taste
1  cup dry white wine
1  cup chicken broth

Insert slivers of garlic into meat. Combine oil, flour, and herbs and rub over meat. Sprinkle with salt and pepper. Pour wine and broth over lamb in roasting pan. Bring liquid to a boil in pan on top of the stove, then place roasting pan in oven. Bake 30 minutes at 325°, basting occasionally. Cover and continue cooking 1½ hours longer or until meat thermometer registers desired degree of doneness. Remove lamb; skim fat from pan juices, bring remaining liquid to a boil, and serve with the sliced meat.

*Bertie M. Deming*

## Herbed Green Beans

2  pounds young, tender green
    beans, snapped
6  tablespoons olive oil
2  cloves garlic, minced
2½ tablespoons chopped fresh
    basil

1¼ teaspoons chopped mint
2½ tablespoons minced parsley
2½ cups tomatoes, peeled and
    chopped
Salt to taste

Soak beans for 15 minutes in water to cover; drain. Cook remaining ingredients together for 5 minutes. Blanch beans in boiling salted water for 1 minute; drain and plunge into cold water. Drain. Add to herbs and cook for 15 minutes.

Variation: Add 4 diced new potatoes. Soak with the beans and proceed as above.

*Bertie M. Deming*

## New Potatoes

4  pounds tiny new potatoes,
    unpeeled
4  tablespoons butter

2  tablespoons cream (optional)
2  tablespoons minced parsley
Salt and pepper to taste

Cook potatoes in boiling water to cover until tender when pricked with a fork (about 20 minutes). Drain and stir in remaining ingredients.

Variation: Add 1 to 2 tablespoons chopped mint.

## Strawberry Molds

| | |
|---|---|
| 1   quart strawberries, mashed | 2   cups milk |
| 3⅓ cups sugar | 1   pint heavy cream, slightly |
| 2   tablespoons Curaçao |     whipped |
| 2   eggs, beaten | 1   pint strawberries |

Combine mashed berries with 1⅓ cups sugar and the liqueur. Set aside. Beat remaining 2 cups sugar with eggs and stir in milk. Combine with fruit mixture, fold in whipped cream, and freeze in a 4-quart freezer. Pack into 2 8-cup molds or bundt pans, cover tightly and freeze. Unmold and decorate with remaining berries.

Yield: 3 to 4 quarts

*Caroline K. Gilliland*

## Lemon Meringue Pie

| | |
|---|---|
| 1   cup sugar | 2   teaspoons grated lemon peel |
| 5   tablespoons cornstarch | ⅛   teaspoon salt |
| ⅛   teaspoon salt | 1   teaspoon warm water |
| 2   cups boiling water | 1   tablespoon sugar |
| 3   eggs, separated | ¼   teaspoon lemon extract |
| 1   tablespoon butter |     (optional) |
| 4   tablespoons lemon juice | 1   9-inch pie shell, baked |

Mix first 3 ingredients; add boiling water and cook over very low heat until thick. Cover and cook 8 minutes longer over lowest possible heat (do not uncover). Mixture should become clear and transparent. Beat the egg yolks and pour in a little of the hot mixture, stirring to blend; add a little more hot mixture, blending well again. Pour egg mixture into hot mixture and cook 1 minute, stirring constantly. Remove from heat; mix in the butter, lemon juice and peel. Cool.

Add ⅛ teaspoon salt and the warm water to the egg whites. Whip *by hand* just until stiff. Add the extract and the 1 tablespoon of sugar and continue beating until very stiff.

Pour lemon filling into pie shell, top with meringue, and bake at 300° about 15 minutes or until lightly browned.

*Ann W. Lowrey*

# EASTER EGG HUNT                          *(Picnic for 25)*

Serve this springtime meal outside on the lawn for young and old to enjoy together.

*\*Marinated Crawfish Tails*
*Chicken Sandwiches*

*\*Quiche Lorraine*

*\*Old Southern Stuffed Baked Ham*
*Asparagus*
*Relishes      Rolls*

*\*Banana Cake      Assorted Cookies*

*Lemonade      Coffee*

## Marinated Crawfish Tails

| | |
|---|---|
| 2 pounds cooked and peeled crawfish tails | 1 teaspoon dry mustard |
| 1 onion, chopped | 1 teaspoon salt |
| 1 cup vegetable oil | ¼ teaspoon pepper |
| 3 tablespoons white vinegar | 2 teaspoons minced parsley |
| 2 tablespoons chopped sweet pickle | 2 teaspoons minced chives |
| | 2 tablespoons drained capers |

Layer crawfish and onions. Heat next 6 ingredients to boiling. Stir in remaining ingredients and pour over crawfish mixture. Cover and refrigerate at least 24 hours. Drain and serve with toothpicks.

*Louise A. Simon*

## Chicken Sandwiches

Make about 50 chicken sandwiches, using 2 pounds sliced chicken and 2 loaves bread spread with mayonnaise. Cut into thirds and serve to hungry egg-hunters.

## Quiche Lorraine

3   9-inch pie shells, baked 5
    minutes at 400°
4½ cups grated Gruyère cheese
    (Swiss or Muenster may be
    substituted)
9   slices bacon, cooked and
    crumbled
1½ cup sliced mushrooms, sautéed
    (optional)

1½ cups chopped green onions,
    sautéed (optional)
9   eggs, beaten
3 to 4 cups milk or cream
1½ teaspoons salt
¼   teaspoon pepper
¼   teaspoon nutmeg
Cayenne to taste
6   tablespoons butter

Sprinkle bacon and cheese (also sautéed vegetables, if included) over bottom of pie shells. Combine milk, eggs, and seasonings and pour over all. Dot with butter. Bake in upper third of oven at 375° for 25 to 30 minutes, until puffed and brown.

*Caroline K. Gilliland*

## Old Southern Stuffed Baked Ham

10 to 12 pound ham, hock
    removed
1   tablespoon vinegar
2   tablespoon brown sugar
1   pound crackers, toasted and
    ground
1   15-ounce loaf of bread, toasted
    and ground
2   tablespoons sugar
1   teaspoon mustard seed

1   teaspoon dry mustard
1   rib celery, ground
2   onions, ground
½   cup pickle relish
1   tablespoon minced parsley
4   eggs, beaten
1   cup sherry
4   dashes Tabasco
Vinegar to combine dressing
    ingredients

Steam ham in water to which the 1 tablespoon vinegar and the brown sugar have been added. Cook until meat is tender enough to feel loose at the bone, about 2 hours. Cool; remove bone and fat. Reserve 1 cup of the fat and grind coarsely. Combine this with all the remaining ingredients, using enough vinegar to make a pastelike consistency; mix well. Stuff cavity in ham with part of the dressing and cover the outside of the ham with the remainder. Wrap securely with cheesecloth and tie tightly with cord. Bake at 300° for 30 minutes. Chill 24 hours; slice thinly.

*Old Southern Tea Room*
*Vicksburg, Mississippi*

## *Banana Cake*

| | |
|---|---|
| ½ pound butter | 2 teaspoons baking soda |
| 2 cups sugar | 1 cup milk |
| 2 eggs | 1¾ cup mashed bananas |
| 3 cups sifted flour | |

Cream butter and sugar; add eggs and beat well. Sift flour and soda together and add to butter mixture alternately with milk. Stir in bananas. Pour into 3 greased and floured 9-inch layer pans. Bake at 350° for 30 minutes or until a cake tester comes out clean. Cool 10 minutes, remove from pans and spread with the following frosting.

### *Cream Cheese Frosting*

| | |
|---|---|
| 8 ounces cream cheese, at room temperature | 1 teaspoon vanilla |
| | 1 to 2 tablespoons milk |
| 1 pound confectioners' sugar, sifted | 1 cup chopped pecans, toasted |

Mix cheese and sugar; add vanilla and milk gradually until spreading consistency is achieved. Spread on partially cooled cake; sprinkle pecans on each frosted layer before stacking.

*Bee H. Randolph*

# LET THE GOOD TIMES ROLL! *(Crawfish Boil for 20)*

*"Laissez les bons temps rouler"* is the catchy phrase that resounds in south Louisiana when it's time for a party. And no occasion calls more for fun and merriment than does a real crawfish boil in bayou country. Large amounts can be cooked outdoors more easily using a butane gas flame, or Cajun Cooker. Newspapers on the tables, large plastic garbage bags and plenty of napkins are a must.

### Crawfish
### Melted Butter and/or Cocktail Sauce
### New Potatoes        Corn on the Cob
### Saltines
### Beer and/or Soft drinks

### Assorted Cookies
### Coffee

| | | | |
|---|---|---|---|
| 80 | pounds live crawfish (2 sacks) | 4 | tablespoons garlic powder (optional) |
| 9 | 3-ounce bags Crab Boil | | |
| 5 | 4-ounce bottles liquid Crab Boil | 4 | tablespoons chili powder (optional) |
| 9 to 10 | 26-ounce boxes salt | | |
| 2 | ounces Tabasco | 12 | lemons, halved |
| 12 | onions, quartered | 50 | new potatoes |
| 4 | tablespoons cayenne (optional) | 30 | ears corn |

In an 8-gallon pot, bring to a boil 4 gallons water, adding 3 bags Crab Boil, 2 bottles Crab Boil, 4 boxes salt, ½ ounce Tabasco, 6 onions, 1 tablespoon cayenne, 1 tablespoon garlic powder and 1 tablespoon chili powder. Squeeze and toss in 6 lemons. Simmer 15 minutes.

Meanwhile, it is necessary to purge the crawfish. While some guests are helping with this chore, let others shuck the corn and set it aside. Empty the crawfish into a wheelbarrow (or tub), sprinkle liberally with salt and fill container with water from the garden hose. Let set about 5 minutes, stirring occasionally with a stick. Pour off water; rinse crawfish thoroughly and repeat purging if water is "too" dirty. Remove any dead crawfish and discard.

Add about 20 pounds of crawfish slowly to pot. Return to boil and let cook about 10 minutes. Turn off heat, cover and let steam 10 to 15 minutes. Remove crawfish and serve. Discard any crawfish whose tail is straight (uncurled).

Reheat stock; add corn and potatoes. Boil 7 minutes or until done. Remove vegetables and serve.

Add 2 bags Crab Boil, 1 bottle Crab Boil, 1 box salt, ½ ounce Tabasco, 2 onions, 1 tablespoon cayenne, 1 tablespoon garlic powder, 1 tablespoon chili powder and 2 lemons. Return to boil. Add about 20 more pounds of crawfish and repeat cooking process. With each additional batch of crawfish, adjust seasonings and cook as directed.

Variation: Substitute shrimp for crawfish, allowing about 2 pounds live shrimp per person. After water has boiled for 15 minutes, add shrimp, turn off heat, cover and let steam for 15 minutes or until shrimp are bright pink.

*Norman J. Chenevert*
*James D. Neilson, Jr.*

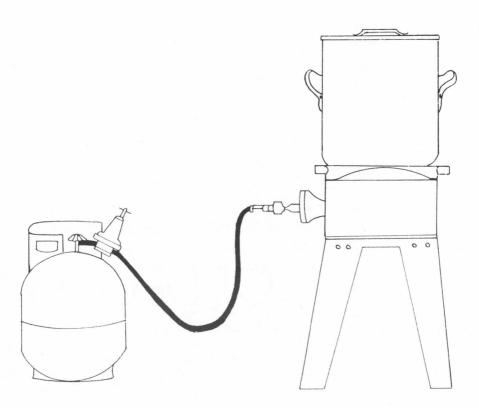

# FÊTE ACCOMPLIE          *(Wedding Reception for 100)*

Large Louisiana families enjoy an informal home celebration when relatives and friends gather to rejoice after a marriage ceremony.

Close friends each bring a specialty to add to the feast. When asked, "What can I do?", request a favorite bread, cake, pickle, or relish. Other friends may be asked to cut flowers from their gardens, to soak them neck-deep in buckets of water overnight, and to deliver them the morning before the party. Enlist your most creative and willing kin to spend half a day arranging and placing these blossoms inside and out (augmented by masses of greenery, also presoaked, from yards or nearby woods). Other relatives and friends may be assigned to help supervise food and drink service. The result is a warm, friendly atmosphere which makes everyone feel a real part of the celebration.

By all means, have music; a group of musicians providing light and lively melodies adds incomparably to the joyousness of mood and spirit at such a fête.

*Champagne Punch        *Wedding Punch*
*or*
*Champagne*

*Turkey      Ham*
*Homemade Breads*
*Mustard and Mayonnaise*

*\*Assorted Pickles*

*Watermelon Basket of Fruit*
*Bride's Cake        \*Groom's Cake*
*\*Variety of Homebaked Cakes*

*Coffee*

Parties of this type vary so in the number of guests that this one is presented for 100 and may serve as a guide for a larger number. If there is music and dancing, and guests are expected to stay for several hours, at least 15 ounces of liquid refreshment should be planned for each person. For a shorter anticipated stay, 10 ounces per guest should be sufficient. If champagne is to be the only liquid refreshment, 5 cases of 12 fifths each would furnish the above mentioned 15 ounces of liquid for 100 guests. Three cases would give each guest 10 ounces.

The following are suggested quantities of the other menu items:

Turkey: One uncarved 10 to 12 pound turkey, baked and garnished, for the center of the platter, to be surrounded by 25 pounds of sliced turkey

Ham: One 6-pound bone-in ham, baked and decorated, plus 10 pounds of ham slices for platter

Breads: 20 loaves of assorted kinds (white, whole wheat, herb, etc.), thinly cut into about 300 slices

Mustard: 2 pints

Mayonnaise: 2 quarts

Pickles: 5 or more pints of various kinds

Fruit: 2 gallons assorted fruits in season to fill watermelon basket

Cakes: 6 to 10 cakes plus a traditional white wedding cake

Coffee: 3 to 4 gallons, plus 2 pounds of sugar and 1 quart of cream

## Champagne Punch

7   fifths champagne, chilled
7   fifths sauterne, chilled

5   quarts club soda, chilled
1   pint strawberries

Fill punch bowl with 1 fifth each champagne and sauterne and ¾ quart of soda. For an attractive garnish, float whole strawberries with hulls. Refill bowls as needed with these same proportions.

Yield: 4 gallons 1 pint, or 104 5-ounce cups

*Molly K. Stagg*

## Wedding Punch

4   cups sugar
1   cup warm water
2   gallons water
48  ounces frozen orange juice
       concentrate

48  ounces frozen lemonade
       concentrate
4   46-ounce cans pineapple juice
6   28-ounce bottles ginger ale

Dissolve sugar in warm water. Mix with juices and water. For each filling of the punch bowl, pour 3 quarts of the juice mixture over the ice cubes or a frozen lemonade ring and add 1 bottle of ginger ale.

Yield: 5½ gallons or 141 5-ounce cups.

*Myrtle M. Montgomery*

## Pickled Okra

7   cloves garlic, peeled
7   hot peppers
7   teaspoons dill seed
4   pounds young, tender okra
       pods, stems removed

1   quart cider vinegar
1   cup water
½   cup salt

Into each hot sterilized jar, place 1 clove garlic, 1 hot pepper and 1 tea-spoon dill seed. Pack each jar firmly with okra. Bring remaining ingredients to a boil and simmer for 5 minutes. Pour over okra and seal immediately.

Yield: 7 pints

*Annie S. Johnson*

## Bread and Butter Pickles

| | | | |
|---|---|---|---|
| 1 | gallon cucumbers, thinly sliced | 5 | cups vinegar |
| 8 | white onions, thinly sliced | 2 | tablespoons mustard seed |
| 2 | green peppers (optional) | 1½ | teaspoons turmeric |
| ½ | cup salt | ½ | teaspoon ground cloves |
| | Ice cubes | | (optional) |
| 5 | cups sugar | 1 | teaspoon celery seed |

Combine cucumbers, onions and peppers with salt. Bury ice cubes in the mixture, cover and let stand for 3 hours. Drain. Bring remaining ingredients to the scalding point but do not boil; pour over cucumbers. Seal in hot sterilized jars.

Yield: 7 to 8 pints

*Jean A. Lafleur*

## Zucchini Pickles

| | | | |
|---|---|---|---|
| 4 | zucchini, thinly sliced | 2 | cups vinegar |
| 3 | white onions, thinly sliced | 1 | teaspoon celery seed |
| ¼ | cup salt | 2 | teaspoons mustard seed |
| 2 | cups sugar | 1 | teaspoon turmeric |

Sprinkle salt on zucchini and onions; add water to cover and let stand 2 hours. Drain. Combine with other ingredients and bring to a simmer. Remove from heat and let stand 2 hours. Return to heat and simmer for 5 minutes. Seal in hot sterilized jars.

Yield: 3 pints

*Lola M. Gilkison*

## Green Tomato Pickles

| | | | |
|---|---|---|---|
| 5 | pounds green tomatoes | 1 | teaspoon mace |
| 7 | white onions, sliced | 1 | teaspoon ground cloves |
| 1 | cup salt | 1 | tablespoon celery seed |
| 2 | quarts white vinegar | 1 | pound brown sugar |
| 1 | teaspoon cayenne | 2 | cups white sugar |
| 1 | teaspoon dry mustard | 4 | ounces mustard seed |
| 1 | teaspoon turmeric | | |

Remove stem end and blemishes from tomatoes and slice. Layer with onions and salt in a large ceramic bowl or crock. Cover with dish towel and let stand overnight. Drain. Cover with 1½ quarts vinegar and boil slowly until tender crisp in a stainless or ceramic pot. Drain. When cool, stir in cayenne, mustard, and turmeric. Add the remaining ingredients to the pint of vinegar and bring just to a rolling boil. Pour immediately over tomatoes and onions. Place in sterilized jars and seal when cold.

Yield: 7 to 8 pints

*Frances B. Davis*

## Squash Pickles

| | |
|---|---|
| 8 cups thinly sliced young, tender yellow squash | 1 tablespoon celery seed |
| ⅔ cup salt | 1 tablespoon mustard seed |
| 3 cups water | 2 cups thinly sliced onions |
| 3 cups sugar | 2 green peppers, sliced into strips |
| 2 cups vinegar | 1 4-ounce jar chopped pimientos, drained (optional) |

Cover squash with salt and water; let stand 1 hour. Drain. Bring next 4 ingredients to a boil. Add squash and remaining ingredients, return to boil and pour into hot sterilized jars. Seal.

Yield: 6 pints

*Betty H. Deumite*

## Sweet Pickle Chunks

| | |
|---|---|
| 6 quarts cucumbers, sliced lengthwise into fingers | 3 pints vinegar |
| 1 cup salt | 1½ teaspoons cinnamon |
| Boiling water as directed | 1 tablespoon celery seed |
| 1½ teaspoons alum | 1 tablespoon pickling spice |
| | 5 cups sugar |

Add the salt to 1 gallon of the boiling water, pour over cucumbers, and allow to stand 1 week. Drain; pour 2 quarts boiling water over cucumbers and let stand 24 hours. Drain; add 2 quarts boiling water and the alum. Let stand 24 hours; drain. Boil together the remaining ingredients and pour over pickles. Seal in hot sterilized jars.

Yield: 4 quarts

*Hope J. Norman*

## Dill Pickles

7  pounds cucumbers, each about       Fresh dill, or 8 to 10 tablespoons
   3 inches long                          dill seed plus 8 to 10 teaspoons
1  whole pod garlic, peeled and          dill weed
   cut into slivers                   1  quart white vinegar
8 to 10 tablespoons pickling spice    1  cup salt
8 to 10 hot peppers (optional)        3  quarts water

Soak cucumbers in cold water about 15 minutes; drain. Pack tightly into quart jars, cutting last few cucumbers to fill spaces at top. Distribute seasonings evenly among jars. Bring vinegar, salt and water to a rolling boil and pour into jars, filling to the top to cover cucumbers completely. Make additional brine if necessary to fill jars. Seal. Let stand 1 to 2 weeks. Refrigerate after opening.
   Yield:  8 to 10 quarts

*J. Herman Katz*


## Groom's Cake

5   tablespoons sifted cocoa          1  teaspoon baking soda
2½ cups sugar                         1  cup buttermilk, at room
½  pound butter or margarine, at         temperature
    room temperature                  3  teaspoons vanilla
5   eggs, separated, at room          2⅓ cups sifted flour
    temperature

Mix cocoa and sugar. Cream butter with this mixture at medium speed until it is the consistency of whipped cream. Add egg yolks. Blend soda with buttermilk and vanilla and add to batter alternately with flour, beginning and ending with flour. By hand, fold in stiffly beaten egg whites. Pour into 4 greased and floured 9-inch layer pans, knocking pans of batter on table to jar out bubbles before putting into oven. Bake at 350° for about 20 minutes or until barely done, not browned. (Layers will be thin.) Cool and frost with the following icing.

### Chocolate Icing

3  cups sugar                         1  teaspoon vanilla
2  tablespoons cocoa                  2  tablespoons butter or margarine
1¼ cups milk

Cook sugar, cocoa and milk until mixture forms a soft ball in cold water (235° on candy thermometer). Remove from heat and, without stirring, cool until lukewarm. Add vanilla and butter. Beat until creamy and spread on cake. It is usually necessary to add additional milk or warm water as cake is being iced to prevent the icing hardening before all layers are covered. This cake is best when made several days before serving. Freezes well.

*Nena M. Love*

## Yellow Cake

3   cups sifted cake flour
3   teaspoons baking powder
½   teaspoon salt
½   pound butter or margarine, softened

2   cups sugar
5   eggs, at room temperature
1   cup milk, at room temperature
3   teaspoons vanilla

Resift cake flour 4 times with baking powder and salt. Cream butter and sugar together until light and fluffy. Add eggs 1 at a time, beating after each addition. Add flour mixture alternately with milk and vanilla combined, beginning and ending with flour. Pour batter into 3 greased and floured 9-inch cake pans; bake at 350° for 25 to 30 minutes. (Arrange pans in oven so that none of the pans touches the sides of the oven or each other, and none sits directly over the other.) Allow cake to stand a minute, then invert onto racks to cool. Frost with Caramel Icing (page 188) or the Chocolate Icing above.

*Nena M. Love*

## Kateland Plantation Lemon Cake

2   tablespoons very soft butter or margarine
¼   cup fine dry bread crumbs
3¾  cups sifted cake flour
2½  teaspoons baking powder
1   teaspoon salt
½   pound plus 4 tablespoons butter or margarine, softened

2½  cups sugar
5   eggs, at room temperature
3   tablespoons grated lemon peel
1¼  cups milk, at room temperature
⅔   cup sugar
⅓   cup lemon juice

Spread the 2 tablespoons soft butter evenly in a 10-inch tube pan and dust with bread crumbs. (This forms a lovely crust when the cake is baked). Sift flour, baking powder and salt together. Beat remaining butter, 2½ cups sugar, eggs and lemon peel at high speed for 3 minutes. Stir in by hand flour mixture alternately with milk, beating after each addition until batter is smooth. Spoon carefully into prepared pan, smooth the top, and bake at 325° for 1¾ hours or until top springs back when lightly pressed with finger tips. Loosen cake at tube edge; turn out onto a wire rack.

To glaze, combine the ⅔ cup sugar and lemon juice in a saucepan. Heat slowly, stirring constantly, just until the sugar is dissolved. Brush some of the glaze onto the sides of the hot cake, then drizzle the remaining glaze evenly over the top. Cool. Freezes well.

*Bee H. Randolph*

# SUMMERTIME                        *(Cookout for 25)*

Perfect for a 4th of July family reunion.

### *Pickled Eggs*
### *Grapes, Cherries, and Melon Wedges*

### *Barbecued Chuck Roast*
### *Potato Salad*
### *Baked Beans*
### *Buns      *Grilled Corn*
### *Pickles      Sliced Tomatoes*

### *Vanilla Ice Cream with Peaches*
### *Iced Tea      Coffee*

*Côte d'or red or California Pinot Noir*

## Pickled Eggs

| | |
|---|---|
| 2 cups white vinegar | 2 slices lemon |
| 2 tablespoons sugar | 1 cayenne pepper (optional) |
| 2 tablespoons salt | Beet juice for coloring (optional) |
| 4 teaspoons pickling spice | 2 dozen hard-boiled eggs |
| 2 cloves garlic, sliced | |

   Simmer first 7 ingredients together for 5 minutes, stirring to blend. Remove from heat and add enough beet juice to make liquid dark red. Pour over the eggs, cover and refrigerate 1 to 2 weeks.

*Claire S. Bordelon*

## Barbecued Chuck Roast

| | |
|---|---|
| 12 to 14 pound boneless rolled chuck roast | 2 tablespoons cracked black pepper |
| 3 tablespoons barbecue spice | ¾ teaspoon celery salt |
| 2 teaspoons hickory smoked salt | 28 ounces catsup |
| 2 cloves garlic, crushed | 12 ounces tomato sauce |
| 2 dried red peppers, crushed (or cayenne to taste) | 1 teaspoon garlic powder |
| 4 tablespoons lemon juice | ¼ pound butter |
| ¼ cup soy sauce | 8 ounces Worcestershire sauce |
| 1½ cup salad oil | 4 tablespoons lemon juice |

   Place roast in a large bowl; combine next 9 ingredients and pour over meat. Refrigerate overnight. Combine remaining ingredients to make sauce and bring to a boil; simmer 30 minutes. Set aside.

Build hot charcoal fire in grill which has a cover. Drain roast, reserving marinade. Sear meat on all sides on grill. Baste with marinade. Cover grill and cook meat 6 to 8 hours, turning and basting frequently with remaining marinade. During last hour or so of cooking, baste with some of the barbecue sauce. Insert meat thermometer and continue cooking to desired degree of doneness. Allow to stand 30 minutes. Slice and serve with remaining barbecue sauce.

*Tom D. Norman*
*Jimmie C. Normand*

## Potato Salad

5 to 8 pounds red potatoes
6 cups mayonnaise
¾ cup wine vinegar
6 tablespoons lemon juice

12 hard-boiled eggs, chopped
9 green onions and tops, minced
3 tablespoons Dijon mustard
Salt and pepper to taste

Boil potatoes in water to cover for 25 to 30 minutes. Drain, chill, peel and chop into 1-inch cubes. Mix remaining ingredients and fold in potatoes. Refrigerate immediately.

*Estha W. Heyman*

## Grilled Corn

40 ears of corn
½ pound butter

Salt and pepper to taste

Shuck corn and remove silks. Wrap each ear in heavy foil, dotting with butter and seasoning before sealing. Place on grill and cook with top closed 30 minutes, turning occasionally.

## Vanilla Ice Cream with Peaches

2 quarts homogenized milk
2 tablespoons cornstarch
2 cups sugar
8 eggs
2 13-ounce cans evaporated milk

3 tablespoons vanilla
½ teaspoon salt
2 quarts peeled and sliced peaches, sugared

Bring homogenized milk to a boil in large saucepan. Blend next 3 ingredients in mixer until smooth. Gradually add some of the hot milk. Pour egg mixture into saucepan with remaining hot milk; cook over low heat, stirring constantly until thick and being careful not to scorch. Remove from heat and stir in evaporated milk, vanilla and salt. Cool immediately in refrigerator. Freeze in 1½ gallon freezer. Serve accompanied by chilled peaches.

Yield: 5 quarts

*Dorothy I. Stuckey*

# COCHON DE LAIT          *(Roast Suckling Pig for 20)*

Central Louisiana parishes (counties to the rest of the United States) are famous for their "cochon de lait" festivals, gala gatherings where piglets are slowly roasted outdoors over hot hickory fires tended by enthusiastic chefs. Perhaps the pig roast is in conjunction with a "coup de main" ("helping hand") when neighbors come to share in a task needing to be done. Whatever the excuse, the succulent pig's tantalizing aroma provokes enormous appetites. "Dirty rice"—spicy, and dingy brown in color—is the traditional accompaniment to this feast.

*Keg of Beer*
*\*Roast Suckling Pig*
*\*Dirty Rice        \*No-toss Salad*
*French Bread*

*Assorted Cookies*
*Coffee*

Equipment:

2   2×3-foot pieces reinforced steel wire or hog fence wire, with 5 to 6-inch square grids

| | |
|---|---|
| Baling wire | Firewood |
| Shovel | 5-foot pipe |
| 8-inch concrete blocks | 2 wood stakes |
| Charcoal | |

## Roast Suckling Pig

| | |
|---|---|
| 40 to 50 pound suckling pig, dressed | 1   tablespoon cayenne |
| 5   tablespoons salt | 1   tablespoon paprika |
| 1   tablespoon black pepper | 1   tablespoon garlic powder |
| | 1   tablespoon chili powder |

Have butcher remove the pig's head and the feet at the knee joints. Stomach cavity should be split open and a vertical cut made on each side of rib cage along inside of backbone—thus enabling pig to be opened flat. Ribs should not be cut all the way through to skin, lest the pig fall apart upon being cooked.

Stretch pig between the 2 pieces of wire. Secure the 4 corners and sides of the 2 grids with the pig between, using baling wire.

Combine the seasonings and sprinkle the powder generously on the pig, rubbing well into the skin. Reserve half of the powder for use later during cooking.

Dig an 8 to 10-inch deep trench measuring about 3 by 4 feet. Stack concrete blocks at each end of pit. Build a brisk fire of charcoal and wood and allow to burn down to make a good bed of hot coals. With a shovel or rake, pull fire to each side of pit.

Wire the pipe lengthwise to the racked pig and place it across pit with each end of rod lying atop the concrete blocks. Pig should be approximately 15 to 20 inches above fire. Balance rack with notched stake on each side of pit.

Turn pig about every 30 to 45 minutes, adding logs to the fire as needed. Sprinkle additional barbecue powder on pig twice more during cooking. After about 4 hours of cooking, back skin becomes brown and crisp and may be cut off and sliced to serve as "cracklings", hot crisp hor d'oeuvres to be eaten on the spot or saved for later use in cooking.

Pierce pig occasionally with a sharp fork to allow fat to drip out. Pig is done when fat stops dripping and leg bones move easily.

Remove meat from rack and carve.

An alternate method of cooking: Suspend racked pig in front of an open fire with a tin backdrop to reflect heat. Cook as above. (Requires more firewood.)

*James D. Neilson, Jr.*

## Dirty Rice

| | | | |
|---|---|---|---|
| 1 | cup cooking oil | 4 | cloves garlic, chopped |
| 1 | pound ground beef | ½ | green pepper, chopped |
| ½ | pound ground pork | | Salt, pepper, and Worcestershire |
| ½ | pound chicken livers and | | sauce to taste |
| | gizzards, ground | 15 | cups cooked rice (2 pounds |
| 4 | onions, chopped | | raw) |
| 4 | ribs celery, chopped | | |

Brown the meats in the oil, mixing together well. Add the chopped vegetables and seasonings and cook until vegetables are soft. Mix with rice. Bake in 2 3-quart casseroles at 350° until hot (10 to 15 minutes).

Meat and vegetable mixture may be made in quantity and kept in freezer, adding freshly steamed rice when ready to heat for serving.

*W. C. Earnest, Jr.*

## No-toss Salad

| | | | |
|---|---|---|---|
| 2 | heads lettuce, torn | 2 | tablespoons sugar |
| ½ | cup chopped green onions | 2 | pounds bacon, cooked and |
| ½ | cup chopped celery | | crumbled (optional) |
| 2 | 10-ounce packages frozen green | 8 | hard-boiled eggs, sliced |
| | peas, partially thawed | ¼ | pound Parmesan or Romano |
| 1 | quart mayonnaise | | cheese, grated |

Place a layer of lettuce in a large rectangular dish. Cover with the next 3 ingredients. Spread mayonnaise on top and sprinkle with sugar. Refrigerate overnight, covered. To serve, scatter bacon and arrange egg slices on top; sprinkle with cheese. Cut into squares.

*Fritzie B. Fine*

# OYSTER ROAST

*(Serves 16)*

An impromptu party which must be held outside for an informal evening of food and fun.

### Raw Oysters    Smoked Sausage
### Cheese and Crackers

### Roasted Oysters
### Clarified Butter and French Bread

### Assorted Cookies
### Coffee

*Beer or Chablis*

Equipment:

8 pairs of work gloves, for handling raw oysters
8 oyster knives
Newspaper
Paper napkins
2 pairs of asbestos gloves, for handling hot oysters
Large outdoor grill with charcoal
Burlap sack
Large washtub, filled with ice
16 cups for sauce
Toothpicks

Grocery List:

2   95-pound sacks of oysters
3   14-ounce bottles tomato catsup
36  lemons
2   8-ounce jars horseradish
2   2-ounce bottles Tabasco
4   16-ounce boxes saltines
3   pounds smoked sausage
4   pounds assorted cheeses
4   loaves French bread

Spread newspapers on picnic tables and forget about plates or utensils. Hose off oysters thoroughly and pack in ice. As guests gather, start charcoal fire in grill. Each person may open his own oysters for eating raw with his individually concocted cocktail sauce. To open raw oysters, put point of oyster knife into hinge of shell and twist sharply.

Cut sausage into 1-inch lengths and heat on grill. Serve with toothpicks accompanied by cheese and crackers.

Steam remaining oysters over hot fire, placing unopened shells directly on grill and covering with damp burlap sack. Roast until they begin to open by themselves or until they open easily when tested with oyster knife, about 20 minutes. Serve with warm clarified butter.

### *Clarified Butter*

2 pounds butter

Heat butter slowly in heavy saucepan. When completely melted, remove from heat carefully. Strain through at least 4 thicknesses of cheesecloth into serving container. Keeps indefinitely without refrigeration.

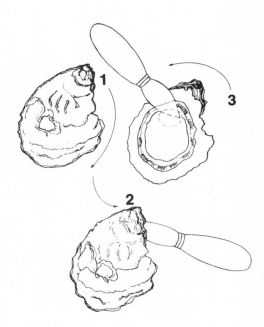

# THANKSGIVING *(Dinner for 12)*

A unique regional method of preparing the traditional turkey, served with a host of seasonal specialties.

### *Artichokes with Lemon Butter*

#### *Turkey Louisiane*
#### *Cranberry Relish*   *Cornbread Dressing*
#### *Cushaw-Stuffed Oranges*   *Scalloped Oysters*
#### *Rolls*

#### *Pumpkin Pie*  or  *Pumpkin Chiffon Pie*
#### *Ambrosia*

#### *Coffee*

*Light Claret or rich white wine*

### Artichokes with Lemon Butter

| | |
|---|---|
| 12 artichokes | 1 teaspoon black pepper |
| 2 ribs celery with leaves | 2 teaspoons cooking oil (optional) |
| 2 onions, quartered | Dash cayenne for each pot |
| 2 cloves garlic | ½ pound butter |
| 2 lemons, halved | Lemon juice and cayenne to taste |
| 2 tablespoons salt | |

Remove tough stem and bottom leaves from artichokes. Place artichokes in 2 large pots, cover with cold water and soak 1 hour. Divide seasonings equally between pots, squeezing lemon pieces upon adding. Simmer about 45 minutes or until an outer leaf is easily removed.

Melt butter in saucepan over medium heat. Skim off foam and pour clear yellow liquid into a bowl; add lemon juice and cayenne to taste. Serve with artichokes.

## Turkey Louisiane

| | |
|---|---|
| 2 onions | ¼ pound butter |
| 1 green pepper | 12 to 15 pound turkey |
| 6 cloves garlic | Salt |
| 1 teaspoon pepper | |

Purée onions, green pepper, garlic and pepper. Sauté in butter to make a paste. Rub turkey all over with salt and pierce skin. Coat with vegetable paste, cover and refrigerate overnight.

Roast breast down at 325° for 15 to 20 minutes per pound or until thermometer registers 185°.

*Lisa L. Norman*

## Cranberry Relish

| | |
|---|---|
| 1 pound cranberries | 2 cups sugar |
| 1 orange, peeled, seeded and sectioned | ½ cup water |
| | 1 teaspoon grated orange peel |

Combine all ingredients in saucepan and simmer about 10 minutes or until berries pop open. Skim foam and cool. Flavor is best if prepared not more than 4 hours prior to serving.

*Lillie G. Sanders*

## Cornbread Dressing

| | |
|---|---|
| Turkey neck and giblets | ½ to 1 cup minced mushrooms |
| 1 carrot | ½ cup chopped pecans (optional) |
| 1 onion | 2 tablespoons minced parsley |
| 1 rib celery, including leaves | 1 tablespoon salt |
| 2 sprigs parsley | Black pepper and cayenne to taste |
| Salt and pepper to taste | Sage, rosemary, savory, thyme |
| ½ pound smoked sausage or bacon | and/or crumbled bay leaf to taste |
| 1 cup minced green pepper | 3 cups crumbled cornbread |
| 1 cup minced onion | 3 cups bread crumbs |
| 1 cup minced celery, including leaves | 4 eggs, beaten |
| 1 clove garlic, minced | 2 tablespoons celery seed (optional) |

Add first 5 ingredients to 1 quart of water. Season and simmer 1 hour. Skim broth, strain and reserve.

Brown sausage or bacon in a large heavy pan. Remove meat and all but 3 tablespoons drippings. Sauté green pepper, onion, celery and garlic over medium heat about 10 minutes or until limp. Add mushrooms, parsley, nuts and seasonings. Cook briefly; remove from heat and stir in combread and bread crumbs. Add remaining ingredients and enough broth so that mixture is moist but not soupy. Pour into 2-quart casserole and bake at 350° for 1 hour.

Doubles easily; freezes well.

*Caroline K. Gilliland*

## Scalloped Oysters

5 cups crushed saltine crackers
2½ quarts oysters, drained, liquor reserved
1½ cups minced parsley
¾ cup minced green onions

½ pound butter or margarine
Seasoned salt or Tony's Creole Seasoning
Pepper
Milk

Place a layer of cracker crumbs in a greased 4-quart casserole; cover with a layer of oysters. Sprinkle with seasonings and dot with butter. Repeat layers, ending with crumbs and butter. Measure oyster liquor and combine with an equal amount of milk. Pour over oysters just before baking at 350° for 20 minutes or until bubbling.

*Mary Jo M. Mansour*

## Cushaw-Stuffed Oranges

4 cups sugar
2 cups water
6 large navel oranges
1 6-pound cushaw

¼ pound butter
½ cup sugar
½ teaspoon nutmeg

Make a simple syrup by dissolving 4 cups sugar in the water and boiling 5 minutes. Halve oranges, remove seeds, scoop out pulp and reserve. Place orange shells in large skillet, cut side up; add simple syrup and orange pulp. Cover and simmer about 1 hour or until candied.

Halve the cushaw, remove seeds, oil the skins and place in shallow pan to bake at 350° about 1 hour or until tender. Scoop out pulp and mash with butter, ½ cup sugar, nutmeg and ½ to 1 cup syrup from candied shells. Fill orange shells with cushaw mixture and bake in shallow pan, coated with enough syrup to cover bottom, for 20 minutes at 350°. (Reserved orange syrup is great in old-fashioneds!)

Variation: 5 cups cooked, mashed sweet potatoes may be substituted for the cushaw.

*Dorothy I. Stuckey*

## Pumpkin Pie

½  cup light brown sugar, packed
½  cup sugar
1   teaspoon cinnamon
1   teaspoon ginger
¼  teaspoon cloves
½  teaspoon salt
1½ cups cooked, mashed pumpkin

2   eggs, beaten
1   cup cream or milk, warmed
1   9-inch pie shell
1   cup heavy cream, whipped with
    1 teaspoon sugar and 1
    tablespoon or more cream
    sherry

Sift dry ingredients and blend with pumpkin. Add eggs and beat until smooth; stir in cream or milk. Pour into pie shell. Bake 10 minutes at 425°, reduce heat to 350° and continue baking 40 minutes or until toothpick comes out clean. Serve warm, topped with flavored whipped cream.

*Kathryn P. Keller*

## Pumpkin Chiffon Pie

1   9-inch pie shell, baked
1   tablespoon gelatin
¼  cup water
2   eggs, separated
¾  cup sugar
1½ cups cooked, mashed pumpkin
⅔  cup milk

½  teaspoon salt
2   teaspoons pumpkin pie spice or
    1 teaspoon cinnamon, ¼
    teaspoon nutmeg, ½ teaspoon
    ginger
½  teaspoon orange extract
1   cup heavy cream, whipped

Soften gelatin in water. In the top of a double boiler, beat egg yolks; stir in ½ cup sugar, pumpkin, milk and salt. Cook over boiling water for 10 minutes, stirring constantly. Remove from heat, stir in gelatin and cool until partially set. Beat egg whites until foamy. Combine ¼ cup sugar and spices, adding gradually to whites. Add extract and beat until stiff. Gently fold pumpkin mixture into egg white mixture and pour into pie shell. Chill until set. Top with whipped cream.

*Mary Frances L. James*

## Ambrosia

6 apples, peeled and cut in wedges
6 to 8 navel oranges, peeled, seeded and sectioned, juice reserved

2 15-ounce cans pineapple chunks, drained, juice reserved
Grated meat of 4 coconuts (approximately 8 cups)
Sugar to taste

In a large crystal bowl layer the apples, oranges and pineapple. Sprinkle with a generous amount of coconut followed by sugar. Repeat layers. Pour orange juice over all, then about ½ cup of the reserved pineapple juice. Cover and refrigerate.

*Jane W. Smith*

# FAMILY HOLIDAY PARTY                    *(Buffet for 60)*

A multigenerational Christmas week gathering that everyone can enjoy. From red-cheeked toddlers to collegiates home from school to their visiting grandparents, whole families mingle in an atmosphere of easy goodwill.

In respect for the bedtimes of both extremes in age, set early hours for the party. Plan the festivities to spread throughout your house: decorate with fresh greenery and well-polished fruits; fill fireplaces with wood for roaring fires; place sturdy nativity scenes within reach of little hands. Besides having your piano ready for caroling, ask musical friends to provide songs and ballads with flute, banjo, or guitar. Let everyone's favorite storyteller delight the children—their parents will be equally wide-eyed.

Arriving guests can sample white wine or cider, which will not harm party clothes if spilled in the excitement. On gleaming wood tables arrange an abundance of meats, fruits, breads, and platters of cheese. Trays of cookies may attract the children, but don't be surprised if a pixy in red velvet samples oysters Rockefeller, while her uncle munches a Santa Claus cookie with his eggnog. Effect a setting in which good cheer will grow; relax, and enjoy it!

*White Wine      Spiced Apple Cider*
*\*Zesty Pecans*
*Cheese and Crackers*
*Bowls of Apples and Tangerines*

*Smithfield Ham      Smoked Turkey*
*Rolls*
*Mayonnaise and Mustard*
*\*Oysters Rockefeller Canapés      \*Sherried Shrimp*

*\*Cherry Nut Cake      \*Lizzies*
*\*Date Nut Cake      \*Spice Cookies*
*\*Raisin Nut Cake      \*Lollipops*

*\*Gala Eggnog*
*Coffee*

To plan adequate amounts, have 2 gallons of cider (recipe page 53), 12 to 15 fifths of chilled white wine, 6 to 8 pounds of assorted cheeses, 4 boxes of crackers, 2 dozen each of apples and tangerines, a 12-pound ham, a 16-pound turkey, 10 dozen rolls, 1 quart mayonnaise, 1 pint mustard, 2 boxes Melba toast rounds, and the following:

## Zesty Pecans

¼ pound butter
4 tablespoons A-1 sauce

1 pound pecan halves
Seasoned salt

Melt butter and A-1 sauce; mix in pecans. Spread on a cookie sheet and bake 1½ hours at 200°, stirring once or twice during cooking time. Spread out on brown paper; sprinkle with salt.

*Henrietta L. Gilliland*

## Oysters Rockefeller Canapés

7 dozen oysters, drained and chopped

Rockefeller Sauce, heated (recipe page 96)

Spread oysters in a shallow dish and bake at 350° for about 7 minutes or until they curl. Drain again and pat dry. Stir into hot sauce. Serve in a chafing dish accompanied by Melba toast.

## Sherried Shrimp

10 pounds shrimp, boiled and peeled
1 pound mushrooms
1 quart olive oil
1 to 1½ cups garlic vinegar
1½ to 2 cups sherry
1 to 2 teaspoons salt

Cayenne to taste
2 lemons, sliced (optional)
6 onions, thinly sliced
1 tablespoon Tony's Creole Seasoning (optional)
1 tablespoon Tabasco (optional)

Layer mushrooms and shrimp in a flat dish; mix next 5 ingredients and pour over shrimp mixture, adding lemons if desired. Cover and refrigerate for 3 days, stirring frequently. Add onions and reseason 12 to 24 hours before serving.

*Suzonne S. Kellogg*

## Cherry Nut Cake

| | |
|---|---|
| 1 pound margarine | 2 ounces lemon extract |
| 2 cups sugar | 1 pound candied cherries |
| 8 eggs | 1 pound candied pineapple, |
| 4 cups flour | chopped |
| 4 teaspoons baking powder | 1 pound chopped pecans |
| ½ teaspoon salt | |

Cream margarine and sugar. Add eggs, 1 at a time, blending well after each. Sift 3½ cups of the flour with the baking powder and salt, using remaining ½ cup of flour for dredging fruit and nuts. Add dry ingredients to margarine mixture alternately with the lemon extract. Fold in fruit-nut mixture. Pour into a greased and floured 9-inch bundt pan and a 9½-inch loaf pan (or 3 9½-inch loaf pans). Bake at 325° for about 1 hour or until a cake tester comes out clean.

*Frances H. Allen*

## Date Nut Cake

| | |
|---|---|
| 4 eggs, separated | 2 ounces lemon extract |
| 2½ cups sugar | 1 quart chopped pecans |
| 1 pound butter, melted | 1 pound dates, chopped |
| 4 cups flour | |

Beat egg yolks with sugar. Add butter gradually and mix at high speed for 2 minutes. Add 3 cups of the flour alternately with the extract. Fold in stiffly beaten egg whites and then the dates and nuts which have been dredged in the remaining cup of flour. Pour batter into 2 9½-inch loaf pans (or a 10-inch tube pan) lined with lightly oiled wax paper. Bake at 275° for 2½ to 3 hours or until cake tester comes out clean. Place a pan of boiling water on the oven shelf below cakes. Cool in pans. Freezes well.

*Daisy W. Watkins*

## Raisin Nut Cake

| | |
|---|---|
| ½ pound butter | 2 teaspoons nutmeg |
| 2 cups sugar | ⅔ cup sherry |
| 6 eggs | 1 pound raisins, washed and |
| 4 cups flour | dried |
| 1 teaspoon baking powder | 1 quart pecan halves |

Cream butter and sugar; add eggs 1 at a time. Combine 3¾ cups flour with baking powder and nutmeg and mix in alternately with sherry. Dredge raisins and pecans in the remaining ¼ cup flour and stir into batter. Pour into a greased 10-inch tube pan with brown paper in the bottom. Bake at 275° for 1 hour 45 minutes or until a cake tester comes out clean.

*Josephine S. Kellogg*

## Lizzies

| | |
|---|---|
| 1 pound chopped, glacéed pineapple, part green, part yellow | 4 eggs, beaten |
| | 3 tablespoons milk |
| | 3 teaspoons baking soda |
| 1 pound chopped, glacéed cherries, part green, part red | 3 cups flour |
| | ½ teaspoon salt |
| 1 pound chopped pitted dates or raisins | 1 teaspoon cloves |
| | 1 teaspoon cinnamon |
| ½ cup bourbon | 1 teaspoon nutmeg |
| ¼ pound butter, softened | 1½ pounds chopped pecans |
| 1 cup brown sugar | |

Soak fruit in bourbon overnight. Cream butter and sugar; add eggs and milk and beat well. Sift together dry ingredients, add to creamed mixture and blend. Stir in fruits and nuts. Drop by the tablespoon onto cookie sheets and bake at 325° for 15 minutes. Cookies will keep 2 to 3 weeks, tightly covered.
Yield: 6 dozen

*Dot P. Davis*

## Spice Cookies

| | |
|---|---|
| ¾ pound butter | ½ teaspoon cloves |
| 2 cups brown sugar | ¼ teaspoon baking soda |
| 1 egg | Colored sugar for decorating |
| 4 cups flour, sifted | cookies before baking or |
| 2 teaspoons cinnamon | frosting for decorating cookies |
| 1 teaspoon nutmeg | after baking (optional) |

Cream butter and sugar; add egg and beat until light and fluffy. Sift remaining ingredients together and stir into batter. Chill about 2 hours until firm.
Roll dough to about ¼-inch thickness. Cut into desired shapes and sprinkle with colored sugar if desired. Bake on foil-lined cookie sheets at 350° for about 12 minutes. Let stand 10 minutes before removing from cookie sheet to rack to cool completely.
Yield: 48 3-inch cookies

*Peggy E. Brian*

## Lollipops

¼ pound butter
1  cup light corn syrup
1½ cups sugar

Food coloring
36 wooden sticks
Marshmallows and gumdrops

Combine first 3 ingredients in a heavy saucepan and cook, stirring occasionally, until mixture boils. Reduce heat and continue cooking to soft crack stage or 270° on a candy thermometer. Remove from heat and add coloring. Drop by the spoonful over ends of wooden sticks placed on greased cookie sheets, until each lollipop is about 2-inches in diameter. Decorate while still hot with marshmallows and gumdrops. Cool completely before removing. Wrap tightly in plastic wrap or wax paper.
    Yield: 36 lollipops

*JoAnn M. Bowers*

## Gala Eggnog

4  cups sugar
2  quarts milk
12 eggs, separated
1  pint brandy

1½ pints dark rum
3  pints bourbon
2  quarts heavy cream, whipped
Nutmeg

Stir sugar and milk together until sugar dissolves. Using low speed on mixer add brandy *very slowly* to beaten egg yolks. Gradually blend in rum, then bourbon. Stir in milk-sugar mixture and gently fold in whipped cream and stiffly beaten egg whites. Refrigerate for at least 24 hours. Sprinkle with freshly ground nutmeg.
    Yield: About 2 gallons

*Elizabeth N. Neilson*

# CHRISTMAS (Dinner for 10)

This memorable holiday meal begins lightly with a small portion of soup; becomes hearty with a magnificent entrée, a delight to both eye and palate; is accented with a tart yet sweet salad and vegetables; and as a finale provides a choice of two elegant desserts. The cranberry pudding was brought to Louisiana from Copenhagen and is an old family recipe. The Southern version of the traditional English plum pudding makes enough not only for this festive occasion but also for gifts for very special friends near and far, since it can even be mailed.

### *Oyster Soup

### *Crown Roast of Pork with Rice Stuffing
### *Scalloped Rutabagas    Steamed Broccoli
### *Orange and Onion Salad
### Dinner Rolls

### *Cranberry Pudding   or   *Plum Pudding
### Coffee

*Champagne or Graves with soup*
*Light Claret with pork*

## Oyster Soup

¼  pound butter
1  cup finely chopped celery
1  cup finely chopped green onions and tops
1  clove garlic, pressed
1  tablespoon flour
2  dozen oysters, drained, liquor reserved

6  cups liquid: oyster liquor plus broth, clam juice, and/or white wine
2  bay leaves
Salt, black pepper, cayenne and Tabasco to taste
Minced parsley

Melt butter in heavy skillet and sauté vegetables until tender. Blend in flour and cook 5 minutes, stirring, over low heat. Add liquids slowly, stirring constantly. Add oysters and seasonings; simmer 20 minutes. Remove bay leaves and sprinkle with parsley.

Yield:  1½ quarts

*Caroline K. Gilliland*

## Crown Roast of Pork with Rice Stuffing

1  cup golden raisins
1  pound bulk pork sausage,
   browned and drained
5  cups cooked rice (1½ cups raw)
1  tablespoon salt
½ tablespoon pepper

¾ tablespoon garlic salt
10 rib crown roast of pork (note
   weight)
Salt, pepper and garlic slivers
10 crabapples

Rinse raisins in hot water; drain. Combine with next 5 ingredients. Allow to stand several hours at room temperature or refrigerate overnight.

Rub roast with salt and pepper, inserting garlic at 1½-inch intervals around fleshy part of crown. Lightly pack stuffing into center and top entire roast loosely with foil. Put any remaining dressing into a buttered casserole; cover and set aside. Preheat oven to 450°; lower to 350° and add roast. Bake 25 to 30 minutes per pound or until a meat thermometer registers 180°. Remove cover for last 30 minutes, at which time additional dressing casserole should be baked. Garnish ribs with crabapples and bring to table uncarved.

*Hope J. Norman*

## Scalloped Rutabagas

3  pounds rutabagas, peeled and
   thinly sliced (about 6 cups)
4  tablespoons butter
2  onions, thinly sliced
1⅓ cups diced green pepper
⅔ cup diced celery
4  tablespoons flour
2  cups milk, at room temperature

1  cup grated sharp Cheddar
   cheese
Salt and freshly ground pepper
   to taste
3 to 6 tablespoons grated
   Parmesan cheese and/or bread
   crumbs

Cover rutabagas with salted water and bring to a boil. Simmer until tender (about 15 minutes); drain. In heavy skillet, melt butter and sauté onions, pepper and celery until wilted. Sprinkle with flour and cook 1 minute. Gradually add the milk; bring to a boil, stirring until mixture thickens. Stir in the Cheddar cheese and seasonings. Add rutabagas and pour mixture into a buttered shallow 2-quart casserole dish. Sprinkle with the Parmesan cheese and/or crumbs and brown under broiler.

*Caroline K. Gilliland*

## Orange and Onion Salad

10 navel oranges, peeled and
   sectioned

2 red onions, sliced into rings
10 Boston lettuce leaves

Fill each lettuce leaf with sections from 1 orange. Top with onion rings. Pour the following dressing over all.

### Lemon Sherry Dressing

1 cup lemon juice
½ teaspoon salt

1 cup sugar
1 cup sherry

Combine ingredients in order listed and refrigerate. Keeps well and is very good on all fruit salads.

## Cranberry Pudding

1 egg, beaten
1 tablespoon sugar
½ cup light molasses (do not
   substitute)
2 teaspoons baking soda
   dissolved in ⅓ cup hot water

1½ cups flour
½ teaspoon salt
2 cups cranberries, washed,
   drained, and halved

Combine all ingredients in order listed. Pour into a greased 8-cup mold until it is about ¾ full. Cover tightly with cheesecloth. Place on rack in large covered pot. Steam for 45 minutes to 1 hour over simmering water until just firm enough to resist pressure. Serve warm in bowls with the following sauce. (No other will do, as this "makes" the pudding.) Doubles easily. Freezes well. Steam again before serving.

### Rum Butter Sauce

1 cup cream
½ pound butter
1 cup sugar

¼ teaspoon salt
1 teaspoon vanilla
1 or 2 tablespoons rum

In a saucepan, simmer cream, butter, sugar and salt until thoroughly heated. Remove from heat; stir in vanilla and rum. Serve warm.

*Nancy R. Struck*

## *Plum Pudding*

1   pound dates, pitted
½  pound candied cherries
1   pound black raisins
1   pound white raisins
1   pound dried prunes, pitted
1   pound dried apricots
2   pounds dried apples
¼  pound each: candied citron,
      lemon, and orange peel
1   pound English walnuts
5   sweet potatoes, peeled and
      grated
2   pounds dark brown sugar
2   cups molasses, sorghum or
      cane syrup (or 1½ cups syrup
      and ½ cup honey)
1   cup bourbon
1   quart grape juice

1   quart sweet pickle juice (from
      spiced peaches, crab apples,
      etc., or homemade sweet
      pickles; use any available
      combination of these juices)
2   teaspoons baking soda
1   teaspoon salt
1   tablespoon of each of the
      following: cinnamon, allspice,
      cloves and ginger
1   quart buttermilk
1   pound sweet white suet, ground
2   pounds dried fine crumbs,
      lightly toasted (any combination
      of breads, cookies, sweetrolls,
      etc.)
12 eggs, beaten
2 to 3 ounces brandy, warmed, for
      each pudding mold

The proportion of fruits may be varied according to your taste.

Finely chop all fruits and nuts. (The use of a food processor is recommended.) In a very large bowl, add the above to the sweet potatoes, brown sugar, syrup and bourbon. This may be allowed to stand for several hours or be refrigerated overnight.

Add the juices and mix well. Whip soda, salt and spices into buttermilk. Stir into pudding mixture. Add suet, crumbs and beaten eggs and mix thoroughly.

Fill greased molds ¾ full; cover with cheesecloth, then aluminum foil and secure with string or rubber bands. Place on a rack in a large roaster containing water reaching one-half the molds' height and steam 1½ to 2½ hours, depending on size of molds. (See chart below.) Cool completely in the molds.

Unmold onto lightly buttered aluminum foil. Wrap securely. These will keep in the refrigerator for a week or may be frozen. When ready to serve, steam pudding again, still wrapped, ½ to 1½ hours (depending upon whether or not it is frozen) or until piping hot.

To serve, place steamed pudding on heatproof platter. Pour warmed brandy over pudding and ignite. Serve with dollop of hard sauce.

Yield:  360 ounces or 11¼ quarts

| Molds | Finished Amount (each) | Steaming Time | Serves (each) |
|---|---|---|---|
| 36  10-ounce | ¾  pound | 1½  hours | 2 to 4 |
| 18  20-ounce | 1¼  pounds | 2½  hours | 6 to 8 |

## Hard Sauce

½ cup unsalted butter, very cold     2 tablespoons sherry or brandy
2 cups confectioners' sugar

   Divide butter into about 6 pieces and, using the steel blade of a food processor, cream with sugar. When fluffy, gradually add the liquor. Chill until firm. If using a mixer, the recipe is the same but butter should be at room temperature.

*Johnie W. Murphy*

# NEW YEAR'S EVE                    *(Cocktail Buffet for 100)*

Make a "Fais-Dodo"—an all night south Louisiana celebration! An extraordinary ending.

## Red and/or White Wine, Liquor, Soft Drinks

### *Spirited Pork      *Smoked Goose
### *Sweet Mustard      Mayonnaise
### Rolls and Bread Slices

### *Jalapeño Quiche      *Red River Pinwheels
### *Creole Oysters      *Sweet and Sour Sausage
### Miniature Pastry Shells

### *Artichoke-Shrimp Spread      *Chicken Liver Pâté
### *Walnut Clam Roll      *Pecan Cheese Ball
### Assorted Crackers

### *Chocolate Bonbons
### *Creamy Fudge
### *Divinity
### Coffee      Champagne

As with any large gathering, the specific guest list will determine the exact quantity of food and drink necessary, so it is important to analyze the expected requirements for any particular crowd. The "rule of thumb" is to allow an average of 3 drinks per person. Wine is usually served in 4-ounce portions and liquor in 1½-ounce jiggers plus about 5 ounces of a mixer. Soft drinks average 6 ounces per glass. For 100 people, the following amounts are a guideline: 4 to 6 magnums (50.7-ounces each) of wine, 15 to 17 fifths of liquor, 20 to 24 quarts of soft drinks and mixers, 4 to 6  10-pound bags of ice (more in hot weather), 4 to 6 lemons and/or limes, a quart of mayonnaise, about 100 slices of bread, 9 to 10 dozen rolls, 4 to 6 boxes of crackers, 8 to 10 dozen miniature pastry shells, 1 pound of sugar and 1 pint of cream to be served with the coffee (1 pound will make 60 cups). Make 3 of the pinwheels, one with each of the fillings. These amounts are only suggestions and to be used as a yardstick. Don't forget lots of toothpicks and napkins, and a myriad of ashtrays.

## Spirited Pork

| | |
|---|---|
| 6 pound boneless pork loin | 3 tablespoons honey |
| ½ cup soy sauce | 1 clove garlic, pressed |
| ½ cup vermouth | |

Marinate meat in a mixture of the remaining ingredients overnight or longer, turning several times. Roast on a rack at 300° for 2 hours or until a meat thermometer registers the desired degree of doneness. Baste often with marinade. Chill thoroughly and have the butcher slice paper thin. Boil the remaining marinade and skimmed pan juices until essence is of desired consistency, adding a small amount of cornstarch to thicken if necessary. Cool and serve with cold meat slices.

Yield: 120 slices

*Wilma H. Uhrich*

## Sweet Mustard

| | |
|---|---|
| 3 teaspoons dry mustard | 1 teaspoon cornstarch |
| ½ cup juice from a fruit preserve | |

Stir mustard into fruit syrup; cook slowly with cornstarch to thicken.

## Smoked Goose

| | |
|---|---|
| 2 wild geese | 2 onions, diced |
| 2 tablespoons olive oil | 4 sprigs parsley, minced |
| 8 lemons, quartered | Salt, pepper and garlic salt |
| 2 apples, diced | 6 strips bacon |

Place each goose, breast side up, on 2 large sheets of heavy foil. Put ½ tablespoon olive oil on each breast and ½ tablespoon inside each cavity. Squeeze juice of 2 lemons inside and 2 outside of each goose. Then dice 4 of these lemons and add to apple, onion and parsley, blending well. Stuff geese with this mixture and sprinkle with seasonings. Place 3 bacon strips on each bird and top with remaining lemon pieces. Pull foil tightly around birds and punch holes in top. Smoke over charcoal for 6 hours.

*M. Lee Jarrell*

## Jalapeño Quiche

1½  pounds extra sharp Cheddar
    cheese, grated
2  tablespoons chopped parsley
3  tablespoons Worcestershire
    sauce
2  dozen eggs, beaten

1  7-ounce can sliced jalapeño
    peppers with onions and
    carrots, drained and finely
    chopped
2  2½-ounce cans real bacon bits
    Paprika

Divide ⅓ of the cheese between 2 greased 9×13-inch baking dishes. Stir parsley, then Worcestershire into eggs and pour ⅓ of this batter over the cheese. Sprinkle with ⅓ of the pepper mixture. Repeat entire process twice. Top with bacon bits and sprinkle with paprika. Bake on top oven rack at 300° for 45 to 60 minutes or until knife inserted into center comes out clean. Cool slightly before cutting into squares. Serve warm; freezes well.

*Isabel G. Useda*

## Red River Pinwheels

4  tablespoons butter
½  cup flour
⅛  teaspoon salt

2  cups milk
4  eggs, separated
1  teaspoon sugar

Melt butter; add flour and salt and cook over medium heat 1 minute. Add milk gradually and cook about 5 minutes, stirring. Remove from heat and blend in egg yolks and sugar; fold in stiffly beaten egg whites. Oil a 10×5-inch jelly roll pan, line with wax paper, and oil again. Spread batter evenly in pan and bake at 325° for 40 to 50 minutes. Turn pan onto additional wax paper, lift pan and peel paper from the soufflé roll. Spread with one of the following fillings and roll across 10-inch side. Slice at ½-inch intervals. Serve hot or cold; freezes well.

Yield: 30 slices; to serve 100, make 3 rolls

### Curried Shrimp Filling

3  ounces cream cheese, at room
    temperature
4  tablespoons sour cream
1  pound cooked peeled shrimp,
    chopped

3  tablespoons chopped chutney
3  tablespoons chopped preserved
    ginger
2  tablespoons curry powder

Beat cream cheese and sour cream together until smooth. Add remaining ingredients and mix well.

### Ham Filling

1 cup heavy cream, whipped
1½ cups chopped ham
½ cup chopped chives

1 teaspoon horseradish
½ teaspoon Dijon mustard

Mix all ingredients together until well blended.

### Caviar Filling

4 ounces cream cheese, at room
   temperature

2 tablespoons sour cream
5 ounces red caviar

Beat cream cheese and sour cream together. Add remaining ingredients and mix well.

*Peggy E. Brian*

## Creole Oysters

10 dozen oysters, drained, liquor
   reserved
4 cups cracker crumbs, soaked in
   1½ cups oyster liquor
3 cups minced celery
3 cups minced parsley
1½ cups minced onion
1½ cups minced green onions
2 green peppers, minced

¼ pound butter
4 eggs, beaten
2 teaspoons salt
3 teaspoons celery salt
2 teaspoons black pepper
1 teaspoon cayenne
6 tablespoons Worcestershire
   sauce
5 tablespoons catsup

Chop or grind oysters and set aside. Mix vegetables with butter and enough water added to remaining oyster liquor to make 2 cups. Cook slowly until vegetables are tender and liquid has evaporated. Blend cracker crumbs and dry seasonings with eggs and add to vegetable mixture. Cook and stir constantly about 25 minutes. Add remaining ingredients and adjust seasonings. Serve hot in a chafing dish accompanied by tiny pastry shells; freezes well.

*Florence B. Crowell*

## Sweet and Sour Sausage

2   13½-ounce cans pineapple
    chunks, drained, juice reserved
8   teaspoons cornstarch
1   teaspoon salt
1   cup maple syrup
⅔   cup water

⅔   cup vinegar
2   pounds smoked sausage, sliced,
    browned and drained
1   cup drained maraschino
    cherries
3   green peppers, cut into chunks

Blend pineapple juice with cornstarch, salt, syrup, water and vinegar. Heat to boiling, stirring. Add sausage, fruits and pepper pieces. Cook 5 minutes over low heat. Serve hot in a chafing dish.

*Marilyn M. Carlton*

## Artichoke-Shrimp Spread

3   egg yolks, at room temperature
1   cup olive oil
1   cup salad oil
6   tablespoons Dijon mustard
6   tablespoons wine vinegar
6   tablespoons lemon juice
Black pepper and cayenne to taste

6   16-ounce cans artichoke hearts,
    drained and chopped
5   pounds cooked peeled shrimp,
    coarsely chopped
3   cups chopped green onions and
    tops

Combine first 6 ingredients in blender or food processor until mixture is the consistency of thin mayonnaise. Season to taste and pour over remaining ingredients. Mix well, cover and refrigerate several hours or overnight. Keeps well for 7 to 10 days.

Variation: Use as a stuffing for a tomato or avocado, or in an omelet.

*Neva K. Sacco*

## Chicken Liver Pâté

5 pounds chicken livers
2½ to 3 dozen eggs, hard-boiled
8 pounds onions, coarsely
   chopped

1 to 2 cups chicken fat (or corn oil)
Salt and pepper to taste

Boil livers in water until tender, 10 to 15 minutes; cool. Sauté 7 pounds of the onions in chicken fat until tender; cool. Grind livers and sautéed onions in a meat grinder (do not use food processor). Grind remaining onions with eggs and add to mixture, blending in well. Add enough chicken fat to form pâté into a smooth paste. Season to taste. Pack into a greased mold and chill. Unmold, garnish, and serve with crackers.

*Blossom K. Hinchin*
*Marilyn W. Silver*

## Walnut Clam Roll

2 7½-ounce cans minced clams,
   drained
32 ounces cream cheese, softened
4 tablespoons minced onion

4 tablespoons lemon juice
Garlic salt, Worcestershire sauce
   and Tabasco to taste
2½ cups chopped toasted walnuts

Beat clams and cheese together until smooth. Mix in onion and lemon juice; season to taste. Stir in 1 cup walnuts. Turn mixture onto a sheet of foil and shape into several "logs" (1¾-inch diameter). Roll in remaining walnuts until surface is well-coated. Wrap and chill.
   Yield: 6 dozen slices

*Mildred S. Chandler*

## Pecan Cheese Ball

16 ounces cream cheese, at room
   temperature
¼ pound butter, softened
16 ounces blue cheese, at room
   temperature
2 4½-ounce cans chopped black
   olives

2 tablespoons minced green
   onions
⅔ cup minced pecans
⅔ cup minced parsley

Blend first 5 ingredients together; chill thoroughly. Shape into a ball; roll in pecans and parsley until well-coated.

*Leta'dele B. DeFee*

## Chocolate Bonbons

| | |
|---|---|
| ¼  pound margarine, melted | 1  cup flaked coconut |
| 2  cups sifted confectioners' sugar | 1  cup finely chopped walnuts or |
| 1  cup crunchy peanut butter | pecans |
| 1  cup chopped dates | 18  ounces semi-sweet chocolate |
| 1  cup mixed candied fruits, | morsels |
| chopped | 2 to 3 ounces paraffin, shredded |

Pour hot margarine over sugar and peanut butter and mix well. Add next 4 ingredients and shape into ½-inch balls. Place on wax paper and refrigerate overnight.

Melt the chocolate and about half of the paraffin, stirring occasionally to blend. Roll each ball in chocolate mixture, adding more paraffin if chocolate is not sticking. Lift out with a fork and return coated balls to wax paper; refrigerate or freeze until ready to serve.

Yield: 5 dozen

*Margaret G. Christensen*

## Creamy Fudge

| | |
|---|---|
| ½  pound butter, cut into pieces | 4½ cups sugar |
| 18  ounces semi-sweet chocolate | 2  teaspoons vanilla |
| morsels | 2  cups chopped pecans or |
| 7  ounces marshmallow creme | walnuts |
| 1  13-ounce can evaporated milk | |

Place butter, chocolate and marshmallow creme into a large bowl. Boil milk and sugar, stirring constantly, until mixture reaches the soft ball stage or 235° on a candy thermometer, about 8 to 10 minutes. Pour over chocolate mixture and beat well. Stir in vanilla and nuts. Pour into a buttered 9×13-inch pan; cool. Cut into pieces.

Yield: 5 dozen 1½-inch pieces

*Josephine S. Kellogg*

## *Divinity*

3   cups sugar
¾  cup white corn syrup
¾  cup hot water

2   egg whites, stiffly beaten
1   teaspoon vanilla
1   cup chopped pecans (optional)

Boil sugar, syrup and water in a heavy saucepan until mixture reaches the soft ball stage or 235° on a candy thermometer. Pour half over the egg whites and mix well. Return remaining mixture to heat and cook almost to hard ball stage or 250° on candy thermometer. Fold into egg white mixture, add vanilla and nuts and beat until nearly cold. Drop by the teaspoon onto wax paper and allow to cool. Do not store in an airtight container. This recipe never fails—even on a rainy Louisiana day.

Yield:  3 to 4 dozen pieces

*Maxine O. Chandler*

# METRIC CONVERSION TABLE

**Volume:**  ¼ teaspoon          1.2 milliliters (ml)
1 teaspoon          5 milliliters
1 tablespoon       15 milliliters
1 fluid ounce      30 milliliters
¼ cup              60 milliliters
⅓ cup              75 milliliters
1 cup              250 milliliters or .25 liters (1)
1 pint             500 milliliters or .5 liters
1 fifth            750 milliliters or .75 liters
1 quart            950 milliliters or .95 liters
1 gallon           3800 milliliters or 3.8 liters

**Weight:**  1 ounce            28 grams (g)
1 pound            450 grams or .45 kilograms (kg)

**Length:**  1 inch             2.5 centimeters (cm)
1 foot             30 centimeters

# BIBLIOGRAPHY

Angers, Trent, ed. *Acadiana Profile*, Lafayette, Louisiana: Acadiana Profile, Inc., First Quarter, 1978. Vol. VI.

Baldridge, Pat. *Headline Recipes*. Baton Rouge, Louisiana: Franklin Press, Inc., 1972.

Brown, Clair A. *Wildflowers of Louisiana and Adjoining States*. Baton Rouge, Louisiana: Louisiana State University Press, 1972.

Collin, Rima and Richard Collin. *The New Orleans Cookbook*. New York: Alfred A. Knopf, Inc., 1975.

Collison, Robert L. *Indexes and Indexing*. London: Ernest Benn Ltd., 1959.

Dozier, Gilbert L. "Louisiana Oysters." *Louisiana Market Bulletin*. 13 July 1978, p. 1. Louisiana Department of Agriculture. Baton Rouge, Louisiana.

Feibleman, Peter S. *American Cooking: Creole and Acadian*. New York: Time-Life Books, 1971.

*Louisiana Conservationist*. Louisiana Wildlife and Fisheries Dept., New Orleans, Louisiana: 1975-78. Vols 27-30.

Louisiana Writers' Project, ed. *Louisiana, A Guide to the State*. New York: Hastings House, 1959.

Lowery, George H. *Louisiana Birds*. Baton Rouge, Louisiana: Louisiana State University Press, 1974.

*MLA Handbook*. New York: Modern Language Assn., 1977.

Montagné, Prosper. *Larousse Gastronomique*. New York: Crown Publishers Inc., 1961.

*The Picayune's Creole Cook Book*. 2nd ed. 1901; rpt. New York: Dover Publications, Inc., 1971.

*Reader's Digest Secrets of Better Cooking*. New York: Reader's Digest Association, 1973.

Rombauer, Irma S. and Marion R. Becker. *The Joy of Cooking*. Indianapolis, Indiana: The Bobbs-Merrill Co., Inc., 1962.

Warriner, John E. *English Grammar and Composition: 11*. New York: Harcourt, Brace and Co., 1958.

*Webster's New Collegiate Dictionary*. 3rd ed. Springfield, Massachusetts: G. and C. Merriam Co., 1963.

*The Wellesley Research Handbook for College Students*. Wellesley, Massachusetts: The Department of English of Wellesley College, 1950.

# Index

RAPIDES SYMPHONY GUILD
P. O. Box 4172
Alexandria, LA. 71301                    Date_____

Please send _____ copies of *Louisiana Entertains* @ $7.95 plus $1.25 postage and handling per copy. Add 3% sales tax in Louisiana ($.24 ea.)

Check if gift wrap is desired _____ ($.50 per copy). _____ Card enclosed.

Make check payable to *Louisiana Entertains* .

            Enclosed is my check or money order for $_____. Sorry, no C.O.D.'s

NAME _____
                              PLEASE PRINT

STREET _____

CITY_____ STATE_____ ZIP_____

All copies will be sent to the same address unless otherwise specified.

Proceeds from the sale of this book support the Rapides Symphony Orchestra.

---

RAPIDES SYMPHONY GUILD
P. O. Box 4172
Alexandria, LA. 71301                    Date_____

Please send _____ copies of *Louisiana Entertains* @ $7.95 plus $1.25 postage and handling per copy. Add 3% sales tax in Louisiana ($.24 ea.)

Check if gift wrap is desired _____ ($.50 per copy). _____ Card enclosed.

Make check payable to *Louisiana Entertains* .

            Enclosed is my check or money order for $_____. Sorry, no C.O.D.'s

NAME _____
                              PLEASE PRINT

STREET _____

CITY_____ STATE_____ ZIP_____

All copies will be sent to the same address unless otherwise specified.

Proceeds from the sale of this book support the Rapides Symphony Orchestra.

---

RAPIDES SYMPHONY GUILD
P. O. Box 4172
Alexandria, LA. 71301                    Date_____

Please send _____ copies of *Louisiana Entertains* @ $7.95 plus $1.25 postage and handling per copy. Add 3% sales tax in Louisiana ($.24 ea.)

Check if gift wrap is desired _____ ($.50 per copy). _____ Card enclosed.

Make check payable to *Louisiana Entertains* .

            Enclosed is my check or money order for $_____. Sorry, no C.O.D.'s

NAME _____
                              PLEASE PRINT

STREET _____

CITY_____ STATE_____ ZIP_____

All copies will be sent to the same address unless otherwise specified.

Proceeds from the sale of this book support the Rapides Symphony Orchestra.

Names and addresses of bookstores, gift shops, etc. in your area would be appreciated.

_____

_____

_____

_____

_____

Names and addresses of bookstores, gift shops, etc. in your area would be appreciated.

_____

_____

_____

_____

_____

Names and addresses of bookstores, gift shops, etc. in your area would be appreciated.

_____

_____

_____

_____

_____

RAPIDES SYMPHONY GUILD
P. O. Box 4172
Alexandria, LA. 71301          Date_____

Please send _____ copies of *Louisiana Entertains* @ $7.95 plus $1.25 postage and handling per copy. Add 3% sales tax in Louisiana ($.24 ea.)

Check if gift wrap is desired _____ ($.50 per copy). _____ Card enclosed.

Make check payable to *Louisiana Entertains* .

Enclosed is my check or money order for $_____. Sorry, no C.O.D.'s

NAME _____
                              PLEASE PRINT

STREET _____

CITY_____ STATE_____ ZIP_____

All copies will be sent to the same address unless otherwise specified.

Proceeds from the sale of this book support the Rapides Symphony Orchestra.

---

RAPIDES SYMPHONY GUILD
P. O. Box 4172
Alexandria, LA. 71301          Date_____

Please send _____ copies of *Louisiana Entertains* @ $7.95 plus $1.25 postage and handling per copy. Add 3% sales tax in Louisiana ($.24 ea.)

Check if gift wrap is desired _____ ($.50 per copy). _____ Card enclosed.

Make check payable to *Louisiana Entertains* .

Enclosed is my check or money order for $_____. Sorry, no C.O.D.'s

NAME _____
                              PLEASE PRINT

STREET _____

CITY_____ STATE_____ ZIP_____

All copies will be sent to the same address unless otherwise specified.

Proceeds from the sale of this book support the Rapides Symphony Orchestra.

---

RAPIDES SYMPHONY GUILD
P. O. Box 4172
Alexandria, LA. 71301          Date_____

Please send _____ copies of *Louisiana Entertains* @ $7.95 plus $1.25 postage and handling per copy. Add 3% sales tax in Louisiana ($.24 ea.)

Check if gift wrap is desired _____ ($.50 per copy). _____ Card enclosed.

Make check payable to *Louisiana Entertains* .

Enclosed is my check or money order for $_____. Sorry, no C.O.D.'s

NAME _____
                              PLEASE PRINT

STREET _____

CITY_____ STATE_____ ZIP_____

All copies will be sent to the same address unless otherwise specified.

Proceeds from the sale of this book support the Rapides Symphony Orchestra.

Names and addresses of bookstores, gift shops, etc. in your area would be appreciated.

_____

_____

_____

_____

_____

Names and addresses of bookstores, gift shops, etc. in your area would be appreciated.

_____

_____

_____

_____

_____

Names and addresses of bookstores, gift shops, etc. in your area would be appreciated.

_____

_____

_____

_____

_____

RAPIDES SYMPHONY GUILD
P. O. Box 4172
Alexandria, LA. 71301                    Date_____

Please send _____ copies of *Louisiana Entertains* @ $7.95 plus $1.25 postage and handling per copy. Add 3% sales tax in Louisiana ($.24 ea.)

Check if gift wrap is desired _____ ($.50 per copy). _____ Card enclosed.

Make check payable to *Louisiana Entertains* .

      Enclosed is my check or money order for $_____. Sorry, no C.O.D.'s

NAME _____
                                 PLEASE PRINT

STREET _____

CITY_____ STATE_____ ZIP_____

All copies will be sent to the same address unless otherwise specified.

Proceeds from the sale of this book support the Rapides Symphony Orchestra.

---

RAPIDES SYMPHONY GUILD
P. O. Box 4172
Alexandria, LA. 71301                    Date_____

Please send _____ copies of *Louisiana Entertains* @ $7.95 plus $1.25 postage and handling per copy. Add 3% sales tax in Louisiana ($.24 ea.)

Check if gift wrap is desired _____ ($.50 per copy). _____ Card enclosed.

Make check payable to *Louisiana Entertains* .

      Enclosed is my check or money order for $_____. Sorry, no C.O.D.'s

NAME _____
                                 PLEASE PRINT

STREET _____

CITY_____ STATE_____ ZIP_____

All copies will be sent to the same address unless otherwise specified.

Proceeds from the sale of this book support the Rapides Symphony Orchestra.

---

RAPIDES SYMPHONY GUILD
P. O. Box 4172
Alexandria, LA. 71301                    Date_____

Please send _____ copies of *Louisiana Entertains* @ $7.95 plus $1.25 postage and handling per copy. Add 3% sales tax in Louisiana ($.24 ea.)

Check if gift wrap is desired _____ ($.50 per copy). _____ Card enclosed.

Make check payable to *Louisiana Entertains* .

      Enclosed is my check or money order for $_____. Sorry, no C.O.D.'s

NAME _____
                                 PLEASE PRINT

STREET _____

CITY_____ STATE_____ ZIP_____

All copies will be sent to the same address unless otherwise specified.

Proceeds from the sale of this book support the Rapides Symphony Orchestra.

Re-OrderAdditionalCopies

Names and addresses of bookstores, gift shops, etc. in your area would be appreciated.

_____

_____

_____

_____

_____

_____

Names and addresses of bookstores, gift shops, etc. in your area would be appreciated.

_____

_____

_____

_____

_____

_____

Names and addresses of bookstores, gift shops, etc. in your area would be appreciated.

_____

_____

_____

_____

_____

_____